The
MEREHURST
CAKE
BOOK

The

MEREHURST

CAKE

BOOK

FOLLOWING THE RECIPES

A standard spoon measurement is used in all recipes.

1 teaspoon (tsp) = one 5 ml spoon
1 tablespoon (tbsp) = one 15 ml spoon
All spoon measures are level.

Ovens should be preheated to the specified temperature.

Eggs used in the recipes are standard size (ie. size 3) unless otherwise stated.

For all recipes, quantities are given in metric, Imperial and cups. Follow one set of measures but not a mixture as they are not interchangeable.

NU

The publisher would like to thank Pat Lock for her valuable assistance in producing this book, also the following authors and photographers for their contributions: Pat Ashby, Lindsay John Bradshaw, Lesley Herbert, Jacqui Hine, Nicholas Lodge, Elaine MacGregor, Anne Smith, Mary Tipton, David Gill, Ken Field, Melvin Grey, John Johnson, Clive Streeter, Graham Tann, and John Todd.

Published in 1992 by Merehurst Limited, Ferry House, 51–57 Lacy Road, Putney, London SW15 1PR.

Copyright © Merehurst Limited 1992

ISBN 1-85391-263-8

A catalogue record of this book is available from the British Library.

Edited by Bridget Jones
Designed by Maggie Aldred
Cover photography by Clive Streeter
Line illustrations by Joyce Tuhill
Typeset by J&L Composition Ltd, Filey, North Yorkshire
Colour separation by J Film Process Ltd., Thailand
Printed in England by BPCC Hazells Ltd

CONTENTS

THE ART AND CRAFT
OF CAKE DESIGN
by Pat Lock

Over the last fifteen years there has been a gradual trend towards a softer, more romantic look in formal cake design and decoration. In the past, the majority of celebration cakes were iced and decorated in white royal icing. The favoured shape was square, making cakes easier to cut into regular pieces. The decoration, mainly consisting of large shells, scrolls and some line work, was piped directly on the surface of the cake, often with the addition of trellis, which was very popular. On many wedding cakes, the only features to contrast with the white were foil leaves, silver horse-shoes and tiny silver slippers; the horse-shoes to bring good luck and the slippers to convey two ancient messages. Firstly, the slippers represented the giving of the bride, by her Father, to the groom and secondly, relating even further back in history, they were used in a ritual related to land ownership. A shoe was placed on a piece of land to indicate its possession by the owner of the footwear.

The Developing Art: Following Social Trends

Taking wedding cakes as an example, and following social as well as practical trends, it is possible to trace the development of cake decorating as an art form. It is not so long ago since the cake was literally the centrepiece at the wedding reception, usually displayed directly in front of the bride and groom and very often obscuring them from view. Gradually, a new approach has evolved to integrate wedding cakes with other aspects of the occasion – the setting, the bridal attire, even the interests of the couple. New-style cakes, with softly curved edges, delicately piped decorations and pretty floral sprays, give a spacious, light impression of the less serious approach to formal celebrations. They are a complete change from the rather heavy, elaborate designs of yesteryear.

In direct contrast to our rather utilitarian approach to everyday wear, wedding dresses have become more romantic with an abundance of satin, silk and lace. Not only does the modern bride take her pick from many glamorous styles when choosing her dress, she looks to the wedding cake to reflect the chosen theme. Flowing lines and ruffled frills are created in sugarwork, and tiny piped designs, reminiscent of embroidery, are painstakingly added by the cake decorator with just as much care and dedication as the dressmaker. There has been a swing away from the tradition of ordering the wedding cake from the local baker and it is now quite common for the bride's mother, a close relative or friend to make the cake. The pre-reception terror, associated with the idea of the couple being unable to pierce the coating on a royal iced cake, is rarely justified as, properly made, this type of icing does not deserve its reputation for setting rock hard.

Alternative Cakes and Different Coatings

Although the majority of wedding cakes are still made from rich fruit cake, occasionally the top tier will be made of sponge as an alternative for those guests who do not like fruit. However, as tastes broaden and become more cosmopolitan it is not unknown for a bride to opt for a chocolate cake or American-style cake as the base for decoration. Since a wide range of tins is available, for sale or on hire, cakes can also be made in many shapes, including, hexagonal, octagonal, horse-shoe, diamond, star, petal and heart shapes.

During the seventies sugarpaste began to rival royal icing as a coating for wedding cakes. Despite its reputation for being a new product, a similar paste was, in fact, being made as far back as the early seventeenth century. By using smoothly rolled paste, the cake can be covered in one operation, eliminating the need for adding repeated layers of royal icing. Soft pastes can also be used for modelling flowers and to make exquisite frills to encircle the cake in one layer or in a series of bewitching ruffles often leaving the uninitiated admirer baffled as to the technique by which the layered effect is achieved.

New Decorating Techniques
This fashion for using soft paste on cakes has allowed for the creation of several new decorating techniques, including smock-ing and ribbon insertion. The latter is popular for wedding cakes and it involves inserting sections of ribbon at equal distances into slits made in the soft icing. This gives the appearance of the ribbon having been threaded in and out of the icing. Among the many innovations in piping, methods of piping decorations separate from the cake, then applying them when dry, have grown in popularity. Fine lace piped in royal icing is a good example. Several hundred tiny pieces may be piped on paper, then attached to the cake with small dabs of icing to secure them in position. The lace provides an interesting combination of textures, as the royal icing and distinct shapes contrast with the smooth surface of the paste-covered cake.

Another modern trend for use on royal icing or paste-covered cakes is the brush embroidery skill. Although very effective, results are achieved quite simply. A piped outline is applied on the icing and while still soft the icing is brushed inwards to give the design a two-dimensional appear-ance. This can be used to great effect when planning a cake to mirror a floral design on a wedding dress.

Attitudes towards colour have also changed and classic white wedding dresses are often replaced by gowns in ivory or even pastel shades. Yet again, cakes may be iced to reflect the chosen colour, thereby providing a harmonious look. The choice of an overall colour scheme for dresses, flowers, table displays and cake is now quite standard and it often puts the skills of the cake decorator to the test. Cake decorating has become as much a method of expressing artistic flair as for displaying craft-based skills, particularly when executing requests for colour co-ordination with appropriate choice of decoration and finishing touches. For example, jewel-bright shades of brides-maids' dresses are sometimes linked with the wedding cake by adding a comple-mentary band of ribbon around the edge of the board and placing tiny bows on the cake surface.

Stands and Supports: New Styles Rival Traditional Pillars
Since we have experienced alternative fashions in icings, decorating techniques and colour, it is not surprising that cake supports and stands have also moved with the times. Pillars are a typical example: in the past, the only pillars available were made of plaster of Paris. Now, a wide variety can be purchased in plastic, perspex and acrylic as well as plaster. There are tapered or Grecian columns, hexagonal pillars to reflect the shape of the cake and even a barley-twist design. Separaters, clear top and base stands, are now used above and below pillars to eliminate the fear of one of the pillars

moving and disturbing the cake, at the same time ensuring an even weight distribution of upper layers. Hollow pillars are designed for paste-covered cakes, with a slim rod of dowelling passed down the pillar and through the cake to rest on the base board. Indeed, the modern tiered cake may be displayed without the use of pillars. Stands in various shapes, and made of different materials, can be hired or purchased to support two or more tiers of cake. One of the most popular types is shaped in the form of an 'S' with a platform on top of each curve to hold a cake. Decorated with ribbons and flowers to complement the decoration, they can look extremely attractive.

High-quality Cakes for All Occasions

The variety of ideas and skills which has broadened the scope of wedding cake design has also enlivened other traditional decorated cakes. Whether for a christening, birthday or anniversary, a decorated cake can be anything the recipient desires and the decorator feels confident to create. The scope and interest is reflected in the increased demand for high-quality cakes and in the number of people who practise the craft at an accomplished level. From small beginnings, the British Sugarcraft Guild has grown into a large organisation with thousands of members countrywide and international outlets ranging as far away from Britain as Australia, South Africa and Japan.

The guild has promoted all aspects of sugar work and cake decorating in particular, providing the general public with an opportunity to gain knowledge or improve basic skills. Through demonstrations, in workshops, exhibitions and the British Sugarcraft Guild magazine, interest in all aspects of sugarcraft has grown and members have acquired extensive and varied skills in many aspects of decorating, such as calligraphy, painting, floristry and modelling.

Cake Decorating Supplies and Courses

This widespread interest has resulted in the broader availability of equipment and ingredients through specialist shops as well as cookshops and many high street outlets. Many specialist companies provide mail order facilities, they often take commissions for cakes and invariably give invaluable advice to their customers. Some better-known companies also run short courses on a range of sugarcraft topics. Courses in cake design and decoration are also popular features of numerous technical college and adult education centre curricula. Privately run classes, increasing in popularity with the growth of the Sugarcraft Guild, also promote an interest in the subject and spread knowledge far and wide. The end result of this initiative is a specialised, yet more individual, approach to the subject of cake decorating.

Since the skill of cake decorating has developed into an art, it has moved on a long way from those stiff-styled white wedding cakes which were heavy in the use of piped adornment. Cake decorating has become a subject for all to enjoy.

NOTES
The Merehurst Cake Book provides an A–Z guide to basic cake making and decorating. The majority of the information is organised in alphabetical order, including hints, tips and essential basic recipes. The symbol * has been used against some terms to indicate that they are explained in a separate entry.

Following the main section, there is a chapter of decorated cakes which includes recipes and instructions for a variety of occasions and different standards of cake decorating skills.

Finally, a quick-reference guide to the quantities and methods for making selected classic cakes completes the text chapters.

A TO Z OF CAKE MAKING AND DECORATING

In this, the main part of the book, you will find a wealth of hints and tips to complement instructions on basic techniques and details of classic methods. From preparing cake tins (pans) to mastering the art of intricate piping, the information is presented in alphabetical order according to subject.

The topic of cake making covers the basic mixtures that are prepared for decoration, among them feather-light sponges used for luscious gâteaux; fine-textured plain cakes for birthday celebrations; airy American sponge cake; and rich fruit cake for traditional British-style wedding feasts – all the recipes needed for the variety of cakes that are ideal for icing and decorating. Towards the end of the book, a glossary-style, quick reference section provides guidelines for making additional classic cakes, many of which are usually served plain, such as Apple Sauce Cake.

Work through this extensive reference section to improve existing skills and to learn new areas of the art of cake design, then turn to the chapter of finished cake designs when you are seeking inspiration for putting the techniques into practice.

A

ACETATE

See papers, coverings and wrappings*.

AIRBRUSH

A precision artist's instrument, which consists of a brush attached to a compressor by a hose. A small cup above the brush is used to hold food colour. A finger trigger regulates the flow of air from the compressor through the hose, cup of colour and a tiny nozzle in the brush to give a fine, even spray. Thin lines are made by holding the nozzle close to the surface and applying gentle pressure on the trigger. By holding the nozzle further away and using more pressure an area of overall colour is achieved. The colour is sprayed on a dry iced surface. Designs or pictures may be created on a cake. Sugar flowers made in white icing may be sprayed with various colours.

The technique is a quick one; however the equipment is expensive and most people require a lot of practice to achieve a reasonable standard, particularly for spraying artistic scenes on cakes. For artists or artistic cake decorators, it is an alternative method for creating elaborate cake designs. Spraying designs on large plaques is useful for beginners.

Remember . . . *Check that the canister of compressed air is full enough to complete the decoration. It's a good idea to keep a spare canister.*

USING AN AIR BRUSH

1 Trace the required outline on oil board, then carefully cut out the shape using a scalpel.

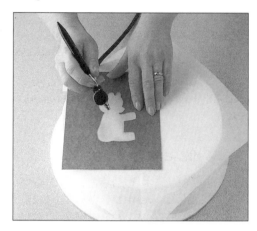

2 Place the oil-board shape on the cake, then mask the surrounding area of cake with paper. Lightly spray the colour over the cut-out shape. Remove the paper and card.

ALBUMEN POWDER

Dried pasteurized egg white in the form of a powder. When dissolved in water it reconstitutes to egg whites and can be used to make royal icing* or meringues.

There are two types: the more readily available, and less expensive, fortified albumen (with added starch and other ingredients) is pale cream in colour and it dissolves easily. Pure hen albumen is a slightly deeper colour cream and it requires more care when mixed with water to ensure it dissolves completely. Both are suitable for use in royal icing. However, the pure hen albumen gives greater bulk to the icing and it is stronger, therefore more suitable for run outs*. The advantages of using albumen powder are that there are no leftover yolks or risk of infection from salmonella bacteria in raw eggs.

Quantities: 22 g (¾ oz/11 tsp) albumen powder to 155 ml (5 fl oz/⅔ cup) water. For a smaller amount use 1 teaspoon albumen powder to 1 tablespoon water.

Use
Place the required amount of lukewarm water in a grease-free bowl (glass, china or metal). Using a fine nylon sieve, sift the albumen into the bowl, whisking well all the time. Whisk until the whites are frothy. Use a clean wooden spoon to gradually beat in sifted icing (confectioners') sugar.

SECRETS OF SUCCESS

If the albumen powder does not dissolve immediately, leave it to stand for a few hours, then whisk it again.

AMERICAN FROSTING

Frosting is quick to make and easily applied to the cake. The frosting sets quickly with a crisp crust and it has a smooth texture produced by boiling the syrup to the correct temperature. Frosting is made by whisking sugar syrup into egg whites. Care must be taken when boiling sugar. Use a small heavy saucepan to make the syrup and melt the sugar over a low heat until it has dissolved completely. Raise the heat and boil the syrup to 115°C (240°F). *Do not stir the syrup while it boils* otherwise it will form white crystals. As soon as the syrup is at the right temperature whisk it into the egg whites. See crème au beurre* for temperature test.

Use
Swirl frosting on plain cakes and Victoria sandwich cakes. Have the cake ready as the frosting sets quickly once made.

Colour and flavour Frosting is usually left plain white but it can be flavoured by adding coffee essence or cocoa powder

dissolved to a smooth thin paste in hot water. Add while whisking in the syrup.

SECRETS OF SUCCESS

If the syrup splashes up the sides of the pan as it boils, sugar crystals will form on the hot pan and drop back into the syrup. These may cause the rest of the syrup to crystallize in which case it will become useless. Keep a cup of water and a pastry brush at hand, then brush the inside of the pan with a very little water to prevent any syrup from forming crystals. When whisking the syrup into the egg whites, use dry, warmed blades in the food mixer. Pour the syrup into the bowl avoiding the blades.

RECIPES

QUICK MERINGUE FROSTING
Sufficient to cover an 18 cm (7 in) cake.

185 g (6 oz/¾ cup) caster (superfine) sugar
1 large egg white
pinch of cream of tartar
●

1 Combine ingredients in a grease-free heatproof bowl. Place over a saucepan of simmering water; whisk constantly until mixture thickens and stands in soft peaks.

2 Remove from heat. Whisk until cool. Use immediately.

AMERICAN FROSTING
Firm outside and soft underneath, this meringue icing may be folded into fruit mousses, custard fillings or buttercreams. Follow the step-by-step method. Sufficient to cover a 20 cm (8 in) cake.

250 g (8 oz/1 cup) granulated sugar
pinch of cream of tartar
60 ml (4 tbsp) water
2 egg whites
●

1 Using the sugar, cream of tartar and measured water, make a syrup and boil the mixture until it registers 115°C/240°F on a sugar (candy) thermometer. Alternatively, test by dropping about 2.5 ml ($\frac{1}{2}$ tsp) syrup into a small bowl of cold water. If you can mould it to a soft ball between your fingers, the syrup is ready.

2 Whisk the egg whites in a clean, grease-free bowl until very stiff. Holding the pan of syrup high above the bowl, pour it in carefully in a steady stream, constantly whisking the mixture with a balloon whisk until all the syrup has been incorporated.

3 Whisk in any flavouring or colouring, then continue to whisk until soft peaks form when the whisk is lifted. Quickly spread the frosting over the prepared cake, drawing it into peaks or swirls with a warm dry palette knife.

ANGELICA

The crystallized stalk from the plant of that name. Angelica grows well in this country and the stalks may be crystallized (or candied) at home but it is a long process, taking about fourteen days.

Commercial angelica is sold in strips and it is often coated in excess sugar. Food colour is also added to most types.

Use
As a decoration on informal cakes, usually with American frosting*, buttercream* and chocolate*. Cut diagonally, angelica is used to resemble leaves.

> *QUICK TIP*
> *Soak angelica very briefly in hot water to make it pliable and to remove surplus sugar. Dry well before use.*

ANGLES

If you are confused by the various angles referred to in cake decorating instructions,

buy a small plastic protractor and draw the angles on paper. Use the drawing as a visual guide. As a rough guide, a perfectly 'square' corner, or upright, has an angle of 90°. An icing ruler held at 45° would come halfway between the flat surface and the upright of a square corner.

APRICOT GLAZE

Apricot glaze is made by boiling apricot jam, then sieving it to remove pieces of fruit. The glaze should be used while it is warm. Bring the jam to the boil in a small saucepan over low heat, then sieve it into a bowl. Apricot jam is used for its delicate flavour which complements marzipan*. Strongly flavoured fruit jams would give the finished cake a distinct taste. Red jam shows up when the cake is cut. Sieved jelly marmalade may be used instead.

Use
The glaze is brushed over cakes before applying marzipan. The jam sets and keeps the marzipan firmly in place. It is also used as a coating for fresh or canned fruit, for example when decorating gâteaux*.

Keeping Qualities Make apricot glaze in small quantities as you need it. Any leftovers may be stored in a covered container in the refrigerator and used up quickly. Do not return the glaze to the jam pot – it is likely to have small crumbs in it and it is no longer sterile so it will not keep well.

> *QUICK TIP*
> *Cheaper jams contain less fruit and are more suitable for making a glaze. Some jams which contain very few pieces of fruit may be boiled and used without sieving. The jam must be boiled and perfectly clean utensils should be used to prevent any risk of a mould forming between the marzipan and cake.*

RECIPE

APRICOT GLAZE
Makes about 250 ml (8 fl oz/1 cup).

250 g (8 oz/1 cup) apricot jam
30 ml (2 tbsp) lemon juice
•

1 Warm the jam in a small saucepan until melted. Press through a sieve into a clean pan and stir in lemon juice.

2 Boil for 30 seconds, then remove from heat. Cool slightly, then apply the glaze to cake with a clean brush.

VARIATIONS

Blackcurrant Glaze A dark glaze is more appropriate for chocolate cakes. Follow recipe above, but substitute blackcurrant jam.

Marmalade Glaze As above, but substitute orange, lime or ginger marmalade for jam.

Strawberry Glaze A rosy glaze with a distinct flavour, this is useful for coating a gâteau decorated with strawberries. As above but substitute good-quality strawberry jam for best flavour.

Honey Glaze As above but substitute clear honey for the jam. The honey does not need sieving but it should be boiled for 1 minute. Do not overboil or the honey will darken. Useful on fruit cakes topped with whole nuts (placed on the mixture before baking). The honey glaze should be applied just before serving.

BAKING TINS

Heavy-duty, well-made tins (pans) will last for years and they will promote even cooking. Heat penetration through thin, inferior tins (pans) can result in cakes with overcooked sides. Strong tins (pans) have even bases which will not warp. Cake decorating shops often hire out good-quality tins (pans) including those of unusual and novelty shapes. Adjustable tins (pans) are also available.

Preparing Tins
● For rich fruit cake, line the tin (pan) with one or two thicknesses of greaseproof paper. Tie a piece of brown paper or corrugated paper around the outside of the tin (pan).
● For Victoria sandwich cake, base-line the tins (pans).
● For Madeira cake, line the tin (pan) with one thickness of greaseproof paper.
● For fatless sponge, ensure the tin (pan) is evenly greased and given a dusting of flour. Do not mark the interior of the prepared tin (pan) with your fingers – one small uncoated area will make the sponge stick.
● For small cakes, place double-thick paper cake cases in patty tins (pans). This will keep the cakes in shape as they cook.

Measuring the Volume of Tins Measure the volume of a tin (pan) to decide on the quantity of mixture required. Take a tin (pan) for which the quantity is known and fill it with water. Pour the water into the tin (pan) you wish to use, then measure the volume of water. If the second tin (pan) holds less water, reduce the quantities of cake mixture proportionally; increase the quantities if the tin (pan) holds more water.

Baking Frames These are tins (pans) without a base, which makes it difficult to judge the quantity of mixture required. A foolproof method is to stand the tin on a level work surface and line it with a large waterproof plastic bag. Pour the water into the lined frame, then compare the volume with that held in a standard tin (pan) and note if more, or less, mixture is necessary. Increase or decrease the quantity of cake mixture proportionally.

STEP-BY-STEP TO SUCCESS

LINING TINS

Double-line the inside of the tin (pan) with greaseproof or non-stick silicone baking paper and the outside with double-thick brown paper. Stand the tin (pan) on a baking sheet lined with 3 or 4 thicknesses of brown paper. This prevents the side and base of a rich fruit cake from being overcooked at the end of the long cooking time. Without this protection the cake will have a dark, dry crust which will not soften on keeping or maturing.

1 Place the tin (pan) on double-thick greaseproof or non-stick silicone baking paper and draw around the base. Cut out the marked shape with a pair of scissors.

2 Cut a strip of double-thick greaseproof or non-stick paper long enough to wrap around the outside of the tin with a small overlap and to stand 2.5 cm (1 in) above the top of the tin (pan).

3 Brush the base and sides of the tin (pan) with melted fat or oil. Place the cut-out shape in the base of the tin (pan) and smooth out the creases.

Place the double strip of paper inside the tin (pan), pressing well against the sides and creasing the corners sharply.

4 Brush the base and side paper well with melted fat or oil. Place a double-thickness strip of brown paper around the outside of the tin (pan) and tie securely with string.

Line a baking sheet with 3 or 4 layers of brown paper and stand the tin (pan) on top.

BASKET WORK

See also Piping*.

Can be piped in royal icing* over marzipan* on a rich fruit cake*, or in stiff buttercream* on a Victoria sandwich or Madeira cake*. Royal icing needs to be well beaten to achieve sufficient bulk to hold its shape and it should be put in a medium piping bag.

Use stiff buttercream (*not* made with soft margarine) to ensure that the pattern shows in the cream. To pipe buttercream, use a bag made with two layers of paper, or you may find it easier to use several small bags, discarding them when they need refilling.

Icing Tube (Tip) Use an icing tube (tip) specially designed for this work. The basket work tube (tip) has a flat piping end with both edges, or sometimes only one edge, finely serrated. A star tube (tip) may be used but it does not give such a realistic effect.

Piping Technique The most commonly used method is to pipe both the horizontal and vertical strokes with the basket work tube (tip). This way, a large area can be covered with each line and with some practice you will soon become accomplished.

Alternatively, the vertical lines may be piped with a writing tube (tip) and the horizontal lines piped with the basket tube (tip). This method takes longer and care is needed to keep the piping neat but it results in a very realistic appearance.

Basket Work Designs The technique is normally used to create a basket of flowers, with moulded flowers* on top and a tilted

lid. Depending on the number of flowers available, the lid can be raised on both sides with flowers underneath or tilted to one side to show fewer flowers. Basket work may also be used for a hat design, with a cluster of flowers at the front of the brim and flowing sugarpaste or ribbon streamers at the back.

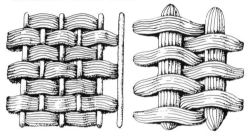

Left: *basket work piped using a basket work tube (tip) and a writing tube (tip)*
Right: *using only the basket work tube (tip)*

QUICK TIP
On a basket of flowers, glue a piece of smooth foil to one side of a cardboard lid and pipe the basket work decoration on the other side. Leave the icing to dry and place the lid in position over the flowers with the foil down. The reflection of the flowers on the foil will add to the beauty and colour of the design.

B

BAS RELIEF

A form of three-dimensional sugarcraft sculpture, with the design standing proud of the background. Bas relief can be modelled directly on the cake surface or made on a plaque. The outline is traced directly on the firm, dry iced surface. Layers of sugarpaste* are moulded within the outline to build up the three-dimensional shape.

If a figure is modelled, make any covering of clothes from pastillage* as this may be rolled out thinly and draped into material-like folds, pleats or flounces. The technique is used on two finished cakes, Easter Egg Cake, pages 185 to 187, and Saint Nicolas Bas Relief, pages 203 to 205, where detailed instructions demonstrate the technique for specific decorations.

BELL MOULD

An extremely useful mould, available in metal or plastic and in a variety of sizes.

Use
To make bells as decoration for a wedding or celebration cake, with sugar or silk flowers spilling out. Also used to make decorations for Christmas cakes. Cut in half, the bells can be applied flat against the sides of cakes.

A bell mould may also be used to shape novelty figures. Long gowns are the perfect covering for the shape, such as on a choir boy, angel or Father Christmas.

Sugar Bells Made in the same way as sand pies! Slightly dampen caster (superfine) sugar with water. To test for the correct consistency, squeeze some dampened sugar in a tightly closed fist and it should show finger impressions. Pack the mould, level off the top and immediately turn out the sugar on to a level surface. Once the outside of the sugar shape is dry enough to be picked up, the middle can be scooped out using the handle of a small spoon. Leave the bells to dry in the sun or in a warm room.

SECRETS OF SUCCESS

Granulated sugar may be used – the bell will not have such a smooth surface as those made with caster (superfine) sugar but the larger sugar crystals add a sparkle. Wipe out the mould with absorbent kitchen paper after moulding each bell, to remove any damp sugar that is clinging to it.

Coloured Bells Colour can be worked into the sugar using the fingertips or the water may be coloured. Remember that the sugar will reduce the strength of the colour.

Lace Bells Grease the outside of a bell mould with white vegetable fat. Using royal icing* and a no. 0 or 1 writing tube (tip), pipe a design of trellis* or cornelli* work over the mould. When dry place near a source of heat to melt the grease, then carefully slip the bell off the mould. Handle carefully as these are very fragile. Make more than the number required for the cake to allow for breakages.

Piped Bells Use a writing tube (tip) and royal icing. Pipe large dots on wax or non-stick paper. While the icing is still wet, pipe smaller dots on top. When the outsides of the bells are firm enough to handle, the centre can be scooped out with a thin, sharp implement.

PROFESSSIONAL TIP

To pipe bells with a perfect circular base, keep the point of the tube (tip) down inside the blob of icing. The blob of icing will then grow in size from the middle, keeping the edges neat.

Moulded Bells Use pastillage* and work a small piece until smooth and free of cracks. Form the pastillage into a rounded, bell-like shape, about half the size of the bell mould. Dust the surface of the paste and the inside of the mould with cornflour (corn starch). Place the rounded end of the paste into the mould and keep smoothing it gently with your fingers and thumb into the centre of the mould until the paste completely covers the inside of the mould. The paste should be thinner towards the edge. Take the bell out of the mould occasionally to ensure the paste is not sticking. Remove any excess paste around the edge by pressing firmly against the rim of the mould.

Black Forest Cake
see page 177

Rose Gâteau
see page 178

ॐ

Petits Fours
see page 179

Chestnut Cream Log
see page 180

BLOSSOM CUTTER

Used to make small flowers which are useful as an individual decoration as well as for combining with larger blossoms. Cutters may be made of metal or plastic and they are used to stamp out flowers in one piece. Some cutters are of the plunger type, incorporating a spring-loaded plunger to curve the flower once it is stamped out.

Stamping Out Flowers Roll out either sugarpaste* or pastillage*. The latter may be rolled thinly to make finer flowers. Use the chosen blossom cutter to stamp out the shapes and immediately place them on a piece of foam. Use a modelling tool* with a rounded end to depress the centre of the flower – this makes the petals curve upwards slightly and look natural.

Varying textures of foam will give a different curve to the flowers depending on how easily it compresses when pressed. Lightly dust the surface of the foam with cornflour (corn starch) to prevent the blossoms from sticking.

Plunger Flowers The plunger cutter with a spring mechanism is quicker to use. Stamp out the flower from the rolled-out paste, then hold the cutter over the foam and depress the spring plunger. The flower will be pushed out of the cutter and the plunger curves the petals at the same time.

BLOSSOM TINTS

Also known as petal dust and dusting powder. Fine powders in pale and deep colours. Used for dusting on flowers or a dry iced surface to give a background tint or variation in shades of colour. They are also useful for dusting the edge of frills. Different powders may be mixed to create a wide variety of colours. Silver and gold lustre add a glamorous sparkle to celebration cakes.

Using Blossom Tints They may be used to colour royal icing* but this is an expensive method best reserved for matching the icing to a dusted decoration.

When piping coloured lace* work, it is better to add powder to royal icing instead of paste colours which generally contain glycerine. They attract moisture from the atmosphere and, in turn, this could soften the lace slightly on standing.

Blossom tints are useful for colouring white chocolate, for example to make moulded roses. Liquid colour is not suitable as it reacts with the chocolate to spoil the texture, causing it to separate, become oily and stiffen.

Applying Blossom Tints A common complaint is that the powder will not stick to the dry icing. This can be due to the fact that there is insufficient powder on the brush. Use a good-quality brush with a rounded end; cheap brushes do not pick up enough powder. Place some blossom tint on a flat surface and load the brush by bouncing it on its side in the powder. When the brush is well loaded apply the powder to the area to be coloured.

SECRETS OF SUCCESS

To soften the colour of a dark blossom tint, mix in a little white blossom tint. If cornflour (corn starch) or icing (confectioners') sugar are used the tint does not adhere as thoroughly to the surface of the icing.

BOARDS

The important point to remember when buying boards is to have the right size and thickness for the cake.

Weight A light cake can be placed on a thin gâteau board or cake card. Heavy fruit cakes need a cake drum, either 1 cm ($\frac{1}{2}$ in) or 1.4 cm ($\frac{5}{8}$ in) thick. Extra large, heavy cakes are best put on two boards of the same size which are stuck together with icing. Attach board edging to cover the seam.

A useful shape of board for either square or round cakes

Size and Shape Buy boards at least 5–7.5 cm (2–3 in) bigger than the cakes. This will keep your hands away from the sides of the cakes, avoiding damaging the icing and decoration as you lift the cakes. Boards used for wedding cakes* must balance with the depth as well as the width of the cakes. Very deep cakes require boards about 13 cm (5 in) larger than their size.

A cake decorated with collars* will require a cake board at least 10 cm (4 in) larger than its size. This will enable the cake to be lifted up without damaging the collar, also the wider board will balance the width of the collar.

On wedding cakes it is important not to overshadow the cakes, so the chosen board should not be larger than the cake of the tier below.

Some manufacturers still make boards to the imperial standard of a half inch. Metric boards are slightly thicker at 2 cm. When making a tiered cake, be sure to use boards of the same thickness throughout. If the boards are to be trimmed with ribbon bands, these should also be of the same thickness.

Fruit cakes should always go on 1 cm ($\frac{1}{2}$ in) thick drum cake boards or wooden

boards to take the weight of the cake. The other boards, known as double-thick and single-thick cards are only suitable for sponge or novelty cakes.

Gone are the days when boards were either round or square; now they are available in many different shapes. They match the shapes of baking tins, for example petal shaped, heart shaped, hexagonal, oval and others. The board that you choose does not always have to be the same shape as the cake; for instance, a round cake can look attractive on a petal-shaped board. It all depends on the effect that you want to achieve. Most of the unusual cake boards come in three or four sizes to match the size of the tins. This is fine for most designs; however, if you are planning runout collars you may find that the collar will extend beyond the board. In this case, it is preferable to make the board yourself.

Jig-saw Boards Unusual and substantial cake boards may be cut with a jig saw and made to your own design from 1 cm ($\frac{1}{2}$ in) thick wood or wood-veneered chipboard. These may then be left plain for some novelty designs decorating the sides with ribbon, or they may be covered to complement the iced cake.

A selection of boards cut to individual designs using templates and a jig saw

Covering Boards Shapes can be cut out of chipboard and covered in embossed silver or gold paper (available from cake decorating suppliers). The easiest way to cover a board is to lay the paper upside down on a clean firm surface. Place the board on top and draw around it. Allow extra paper outside the shape for the depth of the board plus 1 cm ($\frac{1}{2}$ in) to turn under.

Paste the paper, leaving the edge unpasted, and place the board on the centre of it. Carefully slide the board to the edge of the table and use the palm of your hand to press the paper against the sides of the board. Turn the excess paper neatly over the board edges.

On a round board make cuts in the paper at 5 cm (2 in) intervals so that it sticks flat on the base.

For squared boards, or other shapes with corners, make slits into the corners of the paper. Paste and press down the overlapping sections neatly.

Cut out a piece of white paper slightly smaller than the board and paste it on the base to cover the edges of embossed paper. Allow the board to dry before use.

QUICK TIP
Do not use cooking foil to cover boards – it tears very easily.

BOUGHT DECORATIONS

Most cake decorating suppliers offer a wide variety of high-quality, ready-made decorations. Use them creatively to enhance simple cakes, avoiding having to practise techniques which are unfamiliar, or simply to save time. Here are just a few examples.

Bride and Groom Top Decoration: Not considered fashionable by many brides; however, some are very pretty.

Crystallized Flowers: Many varieties are available and they are usually sold by weight.

Crystallized or Candied Orange or Lemon Slices: Useful as a decoration on buttercream*. These vary from 'jellied' sugar-coated orange and lemon decorations to slices of fruit that have been candied (recognize these by their size) and may be cut up.

Dragee: A small, hard sugar ball available in colours but usually silver. The surface of dragees can melt if placed on moist icing.

Heather Sprays: Attractive for decorating a man's cake as they are not too feminine.

Pastillage Flowers: Expensive due to the time involved in making them. Usually sold in a spray, they add a professional touch to a cake covered with sugarpaste* or royal icing*.

Piped Flowers: Royal icing flowers are available in many varieties and colours. Useful when time is short or if you are not skilled at piping flowers. May be used on formal cakes.

Silk Flowers: A quick, attractive form of decoration. Place different shapes together to create interesting sprays and add some small flowers. As well as those on sale in cake decorating shops, look out for flower sprays in gift shops and garden centres. Large sprays may be split to give lots of tiny flower heads.

Silver Horseshoes: Not particularly fashionable; however, they are used on simple cakes. Made in different sizes, the smaller ones may be added discreetly as part of piped decorations.

BRIAR ROSES

These flowers are easy to make. Use a briar rose cutter to cut the petals to make briar roses. Available in different sizes, a cutter will always give a better result than a template because of the sharp cutting edge.

Do not cut too many petals out at once or they will dry out. Soften the edges of the petals with a modelling tool to thin and gently flute them. Place in a mould to dry. Lift some of the petals in the mould and place tiny balls of plastic wrap between the petals. This will make the flowers look more lifelike by lifting and curving the petals instead of leaving them flat and lacking natural movement. When dry, use tweezers to remove the balls of plastic wrap taking care not to break the petals.

Making a Mould Cut out a 7.5 cm (3 in) circle of greaseproof or non-stick paper. Fold the paper into four and crease the folds. Open out and cut along one of the creases to the centre of the paper. Overlap the two cut edges and stick down. The mould can be adjusted to make it smaller or larger by reducing or increasing the overlap.

Stamens The stamens need to be added with care. The quickest way to make a flower centre is to press a small ball of paste on a piece of tulle, or on a nylon sieve, to make an impression of the pattern. Place this paste in the centre of the rose.

Commercial stamens need to be curved to follow the movement of the petals. Take a few stamens, fold them in two and bend their stalks over your forefinger before cutting off the excess stem.

QUICK TIP

Yellow cotton makes very realistic stamens. Wind the cotton about sixty times around the end of a pencil. Slide the cotton off and slip a piece of thin wire through the centre hole, then twist it together securely. Tie a double thickness of cotton around the base of the shank of cotton, as near to the wire as possible. This will keep the threads together. Cut the opposite end of the loop of threads, curving the cut down slightly at either side. Moisten the tip of the threads and dip them carefully into brown food colouring or cocoa powder.

BRIDGE WORK

The basis for extension work*, bridge work supports the lines of icing (curtain work*) keeping them away from the cake.

Bridge work is a technique for the more experienced decorator. It takes time, patience, good eyesight and a steady hand. It is the name given to the overpiped scalloping that lies under the vertically piped curtain work which makes up the edging known as extension work.

Marking the Scallops Cut a template to the exact size and shape of the scallops to fit the cake. The marked line for the scallops should leave sufficient space for a row of small shells to be piped around the base of the cake.

Piping Bridge Work Pipe a row of shells around the base of the cake and leave to dry. Pipe the first line of icing on the scallops and leave to dry before attempting to pipe another row on top. Leave each row to dry otherwise the built-up scallop could collapse.

The choice of writing tube (tip) to pipe the lines depends on your skill, the time available and patience.

SECRETS OF SUCCESS

Once the bridge work is dry, carefully brush thinned-down royal icing over it to strengthen any weak areas.

STEP-BY-STEP TO SUCCESS

BRIDGE WORK

When planning the cake design, remember that long extension lines are more difficult to pipe without breaking. Cut a piece of greaseproof paper the same length and depth as the circumference and height of the cake. Fold the paper into the required number of sections. Unfold the paper and design the first section.

Tilt the cake away from you when piping bridge work; towards you when piping extension work. Work with the cake at eye level.

1 Tilt the cake away from you. Using fresh royal icing and a no. 2 tube, pipe a loop between two dot marks. The loop must lie flat against the side of the cake and it must not touch the board. Use a damp brush to touch the icing into place.

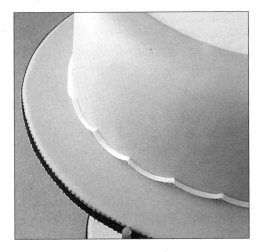

2 Build out the bridge using a no. 1 tube, adding a further three layers of loops. Allow each layer to dry to prevent sagging or breaking. Pipe each layer directly on the one below to create an even bridge. Pipe a further three layers using a no. 0 tube.

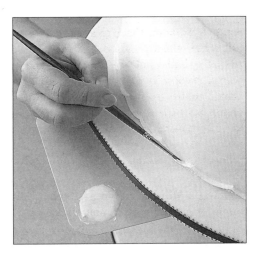

3 When the bridge work is complete, icing of runout consistency can be painted on the loops to neaten and strengthen the bridge. Attractive effects can be achieved by painting with coloured icing or by adding petal dust when dry.

BRODERIE ANGLAISE

An embroidery technique which forms a successful basis for a cake decorating design. Small holes of different shapes are cut into soft paste and later royal icing* is piped around them. The designs are marked and cut in thinly rolled sugar-paste*. The paste is then applied to the surface of an iced cake. Broderie anglaise and ribbon insertion* go together well.

Equipment Sets of cutters may be bought to stamp out designs, giving a sharp, exact cut out. Alternatively, holes can be made with a paint brush handle, a knitting needle, the end of a writing tube (tip), aspic cutters, a tiny blossom cutter or a metal skewer.

Uses
- On a frill around a cake.
- As bands of embroidery on the top or around the side of a cake.
- To decorate a bib for a christening cake.
- To surround a plaque*.

Applying Broderie Anglaise to a Cake
Be careful not to stretch the paste when picking it up. It is a good idea to roll out the paste on a thin piece of card and use this to assist in lifting the paste.

Piping When the paste is dry, use a fine writing tube (tip) to pipe fine lines close to the edge of each cut-out shape. Use the same tube (tip) to pipe a linking pattern of embroidery work directly on the surface of the paste. Use a fine, damp paint brush to take away any surplus ends of icing.

DESIGN IDEA
Stamp out broderie anglaise shapes on a piece of white sugarpaste, trimmed to overhang the cake loosely like a tablecloth. Arrange this as an overlay on a base covering of coloured sugarpaste.

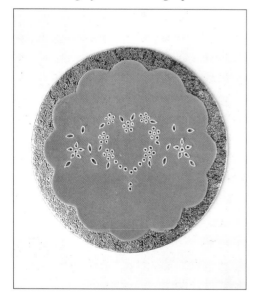

All holes are made with a paint brush handle, then outlined with a no. 0 icing tube (tip)

BRUSH EMBROIDERY

A technique used mainly to create floral designs. A piped royal icing* outline is brushed inwards while still soft, to resemble petals and leaves. The technique is illustrated in the step-by-step instructions which accompany the Basket Cake recipe, see page 207.

Marking the Design Trace the design on greaseproof paper or non-stick paper. Hold the paper firmly on top of the iced cake or plaque* and scribe the design through the paper.

QUICK TIP
Use a lipstick pencil to trace over the outline showing through on the back of the paper. Place on cake with the lipstick lines underneath and draw the outline on top using a HB pencil.

Semi-Permanent Transfer Use for embossing designs on a soft sugarpaste* or pastillage* surface. Trace the reverse image of the design on firm card. Use a no. 1 icing tube (tip) and royal icing to outline the pattern, erasing any ends of icing with a fine, damp paint brush. Leave to dry. Press into the surface of soft sugarpaste or pastillage to make an impression of the piped design.

Instead of piping on card, place the drawn design under a piece of glass or perspex and pipe the outline to use as above.

Piping and Brushing When piping on the cake, add a small amount of piping gel* to the royal icing to give a smooth texture and to stop it from drying out too quickly.

Always start on the outside edge of the design and work on one section at a time. Pipe the outline and brush it immediately with a dampened brush. The brush must be good quality and have a rounded edge. A brush with a pointed tip will make sharp lines in the icing. Brush the icing down the whole of the petal to cover it completely with a thin film. Pipe areas of the flower or design that are meant to be further away thinly, and the foreground area slightly thicker. This gives the design a three-dimensional effect.

Colour Pipe using white icing and moisten the brush with coloured water to achieve a variegated effect. Alternatively, once dry the brush embroidery can be dusted with blossom tint*. Brush embroidery designs show up well by piping white on a coloured base.

> *QUICK TIP*
> *When practising this technique, pipe in icing coloured differently from the base. This way you will be able to see if you are brushing the icing correctly.*

BUTTERCREAM

Also known as butter icing. Buttercream is made by creaming sifted icing (confectioners') sugar with either unsalted butter or soft margarine. This may be done by hand or by using a food mixer. The longer the buttercream is beaten the lighter it will become, both in colour and texture, as more air is incorporated.

Equal quantities of fat and sugar will give a buttercream which is easy to use both as a coating and for piping, and which is not too sweet. However, increasing the quantity of icing (confectioners') sugar gives greater bulk. The resulting icing is very sweet but not as rich in fat as when made with equal quantities. Up to double the quantity of icing (confectioners') sugar may be used to fat, especially when adding fruit juice.

STEP-BY-STEP TO SUCCESS

BASIC BUTTERCREAM
A simple butter icing which may be made in advance. The only drawback with buttercream is that its natural colour makes some tints difficult to achieve. Follow the step-by-step method opposite.

Sufficient to fill and coat a 20 cm (8 in) layer cake.

185 g (6 oz/¾ cup) butter, softened
375 g (12 oz/2¼ cups) icing
(confectioners') sugar
30 ml (2 tbsp) milk or fruit juice

1 Place the softened butter in a large bowl. For a less rich icing, a soft butter and vegetable spread may be used. Grated citrus rind may be mixed in at this stage. Gradually stir in sugar, sifting it over the butter, then beat hard with a wooden spoon or electric mixer until pale, light and fluffy. A little liquid – milk, or orange or lemon juice – may be needed if a soft or flavoured icing is required.

2 A little flavouring or food colouring may be added during the final beating. Pale colours may be altered slightly by the butter content of the icing. If chopped glacé (candied) fruits or nuts are added, fold them in at the end with a metal spoon.

Uses
Buttercream can be used to fill cakes and to coat the top and sides of gâteaux*. It can also be used to cover and decorate small fancies. A smooth, thin undercoat of buttercream may be spread on cakes before they are covered with sugarpaste*. As a general rule, depending on the depth of the cake, 250 g (8 oz/1 cup) fat and 250 g (8 oz/1½ cups) icing (confectioners') sugar will make sufficient buttercream to fill and coat the top and sides of a 20 cm (8 in) round cake, leaving enough for piping a simple border.

Colour and Flavour When colouring buttercream, you may like to complement the flavour with a matching shade. For example, pale green with peppermint, yellow with lemon juice and finely grated peel. Alternatively, vanilla essence gives a good flavour. Lemon curd blends well with buttercream to give a delicate flavour.

Melted chocolate can be added but do make sure the buttercream is at room temperature otherwise the chocolate may set as it is mixed in. If this does happen, gently warm the buttercream over hot water to soften the chocolate, mix well, then leave until it cools to a usable consistency. Coffee, chocolate and cocoa powder impart both colour and flavour.

SECRETS OF SUCCESS

Do not add dry cocoa powder to buttercream. Blend 1–2 tablespoons cocoa powder with a little hot water to make a smooth, creamy paste. When cool, add to the buttercream. This method ensures a superior flavour.

Applying Buttercream to Cakes The buttercream must be at room temperature. If it is too firm it will pull crumbs away from the cake. Soften the buttercream by beating it over warm water or beat in a very small amount of hot water. The buttercream must be soft enough to spread easily. Use a firm palette knife and first coat the top of the cake with a smooth layer of buttercream, then lift the cake on the palm of your hand and carefully spread buttercream around the side. A second coat may be applied if necessary, in which case chill the first layer of buttercream to firm up first.

Piping with Buttercream Use an open star tube (tip) and a large piping bag. Buttercream is the easiest medium to use for piping. However, when piping a large area, buttercream may begin to melt from the heat of the hands. To prevent this use two thicknesses of paper when making the piping bag or use a fabric bag. Keep your hands as cool as possible.

If a paper piping bag softens around the tube (tip) the edge of the paper can slip between the grooves in the metal. This 'smudges' the piping so that the pattern does not show clearly. Similarly, if the buttercream is too warm and the fat begins to soften or melt the piping will not have a clearly defined pattern.

Decorating Ideas Apply the design to the top of the cake first. Use a palette knife held with the index finger firmly placed on the blade.
Swirled Effect: Draw the tip of the knife through the buttercream swirling it from side to side.
Snow Scene: Use the back of the knife to pull up the buttercream into peaks.
Ridges: Use the handle of a spoon to make ridges in the buttercream, working in diamond or square patterns.
Serrated Scraper: Use this to make fine, even ridges around the side or over the top of a cake.

Freezing Freeze for up to 3 months. Take buttercream out of the freezer the day before it is needed and soften once defrosted.

AMERICAN PARFAIT

American Parfait is preferable to butter-cream for coloured icings, since the vegetable fat (shortening) has no definite colour of its own. Sufficient to fill and coat a 20 cm (8 in) cake.

185 g (6 oz/³⁄₄ cup) white vegetable fat (shortening), softened
375 g (12 oz/2¼ cups) icing (confectioners') sugar
30 ml (2 tbsp) milk

•

1 Make the icing following the step-by-step instructions for Basic Buttercream.

2 Remember to add colouring sparingly (if used).

MERINGUE BUTTERCREAM

Sufficient to cover a 20 cm (8 in) cake.

125 g (4 oz/½ cup) butter, softened
1 quantity Quick Meringue Frosting, see page 11

•

1 Beat the butter until pale and creamy.

2 Gradually add the meringue mixture, beating until smooth and fluffy.

BUTTERCREAM PASTE

This versatile icing can be rolled out like marzipan and used to cover the top of a cake, making a dry, flat surface for piping and decorating. If a white fat (shortening) is used, the paste can be tinted for special occasion cakes and the trimmings can be moulded to make flowers. It may be made in advance and briefly stored but should not be refrigerated.

SECRETS OF SUCCESS

Wrap buttercream paste in greaseproof paper, then place in a polythene bag. If paste becomes too dry to handle, sprinkle surface with cooled boiled water and leave well wrapped for several hours. Knead well before use.

BUTTERCREAM PASTE
Makes about 750 g (1½ lb).

60 g (2 oz/¼ cup) butter or white vegetable fat (shortening)
30 ml (2 tbsp) lemon juice
30 ml (2 tbsp) water
625–750 g (1¼–1½ lb/3¼–4½ cups) icing (confectioners') sugar

•

1 Melt the fat with the lemon juice and measured water in a saucepan over low heat. Stir in 185 g (6 oz/1¼ cups) of the icing (confectioners') sugar. Continue to heat, stirring occasionally, for 2–3 minutes or until a few bubbles begin to rise to the surface of the mixture. Do not allow the mixture to boil.

2 Stir in a further 185 g (6 oz/1¼ cups) icing (confectioners') sugar. Remove from heat and pour the mixture into a bowl. Cool slightly, then gradually beat in enough of the remaining sugar to make a soft pliable paste. Beat in colouring and or flavouring, if used, at this stage.

3 Knead paste in the bowl for a few moments, then transfer it to a clean surface which has been lightly dusted with icing (confectioners') sugar. Knead paste until smooth and elastic. The longer the paste is kneaded, the lighter it will become. If not using at once, wrap thoroughly.

BUTTERCREAM ROSES

Make up a stiff buttercream* using unsalted butter and double the quantity of icing (confectioners') sugar to butter. Follow the instructions for piped flowers*. A pretty effect is obtained by using buttercream in two shades, placed side by side in the piping bag, to make a variegated rose.

Leave the roses to firm up in the refrigerator before placing them carefully on the cake. To use the roses straight away, cut out circles of thin marzipan* and slide these up the cocktail stick to form the base of the rose. Pale green marzipan bases make an attractive addition to the roses.

Use Buttercream roses may be used on gâteaux coated with buttercream. Chocolate buttercream may also be used to pipe roses for a chocolate gâteau.

Freezing Open freeze the roses on their backing paper, on a baking tray lined with plastic wrap. Store in a rigid container. When required, peel off the backing paper and immediately place the frozen roses on the cake. Allow to defrost slowly, preferably in the refrigerator. This prevents the roses from being damaged.

SECRETS OF SUCCESS

Soft-textured margarine is not suitable for making buttercream which is to be used for piping roses. Butter sets to a firmer texture when chilled, making the roses easier to handle.

C

CAKES

See also Rich Fruit Cakes.

The basis of good cake decorating is to have a well-made cake of a good shape. Like clothes on a fashion model, icing looks good on a cake that has a good shape. It is disappointing if a high standard of decoration is not matched by eating quality. Here are some suggestions that may help with cake making.

Temperature Keep all ingredients warm. Although recipes use the phrase 'at room temperature', kitchens vary. Consider the heat in a bakery — one reason why the professional baker achieves good results. Warm the bowl and beater in hot water and dry well. Soften the butter or margarine. Never take eggs, butter or margarine straight out of the refrigerator to use, and warm the sugar in the oven for a few minutes.

SECRETS OF SUCCESS

Cold eggs can cause the mixture to curdle. To prevent this happening, place whole eggs in a bowl of hand-hot water for about 5 minutes until they are warmed through.

Eggs Use the size stated in the recipe or in the notes at the front of some cookbooks. Using a different size will give either more or less liquid in proportion to the dry ingredients and change the consistency of the batter. If the recipe or book does not state a size, use standard size 3.

Tins Prepare tins (pans) before mixing a cake. This is particularly important when making a whisked sponge as the mixture must go into the oven directly it is ready or it will collapse.

For sponges and Victoria sandwich mixtures, buy tins (pans) with straight sides and about 3.5 cm (1½ in) deep. This depth will prevent the heat reaching the surface of the cake and causing it to crust over before it has risen properly.

Use the size of tin (pan) stated in the recipe. To ensure equal amounts of mixture are put in two tins (pans), add up the total weight of ingredients, then divide the weight by two. Weigh one empty tin (pan), then add this amount to the half weight of ingredients. Place the tin (pan) on the scale and add mixture until the total weight is reached.

Remember . . . *Baking more than one cake in the oven will create additional steam and increase the cooking time slightly.*

Flour Always sift flour. This is not just to remove lumps – most flour is not lumpy – it lightens the flour by incorporating air. For example, try sifting a cup full of flour into a basin, then pour the flour back into the cup and you will find that there is some left over. The volume of flour has increased because of the air incorporated.

Chocolate Cakes Cocoa powder will give a better flavour if it is blended with boiling water, to make a smooth cream, then cooled before adding to the cake mixture.

Melted chocolate gives a delicious flavour but because of its weight and fat content the resulting cake is usually of the heavier type and not as well risen as those flavoured with cocoa powder.

Keeping Qualities
● One-stage cake or quick-mix cake will keep for about 5 days but it dries out gradually because extra baking powder is used.

● Whisked sponge is best eaten within a day. Being fatless, or containing little fat, it dries out very quickly. However this type of cake freezes well.
● Madeira and Victoria sandwich cakes will keep for up to 2 weeks in an airtight container.
● Rich fruit cake will keep for months. Leave the cake packed in the lining paper from baking. Overwrap in clean greaseproof paper and pack in a polythene bag, plastic wrap, foil or an airtight container.

QUICK TIP
Do not wrap fruit cake directly in foil. The acid content of the fruit will react with the foil, causing it to disintegrate in tiny particles on the surface of the cake.

STEP-BY-STEP TO SUCCESS

VICTORIA SANDWICH

Preheat oven, prepare tins (pans) and set out ingredients, with chosen flavouring. The quantities are suitable for two 20 cm (8 in) round layers or an 18 cm (7 in) square cake. For two 23 cm (9 in) layers or a 20 cm (8 in) square cake, increase quantity of butter to 250 g (8 oz/ 1 cup), caster (superfine) sugar to 250 g (8 oz/1 cup), eggs to 4 and flour to 250 g (8 oz/2 cups).

185 g (6 oz/¾ cup) butter, softened
185 g (6 oz/¾ cup) caster (superfine) sugar
3 eggs, beaten
185 g (6 oz/1½ cups) self-raising flour
●

FLAVOURINGS
Chocolate Replace 30 g (1 oz/¼ cup) flour with an equal weight of cocoa (unsweetened cocoa powder).
Coffee Add 3 tsp instant coffee with flour.
Citrus Add finely grated rind of 1 lemon, lime or orange before adding eggs.

1 Preheat oven to 190°C (375°F/Gas 5). Beat softened butter and sugar together in a bowl, using either a wooden spoon or an electric mixer. When ready, mixture will be pale, light and fluffy. Grated citrus rind may be added at this stage.

2 Add a little egg at a time, beating hard between each addition, until mixture has slackened, then add remaining egg a little more quickly. If eggs are cold or added too quickly, the mixture may curdle. If so, add 1–2 tbsp flour to stabilize mixture.

3 Sift half the flour into the bowl with coffee or cocoa, if using. Fold gently into mixture, using a large metal spoon. Cut through to the bottom of the bowl employing a figure-of-eight action. Repeat with remaining flour. Do not overmix, but stop when all flour has been incorporated.

4 Scrape mixture into prepared cake tins (pans). Spread out evenly. Level surface of mixture with the back of a metal spoon, taking care not to pack it too firmly.

5 Place cake tins on a shelf just above the centre of the oven. Check that tins do not touch each other or the sides of the oven. Bake 3-egg mixture for 20–25 minutes; 4-egg mixture for 25–30 minutes. When cooked, cakes will be golden in colour and they will spring back when gently pressed.

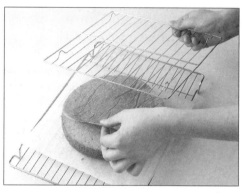

6 Put a piece of greaseproof paper on top of the cake and invert a wire rack on top. Turn cake out onto rack, carefully peel off lining paper and then replace it lightly. Using a second rack, repeat the process to turn the cake the right way up. Remove top paper; and leave the cake to cool. Repeat with second cake.

RECIPE

QUICK MIX SPONGE

The mixture is suitable for a 20 × 30 cm (8 × 12 in) rectangular cake or two 23 cm (9 in) round cakes.

250 g (8 oz/1 cup) soft margarine
250 g (8 oz/1 cup) caster (superfine)
sugar
4 eggs, beaten
250 g (8 oz/2 cups) self-raising flour
3.75 ml (1½ tsp) baking powder
30 ml (2 tbsp) hot water

●

1 Preheat oven to 180°C (350°F/Gas 4) and prepare tins (pans).

2 Beat ingredients for 2–3 minutes with an electric mixer until light and fluffy. Spoon into tin and bake for 25–30 minutes, until golden and firm to touch.

STEP-BY-STEP TO SUCCESS

WHISKED SPONGES

These recipes for whisked sponges are beautifully light, but should be eaten within two days of being baked. Before preparing mixture, preheat oven, prepare tins (pans) and set out ingredients.

GENOESE SPONGE

The quantities below are for two 20 cm (8 in) round layers or an 18 cm (7 in) square cake. For two 23 cm (9 in) layers or a 20 cm (8 in) square cake, increase caster (superfine) sugar to 185 g (6 oz/$\frac{3}{4}$ cup), eggs to 6, plain (all-purpose) flour to 185 g (6 oz/1$\frac{1}{2}$ cups) and butter to 90 g (3 oz/$\frac{1}{3}$ cup).

125 g (4 oz/$\frac{1}{2}$ cup) caster (superfine) sugar
4 eggs
125 g (4 oz/1 cup) plain (all-purpose) flour
50 g (2 oz/$\frac{1}{4}$ cup) butter, melted

•

1 Preheat oven to 180°C (350°F/Gas 4). Combine sugar and eggs in a heatproof bowl. Whisk over hot water until mixture is very thick, pale and creamy. When whisk is lifted, its trail should be visible on the surface of the mixture for a few seconds. Remove bowl from heat and continue whisking for 3–5 minutes more.

2 Sift flour and any dry flavourings. Sift again over the surface of the mixture.

Drizzle the warm butter around the edge of the bowl. Gently fold in, using a figure-of-eight movement to ensure that all flour has been incorporated. Take care not to overbeat or mixture will deflate.

3 Divide mixture between prepared tins (pans), gently tapping the sides against your hand to level the mixture into the corners. Try to avoid using a knife or spoon to spread the mixture. Bake at once. A 4-egg mixture will require 15–20 minutes; a 6-egg mixture 20–25 minutes.

VARIATIONS

The following flavourings may be added to whisked sponges:
Chocolate Replace 15 g ($\frac{1}{2}$ oz/2 tbsp) flour with cocoa (unsweetened cocoa powder).
Coffee Add 2 tsp instant coffee with flour.
Nut Add 1 tbsp ground nuts with flour.

SWISS ROLL

Swiss (jelly) rolls can be prepared in next to no time. The quantities below are suitable for a 20 × 30 cm (8 × 12 in) Swiss roll tin (jelly roll pan).

90 g (3 oz/$\frac{1}{3}$ cup) caster (superfine) sugar
3 eggs
90 g (3 oz/$\frac{3}{4}$ cup) plain (all-purpose) flour
2.5 ml ($\frac{1}{2}$ tsp) baking powder

•

1 Preheat oven to 220°C (425°F/Gas 7). Prepare mixture as for genoese, sifting

C

baking powder with flour. Omit butter. Bake for 7–8 minutes, until firm. Spread out a clean, damp tea-towel. Top with greaseproof paper dusted with caster (superfine) sugar. Have ready filling, or second sheet of paper.

2 Invert cooked sponge onto sugared paper and carefully peel off lining paper. Trim edges all around cake. To assist in rolling, make a shallow cut along one short side of the cake. If using a filling such as jam or fruit butter, warm gently and spread over warm cake. Alternatively, place second sheet of paper on top of sponge.

3 Fold sponge on cut line and roll up, with filling or paper inside. Use sugared paper underneath cake as a guide. Hold rolled sponge in position for a few seconds with join underneath. Peel cake off sugared paper; cool on wire rack. When cold, unroll, remove inner paper and

spread with cream, fudge filling or buttercream. Re-roll.

RECIPES

AMERICAN SPONGE

This is a firm white sponge which is a good base for novelty cakes or petits fours. In advance, preheat oven, prepare tin (pan), and set out ingredients. The quantities below are suitable for a 20 cm (8 in) round or 18 cm (7 in) square cake. Double all quantities for a 23 cm (9 in) round or a 20 cm (8 in) square cake.

125 g (4oz/$\frac{1}{2}$ cup) butter
185 g (6 oz/$\frac{3}{4}$ cup) caster (superfine) sugar
2·5 ml ($\frac{1}{2}$ tsp) vanilla essence (extract)
220 g (7 oz/1$\frac{3}{4}$ cups) plain (all-purpose) flour
10 ml (2 tsp) baking powder
125 ml (4 fl oz/$\frac{1}{2}$ cup) water
4 egg whites

●

1 Preheat oven to 180°C (350°F/Gas 4). Beat butter, caster (superfine) sugar and vanilla together in a bowl until light and fluffy, using either a wooden spoon or an electric mixer. Vanilla sugar may be used instead of caster sugar, in which case omit the essence (extract).

2 Sift flour and baking powder together. Add to creamed mixture alternately with water, beating well between each addition, until smooth. Break down any lumps of flour immediately by pressing them against the side of the bowl. In a clean, dry, grease-free bowl, whisk egg whites until stiff but not dry.

3 Add egg whites to cake mixture a little at a time, folding them in with a clean metal spoon. Use a figure-of-eight action, taking care not to overmix. Scrape mixture into cake tin (pan). Bake 4-egg white mixture for 35–45 minutes; 8-egg white mixture for 55–65 minutes. Remove from tin (pan) as for Victoria Sandwich and leave to cool on a wire rack.

MADEIRA CAKE

A traditional cake with a firm texture. A strip of candied citron peel may be placed on the mixture before cooking the cake. The quantities below are suitable for a 20 cm (8 in) round or an 18 cm (7 in) square cake. For a 23 cm (9 in) or shallow 25 cm (10 in) round or a 20 cm (8 in) square cake, increase butter to 315 g (10 oz), caster (superfine) sugar to 315 g (10 oz/1¼ cups), eggs to 6, self-raising flour to 280 g (9 oz/2¼ cups) and plain (all-purpose) flour to 125 g (4 oz/1 cup).

250 g (8 oz/1 cup) butter, softened
250 g (8 oz/1 cup) caster (superfine) sugar
grated rind and juice of 1 lemon
5 eggs, beaten
220 g (7 oz/1¾ cups) self-raising flour
90 g (3 oz/¾ cup) plain (all-purpose) flour

•

1 Preheat oven to 160°C (325°F/Gas 3). In a warm bowl, cream butter and sugar with lemon rind, using either a wooden spoon or an electric mixer. When ready, mixture will be pale in colour and light and fluffy in consistency. Gradually add eggs, beating well between each addition. Add a little flour, if necessary, to prevent curdling.

2 Sift flours together into a bowl. Sift again into the creamed mixture, adding about one third at a time and folding in carefully with a large metal spoon. Cut through to the bottom of the bowl with a figure-of-eight action. Add sufficient lemon juice to make a soft dropping consistency. If more liquid is needed, add water or milk.

3 Scrape mixture into tin (pan). Bake 5-egg mixture for 1½–1¾ hours; 6-egg mixture for 1¾–2 hours, covering cake with greaseproof paper after about 1 hour to prevent overbrowning. When cooked, a warm skewer inserted into the cake should come out clean. Cool in tin, then invert onto a wire rack.

LIGHT FRUIT CAKE

Makes a 20 cm (8 in) round cake.

225 g (8 oz/1½ cups) mixed dried fruit
75 ml (2½ fl oz/⅓ cup) orange juice or sherry
225 g (8 oz/1 cup) butter
225 g (8 oz/1 cup) caster (superfine) sugar
3 eggs, lightly beaten
250 g (8 oz/2 cups) plain (all-purpose) flour

•

1 Soak the dried fruit in the orange juice or sherry overnight.

2 Set the oven at 160°C (325°F/Gas 3). Cream together the butter and sugar, then gradually add the eggs. If they separate, stir in a little flour before adding more egg mixture.

3 Stir in the fruit, then fold in the flour. Turn the mixture into a well greased 20 cm (8 in) round tin (pan). Bake for 2½ hours or until risen, browned, firm to the touch and cooked through.

VARIATIONS

Light Fruit and Nut Cake Add 60 g (2 oz/½ cup) chopped walnuts with the flour.
Angelica and Fruit Cake Chop a 5 cm (2 in) strip of angelica, then place in a sieve and rinse well with boiling water. Drain and dry on absorbent kitchen paper. Add to the mixture with the fruit.

VICTORIA SANDWICH
AND QUICK MIX TYPE SPONGE CAKES

Tin (pan) Sizes	17.5 cm (7 in) shallow square tin (pan) 20 cm (8 in) round sandwich (shallow) tin (pan)	1 kg (2 lb) loaf tin (pan) 22.5 cm (9 in) ring mould (tube pan)	940 ml (30 fl oz/ 3¾ cups) pudding basin (bowl) or mould	Two 17.5 cm (7 in) shallow square tins (pans) Two 20 cm (8 in) sandwich (shallow) tins (pans)
Self-raising Flour	125 g (4 oz/1 cup)	125 g (4 oz/1 cup)	125 g (4 oz/1 cup)	185 g (6 oz/1½ cups)
Baking Powder	5 ml (1 tsp)	5 ml (1 tsp)	5 ml (1 tsp)	7.5 ml (1½ tsp)
Caster (superfine) sugar	125 g (4 oz/½ cup)	125 g (4 oz/½ cup)	125 g (4 oz/½ cup)	185 g (6 oz/¾ cup)
Soft Margarine	125 g (4 oz/½ cup)	125 g (4 oz/½ cup)	125 g (4 oz/½ cup)	185 g (6 oz/¾ cup)
Medium Eggs	2	2	2	3
Approximate Cooking Time	35 to 40 minutes	30 to 35 minutes	50 to 55 minutes	30 to 35 minutes

Tin (pan) Sizes	1 litre (32 fl oz/ 4 cups) pudding basin (bowl) 17.5 cm (7 in) mould	1 kg (2 lb) loaf tin (pan) 27.5 cm × 17.5 cm (11 in × 7 in) oblong tin (pan)	Two 20 cm (8 in) round sandwich (shallow) tins (pans) Two 22.5 cm (9 in) round sandwich (shallow) tins (pans)	22.5 cm (9 in) deep round or square cake tin (pan)
Self-raising Flour	185 g (6 oz/1½ cups)	185 g (6 oz/1½ cups)	250 g (8 oz/2 cups)	250 g (8 oz/2 cups)
Baking Powder	7.5 ml (1½ tsp)	7.5 ml (1½ tsp)	10 ml (2 tsp)	10 ml (2 tsp)
Caster (superfine) Sugar	185 g (6 oz/¾ cup)	185 g (6 oz/¾ cup)	250 g (8 oz/1 cup)	250 g (8 oz/1 cup)
Soft Margarine	185 g (6 oz/¾ cup)	185 g (6 oz/¾ cup)	250 g (8 oz/1 cup)	250 g (8 oz/1 cup)
Medium Eggs	3	3	4	4
Approximate Cooking Time	60 to 70 minutes	45 to 55 minutes	35 to 40 minutes	55 to 65 minutes

WHISKED SPONGE CAKE

Tin (pan) Sizes	27.5 cm × 17.5 cm (11 in × 7 in) Swiss (jelly) roll tin (pan)	17.5 cm (7 in) shallow square tin (pan) 20 cm (8 in) round sandwich (shallow) tin (pan)	32.5 cm × 22.5 cm (13 in × 9 in) Swiss (jelly) roll tin (pan) Two 17.5 cm (7 in) shallow square tins (pans)	20 cm (8 in) round cake tin (pan)	Two 20 cm (8 in) round sandwich (shallow) tins (pans) Two 17.5 cm (7 in) shallow square tins (pans)	17.5 cm (7 in) square cake tin (pan)
Medium Eggs	2	2	3	3	4	4
Caster (superfine) Sugar	50 g (2 oz/ $\frac{1}{4}$ cup)	50 g (2 oz/ $\frac{1}{4}$ cup)	90 g (3 oz/ $\frac{1}{3}$ cup)	90 g (3 oz/ $\frac{1}{3}$ cup)	125 g (4 oz/ $\frac{1}{2}$ cup)	125 g (4 oz/ $\frac{1}{2}$ cup)
Plain (all-purpose) Flour	50 g (2 oz/ $\frac{1}{2}$ cup)	50 g (2 oz/ $\frac{1}{2}$ cup)	90 g (3 oz/ $\frac{3}{4}$ cup)	90 g (3 oz/ $\frac{3}{4}$ cup)	125 g (4 oz/ 1 cup)	125 g (4 oz/ 1 cup)
Baking Powder	2.5 ml ($\frac{1}{2}$ tsp)	2.5 ml ($\frac{1}{2}$ tsp)	2.5 ml ($\frac{1}{2}$ tsp)	2.5 ml ($\frac{1}{2}$ tsp)	2.5 ml ($\frac{1}{2}$ tsp)	2.5 ml ($\frac{1}{2}$ tsp)
Approximate Cooking Time	10 to 15 minutes	20 to 25 minutes	10 to 15 minutes	30 to 35 minutes	20 to 25 minutes	30 to 35 minutes

QUICK MADEIRA CAKE

These ingredients can be used for a one-stage cake as an alternative to the traditional recipe.

Tin (pan) Sizes	15.5 cm (6 in) square 17.5 cm (7 in) round	17.5 cm (7 in) square 20 cm (8 in) round	20 cm (8 in) square 22.5 cm (9 in) round	22.5 cm (9 in) square 25 cm (10 in) round
Plain (all-purpose) Flour	250g (8 oz/2 cups)	375g (12 oz/3 cups)	500g (1 lb/4 cups)	560g (1 lb 2 oz/4$\frac{1}{4}$ cups)
Baking Powder	5 ml (1 tsp)	7.5 ml (1$\frac{1}{2}$ tsp)	10 ml (2 tsp)	12.5 ml (2$\frac{1}{2}$ tsp)
Caster (superfine) Sugar	185 g (6 oz/$\frac{3}{4}$ cup)	315 g (10 oz/1$\frac{1}{4}$ cups)	440 g (14 oz/1$\frac{3}{4}$ cups)	500 g (1 lb/2 cups)
Soft Margarine	185 g (6 oz/$\frac{3}{4}$ cup)	315 g (10 oz/1$\frac{1}{4}$ cups)	440 g (14 oz/1$\frac{3}{4}$ cups)	500 g (1 lb/2 cups)
Medium Eggs	3	5	7	8
Milk or Citrus Juice	30 ml (2 tbsp)	45 ml (3 tbsp)	52.5 ml (3$\frac{1}{2}$ tbsp)	60 ml (4 tbsp)
Approximate Cooking Time	1$\frac{1}{4}$ to 1$\frac{1}{2}$ hours	1$\frac{1}{2}$ to 1$\frac{3}{4}$ hours	1$\frac{3}{4}$ to 2 hours	1$\frac{3}{4}$ to 2 hours

GENOESE SPONGE CAKE

Tin (pan) Sizes	32.5 cm × 22.5 cm (13 in × 9 in) Two 17.5 cm (7 in) square Two 20 cm (8 in) round sandwich	Two 20 cm (8 in) shallow square Two 22.5 cm (9 in) round sandwich (shallow)	22.5 cm (9 in) deep square 25 cm (10 in) deep round
Medium Eggs	4	6	8
Caster (superfine) Sugar	125 g (4 oz/$\frac{1}{2}$ cup)	185 g (6 oz/$\frac{3}{4}$ cup)	250 g (8 oz/1 cup)
Plain (all-purpose) Flour	125 g (4 oz/1 cup)	185 g (6 oz/1$\frac{1}{2}$ cups)	250 g (8 oz/2 cups)
Unsalted (sweet) Butter, melted	50 g (2 oz/$\frac{1}{4}$ cup)	90 g (3 oz/$\frac{1}{3}$ cup)	125 g (4 oz/$\frac{1}{2}$ cup)
Approximate Cooking Time	15 minutes to 20 minutes	25 to 30 minutes	35 to 40 minutes

AMERICAN SPONGE CAKE

Tin (pan) Sizes	17.5 cm (7 in) square 20 cm (8 in) round 22.5 cm (9 in) ring (tube) tin (pan)	20 cm (8 in) square 22.5 cm (9 in) round	22.5 cm (9 in) square 25 cm (10 in) round
Butter, softened	125 g (4 oz/$\frac{1}{2}$ cup)	250 g (8 oz/1 cup)	375 g (12 oz/1$\frac{1}{2}$ cups)
Caster (superfine) Sugar	185 g (6 oz/$\frac{3}{4}$ cup)	375 g (12 oz/1$\frac{1}{4}$ cups)	560 g (1lb 2oz/2 cups)
Plain (all-purpose) Flour	220 g (7 oz/1$\frac{3}{4}$ cups)	440 g (14 oz/3$\frac{1}{2}$ cups)	655 g (1 lb 5oz/5$\frac{1}{4}$ cups)
Baking Powder	10 ml (2 tsp)	20 ml (4 tsp)	30 ml (6 tsp)
Water	125 ml (4 fl oz/$\frac{1}{2}$ cup)	250 ml (8 fl oz/1 cup)	375 ml (12 fl oz/1$\frac{1}{2}$ cups)
Vanilla Essence (extract)	2.5 ml ($\frac{1}{2}$ tsp)	5 ml (1 tsp)	7.5 ml (1$\frac{1}{2}$ tsp)
Medium Egg Whites	4	8	12
Approximate Cooking Time	35 to 45 minutes	60 to 65 minutes	60 to 65 minutes

CALYX CUTTER

Made of metal or plastic, in a variety of sizes and slightly different shapes. For use with sugarpaste* or pastillage*. Place a calyx on the back of a moulded* or cutter* flower while still soft. Alternatively, place the calyx in a greased mould and arrange the petals over it. The calyx supports the petals in the second method.

QUICK TIP
As well as for cutting out a calyx for a flower, use the calyx cutter to cut out flowers. Mould a small piece of pastillage into a Mexican-hat shape, with a wide brim and tall, thin crown. Place the calyx cutter over the hat and cut out the paste. Model the centre to make a flower with five petals, using the thin crown as the base.

CANDLES

Even adults love to blow out candles! Look out for trick candles which will not blow out. The candles re-light after a few seconds and they can eventually be extinguished by snuffing them out.

Candles of equal height can be rather dull – particularly if there are a lot of them! They look more interesting if graduated in size, for example, placing the tallest in the middle of a cake and graduating the size down towards the side. To cut candles mark a line and cut with scissors.

Novelty Candles Small animal-shaped candles for children's cakes. Number candles for adults as well as children, birthdays or anniversaries.

Attaching Candles to a Cake
● Pipe a rose in royal icing* on backing paper and place a candle through the centre.
● Mark a hole in sugarpaste* while the surface is soft, remove the candle and replace it when the cake is decorated.
● Use marshmallows as bases for candles.
● Use a skewer or fine-pointed knife to make a hole in a cork. Cover most of the cork with tiny flowers and position the candle in the hole.

CARBOXYMETHYL CELLULOSE

Known as CMC, this light-textured white powder is a synthetic cellulose which expands when wet. It is used to replace some or all of gum tragacanth* in pastillage* recipes. It is a cheaper alternative to gum tragacanth.

CELLOPHANE

See papers, coverings and wrappings.*

CHANTILLY CREAM

This is slightly sweetened whipped cream which may be flavoured with vanilla.

Use
As well as being served as an accompaniment for desserts, chantilly cream is used to fill light cakes and to decorate gateaux*.

RECIPE

CHANTILLY CREAM
Sufficient to fill and thinly coat an 18 cm (7 in) layer cake.

250 ml (8 fl oz/1 cup) double (heavy) cream
30 g (1 oz/2 tbsp) icing (confectioners') sugar
few drops of vanilla essence (extract)
●

Whip the cream lightly in a bowl. Sift in icing (confectioners') sugar and vanilla. Whip again until soft peaks form.

CHOCOLATE

A versatile ingredient available as either plain, milk or white chocolate. Confusion is sometimes caused by the many types. Here is a quick guide.

Dessert Chocolate: Manufactured for eating (and delicious) but difficult to work with if melting and using for cake decorating.

Cooking Chocolate: High-quality chocolate available from some good supermarkets, for example as Menier or own brands. Used for all forms of chocolate cookery, such as sauces, cakes and desserts but not easy to use for decorating purposes. This product has a good flavour.

Couverture: Good-quality chocolate, this needs to be tempered before use.

Chocolate-flavoured Cake Covering: Not a true chocolate, this contains vegetable fat to replace the cocoa butter. This is inexpensive, easy to use, it melts and sets well; however it does not have such a good flavour. Useful for everyday cakes or children's cakes but not for high-quality results.

Cocoa Butter Fat present in the cocoa bean when it is harvested. The more cocoa butter in the chocolate product, the better it tastes but the less easily it will melt and set. Check the percentage of cocoa butter (or solids) on the label. Cake decorating shops sell a type of chocolate specially prepared for cake decorating. It has a balance of cocoa butter for flavour with added vegetable fat so it is easy to use.

Melting Chocolate Chocolate melts at blood heat so little heat is required to soften it. Put the broken chocolate in a bowl over a saucepan of hot water, away from the heat source. Do not allow the base of the bowl to touch the water. Leave until melted. This will depend on the size of the pieces of chocolate and the amount in the bowl. Chocolate retains its shape as it melts and needs a gentle stir to become fluid.

Always wipe the base of the bowl when taking it away from the water. Do not allow any moisture to enter the bowl of chocolate as the two react to cause the chocolate to stiffen and separate slightly.

Microwave Method Chocolate may be melted successfully in a microwave on low or defrost setting. The timing depends on the thickness of the chocolate and the amount. Check frequently: it is better to check every 30–50 seconds than to find separated or even scorched chocolate.

> *QUICK TIP*
> *Pour leftover melted chocolate into an airtight container. Cover when cool and store in the refrigerator. Re-melt as required.*

Carob The carob bean is taken from a tree grown in the Mediterranean area. Carob is processed into a chocolate-like substance but without the caffeine which is naturally present in the cocoa bean. Ideal for migraine sufferers who avoid caffeine.

Available as dairy milk carob or in a variety of forms – for example as Easter eggs or bars with fruits and nuts. Soya bean carob is available for those allergic to dairy milk carob.

Chocolate Varnish A tasteless varnish based on alcohol. Used to give a gloss to set chocolate. The smell which is evident when the container of varnish is opened dissipates on use.

Tempering Chocolate Couverture chocolate contains different fats which melt at various temperatures. These need to be worked so that they set at the same temperature and in the form of small crystals. This gives the chocolate its gloss and 'snap' which is characteristic of expensive chocolates.

The chocolate is melted down to an exact degree, for which a chocolate thermometer is necessary. Pâtisserie chefs who are adept at this work test the temperature of chocolate on their lower lip which is particularly heat sensitive. Once melted, the chocolate must be cooled quickly, either by standing it over ice or by pouring it on a marble slab and using a palette knife to fold and spread it. It is then reheated to an exact degree for working. If the process is not carried out properly, the chocolate will not set well and the fat will separate, causing a film to spoil the gloss when set.

This method of tempering works for quantities up to 450 g (1 lb) of plain chocolate. Break the chocolate into small pieces and melt in the top of a double saucepan over simmering, not boiling, water. When the chocolate reaches 46°C (115°F), remove the pan from the hot water and place in a bowl of cold water. Stir until the chocolate cools to 27–28°C (80–82°F). Return the chocolate to the pan of hot water and heat it again to 31°C (88°F), when it is tempered and ready for use. If tempering milk chocolate, the temperatures should be 1°C (2°F) lower at all stages.

Another method is to melt the chocolate in a double saucepan as above and heat to 46°C (115°F) for plain chocolate or 43°C (110°F) for milk. Pour two-thirds of the chocolate onto a cold marble slab and spread out with a palette knife. Work with a plastic scraper to bring the temperature down. The chocolate will begin to set at this point. Return it to the pan and reheat to 31°C (88°F) for plain or 29°C (84°F) for milk which will take a very short time. The chocolate is ready for use.

Chocolate which is not tempered correctly will not set well, and unmoulding will be difficult. There may also be a white or grey bloom on the surface.

Common Faults in Chocolate Work
Fat Bloom: White surface on chocolate. Caused by the set surface melting slightly when left in over-warm conditions and setting again to leave a film of fat on the surface.
Sugar Bloom: When chocolate becomes damp some of its sugar content dissolves. When dried again the sugar crystals re-

form into a larger pattern leaving a white bloom on the surface of the chocolate.

Chocolate Caraque Pour melted chocolate on a flat surface and leave to set. Use a chef's knife to scrape off long, rolled curls of chocolate. Hold the knife at an acute angle, gripping the blade firmly with both hands. Leave the caraque in a cool place until using.

Caraque may be made from white chocolate as well as dark chocolate. Combining both types of caraque makes an attractive decoration on a gâteau. Always use caraque lavishly for a luscious effect, piling only less-than-perfect caraque under prize examples arranged on top.

STEP-BY-STEP TO SUCCESS

CHOCOLATE CARAQUE
Chocolate Caraque can be used to decorate cakes or desserts. It is the traditional decoration on a Black Forest Gâteau. Pour the melted chocolate onto a marble slab or follow the method here. Handle the caraque carefully, as it is fragile and melts easily.

1 Pour the melted chocolate onto greaseproof paper. Pick up and drop the paper several times, or spread the chocolate backwards and forwards with a palette knife until it just sets.

2 Use a sharp knife held at a 45° angle to the chocolate. Shave the chocolate off the surface with a shearing action. The chocolate will form curls. The thickness depends on the length of the shearing action and the angle of the knife. Make chocolate shavings in the same way, but let the chocolate set until firm before working with it.

Chocolate Curls Use a potato peeler to curl thin strips off the side of a block of chocolate. Dessert chocolate will need to be softened at room temperature for a few hours first. Place the curls in the refrigerator to firm up before use.

Chocolate Leaves Wash and dry rose leaves with small stalks. Use a palette knife to spread melted chocolate on the back of the leaves and leave to dry. Apply a second coat. Hold the stalks, then peel the leaves away from the chocolate.

Chocolate Roses Use just over half the weight of liquid glucose* to melted couverture chocolate. Stir gently together and leave until set. If the chocolate mixture is too soft to mould, then re-melt it adding more melted chocolate. Mould the roses using the same technique as for moulded flowers*. If the paste becomes sticky, dust it with a little cocoa powder. To thin the petals

place them inside a plastic bag. Delicately coloured chocolate flowers can be made by adding blossom tints* to white couverture chocolate. Keep your hands as cool as possible; holding them under cold running water and drying occasionally helps.

PROFESSIONAL TIP

Weigh the jar of liquid glucose (clear corn syrup) without the lid. With the jar on the scales, use a hot, wet spoon to remove the required weight of glucose.

Chocolate Shapes Pour melted chocolate on non-stick paper and quickly spread it out evenly to a depth of about 2.5 mm ($\frac{1}{8}$ in). If the paper shows through the chocolate, cover the patches with more melted chocolate. Chocolate contracts as it dries, so weight down the corners of the paper to keep it flat. When the chocolate is firm, but before it sets hard, cut it into squares, triangles and diamonds. Use a large, sharp knife to make long, neat cuts.

SECRETS OF SUCCESS

For glossy shapes, use a shiny surface to set chocolate. Matt paper, such as grease-proof, does not give the chocolate a glossy finish.

Chocolate Cutouts Simple designs can be made by making chocolate cutouts using biscuit, cookie or aspic cutters, or by cutting the chocolate with a sharp knife around a template. Be sure that the chocolate is smooth and an even thickness without any air bubbles, or the cutouts will not look attractive and may break.

Pour melted chocolate onto greaseproof paper. Pick up and drop the paper a few times so that the chocolate runs level and any air bubbles break. Leave until it starts to set.

Use biscuit cutters to cut out the

shapes. Press in firmly without twisting to make a clean cut. Leave to harden on greaseproof paper before using as decorations.

Piping Chocolate Use a small paper piping bag. Add a few drops of glycerine to 30–60 g (1–2 oz/1–2 squares) melted chocolate. Stir gently until it starts to stiffen. Place in the piping bag and cut a small hole in the tip of the bag. Start to pipe immediately. The chocolate has a limited working time before it starts to set.

Spinning Chocolate Place melted chocolate in a small paper piping bag. Cut a tiny hole in the bag and quickly flick the bag back and forth over the top of a cake. Be sure to apply equal pressure on the bag as you work.

Uses for Spinning Chocolate
● Spin milk chocolate on a coat of dark chocolate.
● Spin chocolate across buttercream or whipped cream.
● Spin chocolate on small fancies.

> *QUICK TIP*
> *If the chocolate stiffens in the piping bag, hold it against the side of a hot saucepan until melted again.*

Chocolate Rice Paper Rice paper cutouts can be dipped into melted choco-late to make unusual decorations. The

main advantage of this technique is that it is possible to make shapes which are more intricate and delicate than those made by cutting melted chocolate with a knife or cutters. The template is on page 242.

Place the design on the table and put the rice paper over it with the shiny side up. Outline the design using a pen with edible ink. Leave a tab of rice paper at the widest point of the design, as shown on the templates. Cut out the design with scissors.

Hold the rice paper by the tab and dip in the melted chocolate. Allow any excess chocolate to drip off, then place the shape on a piece of greaseproof paper to dry. A single dipping is sufficient for a design to lie flat, but if the shape is to stand up, dip it a second time.

When the shape is completely dry, cut off the tab with scissors. Dip the end where the rice paper shows and leave to dry. For a standing figure, place the dipped end on the place where it is to stand and count to ten for it to harden off.

If the finished shape is to be curved, place it to dry on a piece of greaseproof paper in an apple tray or cut a washing-up liquid bottle in half and dry on the curved side.

To make the turbans on the three kings, marble together some white and dark chocolate, then dip just the heads in this

Three Kings

when the first coats have dried. This could be done for any parts of figures which need to be three-dimensional.

RECIPES

CHOCOLATE GLAZE
Sufficient to top a 20 cm (8 in) cake.

185 g (6 oz/6 squares) dark dessert chocolate, chopped
10 ml (2 tsp) vegetable oil
60 g (2 oz/¼ cup) caster (superfine) sugar
60 ml (4 tbsp) boiling water

•

1 Combine all the ingredients in a heatproof bowl. Place over hot (not boiling) water and stir until melted.

2 Remove from the heat and stir occasionally until the icing begins to thicken. Pour the glaze slowly over the cake.

CHOCOLATE FUDGE ICING
Swirls of this delicious icing turn a Victoria Sandwich into a special treat. Have the cake filled and glazed before making the icing, which sets quickly. Sufficient to cover a 20 cm (8 in) cake.

125 g (4 oz/4 squares) dark dessert chocolate, broken up
60 g (2 oz) butter
1 egg
185 g (6 oz/1¼ cups) icing (confectioners') sugar

1 Combine chocolate and butter in a large heatproof bowl. Set bowl over a

saucepan of hot water and leave until chocolate and butter have melted. Alternatively, place bowl in microwave oven on medium power for 1–2 minutes. The chocolate will soften while retaining its shape; stir into the melted butter.

2 Cool chocolate mixture slightly, then beat in egg. Beat vigorously for about 30 seconds, then stir in icing (confectioners') sugar. Beat mixture until it begins to thicken. When ready, it should coat the back of the spoon.

3 Pour icing quickly over glazed cake, smoothing it with a warmed knife. Alternatively, continue beating until the icing forms soft peaks. Swirl it quickly over glazed cake with a small palette knife, using small circular movements that create soft peaks when the knife is lifted.

WHITE CHOCOLATE FUDGE ICING

Have the cake ready before starting to make this icing. Sufficient to coat a 20 cm (8 in) cake.

125 g (4 oz/4 squares) white chocolate
60 g (2 oz/¼ cup) butter
185 g (6 oz/1¼ cups) icing
(confectioners') sugar
15–30 ml (1–2 tbsp) milk

●

1 Melt the chocolate in a heatproof bowl set over a saucepan of hot water. Melt the butter separately in a small saucepan.

2 Let both ingredients cool slightly, then mix them together and beat vigorously for about 30 seconds. Stir in icing (confectioners') sugar, with 1 tbsp milk.

3 Beat the mixture until thick enough to coat the back of the spoon, adding the remaining milk if necessary. Use at once.

CLAY GUN

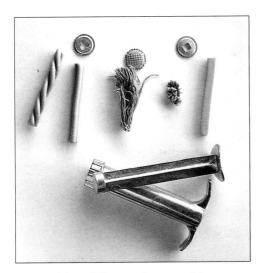

This useful modelling tool comes with a selection of tops to create various shapes. To use, soften some modelling paste with white vegetable fat (shortening), place in gun and push down to extrude paste. Twisting paste can introduce a variety of effects.

COCOA PAINTING

A technique using cocoa powder combined with melted cocoa butter. The cocoa butter is melted and varying amounts of cocoa powder are added to obtain different shades of brown.

Uses
The cocoa mixture can be painted on sugarpaste*, pastillage* or marzipan*. The paste must be firm and dry before applying the decoration. A cream-coloured base, and varying shades of brown cocoa paint, are used to produce pictures resembling old sepia (a dye obtained from cuttlefish) photographs.

Mastering the Technique Unless you are good at drawing it is better to trace the picture and mark it on the base. Keep the liquid warm. Use good quality brushes: a medium size for larger areas and a fine brush for painting thin lines. Start painting the background and the lighter shades first, adding the dark tones later.

Texture and highlights can be added by using a sharp knife to scrape away small areas once the cocoa paint has set.

> *QUICK TIP*
> *If cocoa butter cannot be obtained use coconut oil or vegetable fat. Add petal dust instead of cocoa powder to create coloured paints.*

COLLARS

See also runouts for reference.*
An icing collar is a fragile royal icing* runout that extends beyond the edge of the cake. The most delicate collars have open sections within the runout, often part filled with piped designs.

Types of Collars One-piece collars completely surround the top of the cake. Collars which surround the base of the cake can also be placed on the board in two ways: by piping an outline on the board and flooding it or by making a separate collar and lowering it down over the cake until it sits on the board. The latter method calls for exact measurements and steady hands. Also, the side of the cake must be perfectly straight – if it slopes out at the base the collar will not fit.

One-piece Collar *This hexagonal collar has a flower and leaf cutout. Once dry, pipe scalloped line with a no. 0 tube, then pipe a small shell from the centre of the scallop outwards. Some fine lines are piped on to show how to finish off the inside edge.*

Collars Made in Sections
Made in sections and positioned around the top edge of the cake, this is an easier method than making a complete collar. Remember that each iced section will usually be slightly bigger than the paper template and allow for this when working out the design. It is better to leave a small space between each section of collar than to find that the finished collars will not fit the cake.

Double Collars
Two collars of equal size, one positioned above the other and supported by means of hidden stars of royal icing.

Floating Collars
Two collars one above the other, supported by very fine lines of icing piped close together. The bottom collar is positioned on the cake and small supports are placed at regular intervals on top of it. The top collar is lowered to rest on the supports, then lines of piping are worked from the top collar down to the bottom collar in sections. Once a section of piping is dry, the support is removed. A space is left when piping for removing the last support later when all the icing is dry. Then the space is completed. These collars are extremely fragile. It is most important that the supports are all exactly the same depth.

Templates
Take exact measurements when the cake has been iced. Allow for the collar to extend 5 mm ($\frac{1}{4}$ in) over the top surface of the cake. Ensure that the collar will not protrude over the board.

Papers
Use smooth wax paper*. Cut a 2.5 cm (1 in) slit in the centre of the paper when making a circular run out to allow for the paper shrinking. Non-stick paper is suitable for small collar sections. Smooth cellophane is easy to remove and clear.

Perspex
Ideally, collars ought to be piped on perspex or glass. These surfaces are rigid, flat and attract warmth which encourages the collars to dry.

Piping
Use a small bag and a fine writing tube (tip) for piping the outline.

Flooding
Thin royal icing with egg white. Bang the bowl of icing on the working surface to bring air bubbles to the surface. Break the bubbles by drawing a knife across the surface of the icing. Leave the icing to stand for 15 minutes, covered with a damp cloth, then repeat the process of banging and pricking bubbles. You will need a large piping bag of icing to flood a large collar. If the design has inserts, a small bag will help to flood the icing into narrow sections.

Have the flooding icing ready in the piping bag before starting to pipe the outline. Once the outline is piped, immediately cut a hole in the bag and start flooding. The size of hole should correspond to the size of the runout. Do not make the hole too large or the icing will flow out too quickly, also air bubbles will flow through large holes. The hole should be about the same size as a no. 2–3 icing tube (tip).

The tip of the bag should be kept down in the icing as the surface is flooded to expel air bubbles.

On a large collar, do not work in one direction only, otherwise the edge of the flooding icing will be dry before you completely flood the collar. Work for short distances in clockwise and anti-clockwise directions alternately until the whole area is flooded and smooth. This way there will not be any indication of where the icing started to flow.

Drying Position a lamp with a flexible arm over the collar at a height of about 15 cm (6 in) to dry the surface and give the icing a gloss. Leave the collar to dry in a warm room, or in the airing cupboard, supporting the base on blocks to allow the warmth to circulate.

Applying the Collar to a Cake To remove the paper from a large collar, place it near the edge of a table and gently peel the paper down, turning the collar around gradually.

Alternatively, turn the collar upside down on a level surface and peel away the paper a little at a time.

Use a star tube (tip) and stiff royal icing to pipe a rope inside the top edge of the cake. Gently lower the collar into position on the rope of icing and leave to set before moving the cake.

QUICK TIP
To repair a small area of broken collar, stick a piece of plastic bag, slightly larger than the break, on the underside of the collar. Repair with icing and leave to dry, then peel away the plastic.

COLOURS

The wide range of edible colours available originates from the three basic colours: red, blue and yellow.

Liquid Colours Easy to mix, these blend well into liquid icing, such as glacé icing*, or buttercream*. However, the colours are not concentrated and they can soften paste icing excessively. It then requires more icing (confectioners') sugar to restore the consistency and this, in turn, lightens the colour.

The bottles are easily knocked over, so look out for the type with a dropper.

Uses
For royal icing* and glacé icing or buttercream. Liquid colours may be used to tint royal icing but if a strong colour is required for piping the liquid colour will spoil the texture of the icing, making it too thin to pipe.

Liquids will give an even blend of colour to flooding icing. Stir the colour into the icing very gently. To remove colour from a bottle use either an eye dropper, obtainable from the chemist, or the tip of a cocktail stick.

Remember . . . *Cochineal is pink not red. When it is in the bottle it may look red, however it will not give a red colour.*

Paste Colours Easy to use and concentrated so only a small amount is needed. Ideal when deep colours are needed and for painting. Care must be taken to blend the colour into the icing to avoid producing streaks.

Uses
For royal icing, marzipan*, sugarpaste*, glacé icing and buttercream.

Powder Colours Referred to in this book as blossom tints, also known as petal dust. Fine powders in a wide range of colours. *See blossom tints*.

Uses

For dusting on flowers, frills and pictures to give a delicate effect. Powders may also be used to colour royal icing – an expensive method, best used when colouring a small quantity of icing to pipe decorations to match a dusted area, for instance, to colour piped roses to match a garrett frill* which is dusted with colour.

Care must be taken when using the powders as they tend to float in the air and land at random on the surface of the cake.

Gold and Silver Lustre Colours Edible powders with added sparkle. These can be moistened to use for painting but only for delicate shades as they do not give a great depth of colour.

Gold and Silver Colours Non-toxic paint for use on plaques* and non-edible items. The paint settles at the base of the bottle and needs to be stirred well before use.

Chalk Colours Ordinary children's colouring chalks, they are non-toxic sticks of colour available from art shops. Scrape a fine powder off the chalks and use for dusting on non-edible decorations.

Colour Wheel Obtainable from art shops, this device is designed to help understand how to mix colours. For example, the colour wheel shows red as the opposite colour to green so by adding red to green it will dull the colour.

Colouring Sugarpaste*, Pastillage* and Marzipan* Add the colour with a cocktail stick. Knead the colour into the paste until it is evenly distributed. Cut the paste in half to check that the colour is even.

> *QUICK TIP*
> *Label the top of each jar of colour, then they can be identified at a glance.*

Colour Combinations Experiment by mixing colours to discover the many effects that can be achieved. Not only is this fascinating but it is an excellent way of producing life-like colours, unusual shades and delicate tints. Here are a few useful basic combinations. Vary the ratio of one colour to another to make quite different shades.

Red + blue	=	purple
Blue + yellow	=	green
Red + yellow	=	orange

COOKED ICINGS

Glaze and fill cakes before making and applying these icings, as they set quickly and must be poured over the cakes while still warm if a smooth effect is to be created. For thicker icings that can be drawn into peaks, continue to beat the icings as they cool.

Use

For light cakes, such as Victoria Sandwich, Madeira or Whisked Sponges, and small cakes or petits fours.

RECIPES

CARAMEL ICING
Sufficient to coat a 20 cm (8 in) cake.

60 ml (4 tbsp) caster (superfine) sugar
10 ml (2 tsp) water
90 g (3 oz/⅓ cup) butter, melted
90 ml (6 tbsp) single (light) cream
375 g (12 oz/2¼ cups) icing
(confectioners') sugar, sifted

•

1 Put the sugar in a small heavy-bottomed saucepan. Add measured water. Stir occasionally over moderate heat until sugar has melted, then increase the heat and boil without stirring until syrup turns pale brown.

2 Immediately add butter and cream, stirring constantly until caramel dissolves. Remove pan from heat and add icing (confectioners') sugar, beating until smooth and creamy.

3 Spread warm icing over cake, smoothing it with a warm dry palette knife. Leave to cool and set before serving.

CHOCOLATE LIQUEUR ICING
Sufficient to coat a 20 cm (8 in) cake.

*125 g (4 oz/4 squares) dark dessert
chocolate, chopped
125 g (4 oz/½ cup) butter
125 g (4 oz/¾ cup) icing
(confectioners') sugar
15 ml (1 tbsp) orange or coffee liqueur*

●

1 Melt chocolate, butter and sugar in a saucepan over low heat, stirring occasionally. Do not overheat.

2 Remove from heat and stir in liqueur. Leave icing to cool and thicken slightly before pouring and smoothing over cake.

CREAMY FUDGE ICING
Sufficient to coat a filled 23 cm (9 in) cake.

*125 g (4 oz/½ cup) butter
125 g (4 oz/⅔ cup) soft dark brown sugar
45 ml (3 tbsp) milk
315 g (10 oz/2 cups) icing
(confectioners') sugar*

●

1 Combine butter and brown sugar in a saucepan. Add milk and stir over moderate heat until butter and sugar have melted.

2 Remove from the heat, add icing (confectioners') sugar and beat until cool and thick.

ORANGE CREAM ICING
Sufficient to coat a 20 cm (8 in) cake.

*3 egg yolks
125 g (4 oz/½ cup) caster (superfine)
sugar
5 ml (1 tsp) grated orange rind
60 ml (4 tbsp) orange juice
125 ml (4 fl oz/½ cup) double
(heavy) cream*

●

1 Combine the egg yolks, sugar and orange rind in the top of a double boiler

(double saucepan). Beat until mixture is pale and light.

2 Set the mixture over simmering water. Gradually add orange juice, beating constantly until mixture thickens. Remove from the heat and set aside until cool. Chill.

3 In a bowl, whip cream until stiff. Fold into orange mixture until evenly combined. Use at once.

COOKING FOIL

See Papers, coverings and wrappings*.

CONFECTIONERY GLAZE

A clear, edible glaze which may be used on plaques*, flowers or other work. The same as chocolate glaze* but lighter in colour, this protects finished work from moisture as well as making it look attractive.

CORNELLI WORK

Also known as scribbling and 'take a line for a walk', a description borrowed from the art world. Cornelli work is not a haphazard technique of piping lines but a tightly controlled design which gives a delicate appearance.

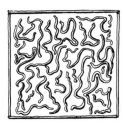

Left: the correct method of piping cornelli work
Right: lines should not be short and broken as they look unattractive

Piping Use royal icing in a small piping bag fitted with a fine writing tube (tip). Hold the tube (tip) at a 45° angle either touching, or very close to, the surface. Pipe the icing to resemble the shapes of jigsaw pieces, with no sharp angles, in a close pattern of curves, near to each other but not touching. The joins must be invisible and a fine, damp, paint brush should be used to eliminate any unwanted ends of icing.

Uses
- To decorate a cake board.
- Piped on the exterior of pastillage* bells.
- As part of a design on a cake or plaque*.

> *QUICK TIP*
> *Cornelli work is useful for hiding small cracks in royal icing* and flaws in sugarpaste*.*

COUVERTURE

See Chocolate.*

CORN SYRUP

American term for liquid glucose*. Also known as clear corn syrup.

CRAFT KNIFE

Small, sharp knife, similar to a scalpel, available from cake decorating shops, this is useful for cutting out paste. One type has two removable blades: a small blade for intricate work and a straight-topped blade for ribbon insertion. Use for cutting around templates, for trimming paste, for cutting fine strips of paste and other delicate work.

Most kitchen knives are either too large to handle for delicate work or not sharp enough to cut the paste without dragging and stretching it.

CREAM

For filling and decorating cakes, usually gâteaux*. Two types of cream can be whipped: whipping cream and double (heavy) cream.

Whipping Cream : Contains 35% butterfat and is pale, almost white, when whipped. Whipping cream takes longer to whip than double (heavy) cream because it contains less fat. It does not give as firm a consistency and it does not hold its shape as well as double (heavy) cream.

Double (Heavy) Cream: Contains 48% butterfat and is cream coloured. Double (heavy) cream whips up very quickly, is firmer and holds its shape longer than whipping cream. It very soon curdles and becomes buttery if overbeaten.

Whipping Cream — Creating Volume An 18th century cookery writer wrote of 'flogging cream until stiff', a term with broader general use in those days but not the way to treat cream!

Chill the cream, bowl and whisk. A hand (balloon or spiral) whisk gives the greatest volume but involves hard work. A rotary whisk or hand-held electric beater is quicker. Do not use a very large electric beater as it is easy to overwhip cream in such a machine. Use a bowl large enough to hold four times the amount of unwhipped cream. This will provide plenty of space for whipping air into the cream. The cream is ready for piping when it is *just* holding its shape in peaks. Do not overwhip the cream or it will have a slightly rough, almost curdled, appearance when piped. The process of spooning the cream into the piping bag and squeezing it out tends to stiffen it slightly, particularly in warm weather.

Piping Bags Paper bags are not suitable as they very soon become soft from the moisture of the cream. A nylon piping bag may be used but some fat or liquid tends to ooze out through the fabric, making it wet and unpleasant to hold. A cloth bag that can be boiled is best for piping cream.

Icing Tube (Tip) Use a large star icing tube (tip). If the opening in the tube (tip) is too small, the cream will separate.

Filling the Piping Bag Place the tube (tip) end of the piping bag in a wide-topped jug and extend the bag over the edge of the jug, down around the outside. This will make it easier to fill the bag by spooning in the cream. Twist the top of the bag to stop the cream from coming out.

Using Whipped Cream Pipe on fatless sponges, genoese sponge or chocolate cakes. Mark a covering of cream by swirling it with a pointed knife or smoothing into even 'waves' with a large palette knife.

Keeping Qualities Cakes decorated with whipped cream should be eaten on the same day as prepared. Cream turns yellow if left and it can pick up flavours from other foods. Store in the refrigerator.

Freezing Whipped cream freezes well for up to 4 months, in a rigid covered container.

> *QUICK TIP*
> *Line a baking sheet with foil. Pipe rosettes of cream on the tray and open freeze until firm. Pack carefully in a rigid container. To use, simply place the rosettes directly on the cake and leave in the refrigerator for a couple of hours or in a cool room until softened.*

Frozen Cream Double (heavy) and whipping cream are available ready frozen, unwhipped. Packed in small chunks or sticks, this is a great standby, also economical, as only a small amount need be thawed as required. For best results thaw the cream in a covered container in the refrigerator, a few hours ahead or the day before using. For quicker thawing leave the sticks at room temperature or

speed the process by placing in the microwave for about 10 seconds on a medium or low setting. Do not heat the cream as it tends to separate, becoming unsuitable for whipping.

CREAM CHEESE ICINGS

These are made from cream cheese or from other soft cheeses, such as curd cheese or quark and they are used instead of buttercream-type icings and frostings. They have a rich and creamy flavour and texture which makes them ideal for use instead of whipped cream; however if made with a low-fat soft cheese they are a useful alternative to rich fillings and toppings.

Use
For filling or topping light cakes, such as Victoria Sandwich, Madeira or whisked sponges. Not suitable for piping if a very soft low-fat cheese is used but most full-fat soft cheeses give a consistency that allows for piping swirls.

RECIPES

CREAM CHEESE ICING
Not strictly a butter icing this, but made in much the same way. It is rich and creamy without being cloying, and is the perfect spread for carrot cake or a Madeira. Sufficient to coat a 20 cm (8 in) cake.

125 g (4 oz/$\frac{1}{2}$ cup) full-fat cream cheese
60 g (2 oz/$\frac{1}{4}$ cup) caster (superfine)
sugar
grated rind of $\frac{1}{2}$ lemon
30 ml (2 tbsp) lemon juice
90 ml (3 fl oz/$\frac{1}{3}$ cup) double (heavy)
cream, whipped
•

1 Cream the cheese with the sugar in a bowl until the sugar has dissolved.

2 Beat in the lemon rind and juice, then fold in the cream.

CITRUS CHEESE CREAM

Sufficient to fill and coat an 18 cm (7 in) layer cake.

125 g (4 oz/$\frac{2}{3}$ cup) curd or quark cheese
60 g (2 oz/$\frac{1}{4}$ cup) caster (superfine)
sugar
grated rind of $\frac{1}{2}$ orange
45 ml (3 tbsp) orange juice
30 ml (2 tbsp) Greek-style yogurt

●

1 Cream the cheese and sugar together in a bowl until the sugar has dissolved completely.

2 Gradually beat in orange rind and juice, then fold in yogurt.

CREME AU BEURRE

Also known as boiled buttercream and continental buttercream. Boiled sugar syrup is whisked into egg yolks, then softened butter is gradually beaten in. A delicious buttercream that should be made with care but the effort is worthwhile. A smooth cream that can be used to fill, coat and pipe on cakes. Keep the syrup away from the beater when pouring it on the eggs. Soften the butter well and add it a small amount at a time.

Temperature Test This test also applies when making American frosting*. For making crème au beurre the sugar syrup must boil to 107°C (225°F). This is known as the thread stage. A sugar thermometer is helpful but not essential. Test the sugar syrup by dipping a wooden spoon into it as it boils. Use your forefinger and thumb to remove some syrup from the edge of the spoon. Press your finger and thumb together, then separate them. A thread of sugar should form if the correct temperature is reached and the syrup boiled sufficiently.

Problem Solving If the mixture curdles, place the bowl over a pan of warm water and stir until the crème is smooth.

Uses

As a filling and covering for light cakes, for example fatless sponges, all-in-one cakes and Victoria Sandwich cakes.

SECRETS OF SUCCESS

When the syrup has boiled sufficiently, dip the base of the saucepan into cold water to prevent the syrup from overcooking.

RECIPE

CREME AU BEURRE

Eggs must be perfectly fresh and all utensils spotlessly clean. The quantity below will cover a 20 cm (8 in) cake.

90 g (3 oz/$\frac{1}{3}$ cup) caster (superfine) sugar
60 ml (4 tbsp) water
2 egg yolks
185 g (6 oz/$\frac{3}{4}$ cup) unsalted butter,
softened
vanilla essence (extract)

●

1 Make a syrup, using caster (superfine) sugar and water, and boil it to 107°C (225°F). Using a balloon whisk, whisk egg yolks in a bowl until pale in colour. Pour in the syrup in a thin, steady stream. Continue to whisk until all the syrup has been incorporated and the mixture is thick and creamy.

2 Beat the softened butter in a separate bowl until light and fluffy. Gradually beat in syrup and egg mixture. Fold or beat in flavourings, if required, or add a little vanilla essence (extract).

CREME PATISSIERE

A rich, thick custard which is stabilized by the addition of flour. It is used, as its title suggests, in pastry items, sweet flans and a wide variety of desserts. It is also excellent

Strawberry Chocolate Gâteau
see page 182

Raspberry Valentine Cake
see page 182

Easter Nest
see page 184

Easter Egg Cake
see page 185

for filling gâteaux* and any other light cakes. A quick alternative to crème pâtissiere is provided in the recipe for crème diplomate, which is simply a cornflower sauce enriched with cream.

RECIPES

CREME PATISSIERE

All recipes on this page yield about 315 ml ($\frac{1}{2}$ pt/1$\frac{1}{4}$ cups).

315 ml ($\frac{1}{2}$ pt/1$\frac{1}{4}$ cups) milk
1 vanilla pod (bean)
2 egg yolks
60 g (2 oz/$\frac{1}{4}$ cup) caster (superfine) sugar
30 g (1 oz/$\frac{1}{4}$ cup) plain (all-purpose) flour
few drops of vanilla essence (extract)

1 Heat the milk with the vanilla pod (bean) to boiling point; remove from heat. Combine egg yolks and sugar in a bowl and beat vigorously for several minutes until light in colour and thick and creamy in texture. Sift in the flour and beat well until mixture is smooth.

2 Remove vanilla pod (bean) and pour warm milk in a steady stream onto egg mixture, stirring constantly until smooth. Return mixture to clean saucepan and bring to the boil over moderate heat stirring all the time. Lower the heat and simmer, stirring, for 2–3 minutes more until smooth and thick.

3 To ensure that Crème Pâtissière is smooth and velvety, press mixture through a sieve into a clean bowl. If vanilla pod (bean) was not used to flavour milk, stir in vanilla or other liquid flavouring. Cover surface of crème lightly with damp greaseproof paper to prevent formation of a skin. Chill before use.

QUICK TIP
When the mixture first begins to thicken it will become lumpy but this is normal and vigorous stirring is the solution.

CREME DIPLOMATE

15 ml (3 tsp) custard powder or 20 ml (4 tsp) cornflour (corn starch)
15 ml (1 tbsp) caster (superfine) sugar
155 ml ($\frac{1}{4}$ pt/$\frac{2}{3}$ cup) milk
155 ml ($\frac{1}{4}$ pt/$\frac{2}{3}$ cup) double (heavy) cream
few drops of vanilla essence (extract)

1 Blend custard powder or cornflour (corn starch) and sugar with a little milk in a saucepan.

2 Stir in remaining milk and cook over moderate heat, stirring constantly, until thick and smooth. Pour into a bowl, cover and chill.

3 Whip cream until thick and fold into chilled custard with vanilla.

CRIMPERS

C

Metal implements obtainable in a variety of designs and used to pinch together soft sugarpaste* to make a pattern. Crimping is a quick and easy way to decorate sugarpaste-covered cakes. Some crimpers have a rubber band around their bases to ensure they do not spring open too wide when in use.

Practise on a small piece of paste. Remember to crimp the paste when the cake is freshly coated or the paste will crack.

Using To ensure complete control, hold the crimpers near to their serrated edge. Use even pressure when pinching the design into the paste. If the crimper sticks in the paste, dip it into cornflour (corn starch) or icing (confectioners') sugar before using, or wash and dry it well. Release the tension gently from the crimper. Do not allow the crimper to open fully in the paste or it will stretch, and spoil, the pattern.

A very effective design can be made – even on wedding cakes – by crimping a pattern around the sides of a cake. Heart or holly designs can be crimped and the design coloured.

Piping The crimped designs can be overpiped with royal icing* either in the same colour or in a contrasting colour.

Uses
- Around the edges of plaques*.
- As a frame for a picture in icing.
- Around the top and sides of a cake.
- As a border for ribbon insertion*.
- Around the edge of a sugarpaste covering on a cake board.

CRYSTALLIZED FLOWERS

A quick and unusual decoration, crystallized flowers are edible, depending on the type of bloom used. Delicate coloured crystallized flowers make an ideal decoration for a Mother's Day cake.

Choose small flowers with smooth petals: primroses, violets, the blossom from fruit trees or rose petals and mint leaves. Leave a small stalk on the flower for ease of handling.

Preparation Colour small amounts of caster (super fine) sugar the same colour as the flowers. Place the sugar in a plastic bag, add the colour and rub the bag between your hands to distribute the colour evenly. Pour out on a plate and dry.

SECRETS OF SUCCESS

Petal dust may be used to colour the sugar. You will need a stand to hold the flowers while they are drying. Cover a cup, or basin depending on the number of flowers, with a circle of greaseproof paper*, secure it down around the side with a rubber band.

Gum Arabic Solution Place 10 ml (2 tsp) rose water in a cup with 5 ml (1 tsp) gum arabic*. Stand the cup in hot water until the gum dissolves, stirring occasionally. Leave to cool.

The flowers must be absolutely fresh and perfect, clean and dry. Using a medium paint brush, lightly coat the whole of the flower with the solution. Sprinkle a thin layer of sugar all over the flower. Pierce a hole in the paper stand to support the flower. Leave to dry in a warm dry room, away from moisture. The flowers are brittle once crystallized and they attract moisture from the atmosphere if kept in a humid place.

Keeping Qualities Store the crystallized flowers between layers of tissue paper in a warm dry place. Do not cover with an airtight lid as they tend to soften. They keep for a few weeks, depending on the type of flowers.

CURTAIN WORK

The term used for fine lines of piping which are part of extension work*. They extend from the side of the cake to the built out bridge work*. They are piped in royal icing* using a small bag fitted with a fine plain writing tube (tip).

Mark the top guideline for the design using a sharp tool: the fine groove is useful when beginning the piped lines of icing, as it provides a 'grip' for attaching them to the side of the cake.

Piping The lines should be piped as close together as possible. Dabbing the opening of the icing tube (tip) on a damp sponge between piping lines can assist in attaching the icing on the cake. This keeps the opening clean and the icing slightly moist.

Place an object under the back of the cake board to lift it slightly and tilt the cake forward. This will ensure that the piped lines hang vertically rather than sagging inwards. Pipe each line past the base of the bridge work and neaten the excess end with a fine damp brush before the icing dries. It helps to work with the cake at eye level, even if this means kneeling down. Be careful when turning the cake: the wet iced lines can stick together.

Board The board must be strong and at least 7.5 cm (3 in) larger than the iced cake to protect the piping. A light board can cause the work to shatter through vibration or flexing.

Designs The top edge of the curtain work may be a straight line, a scalloped edge or pointed edge. Heart and bell shapes may also be used. When the curtain work is dry, staggered tiny dots of icing may be piped on the lines. Pieces of deep lace can be made separately and attached to the bridge work.

SECRETS OF SUCCESS

The longer the lines of piping, or the deeper the curtain, the more difficult the work. Practise the technique on small, short examples of the design.

STEP-BY-STEP TO SUCCESS

CURTAIN WORK

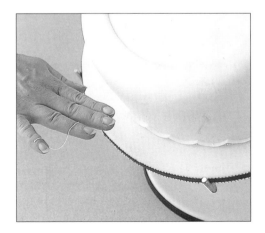

1 Tilt the cake towards you to prevent the piped thread from sagging. Pipe a thread of icing between two parted fingers, then try moving your fingers slightly. It should be possible to gently move your fingers apart to stretch, but without breaking, the thread of icing.

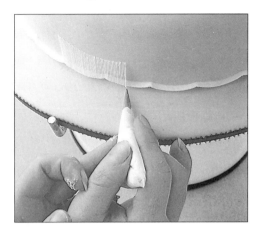

2 Using a no. 0 or 00 tube, pipe a straight line from the cake to just below the bridge work, carefully tuck the tube under the bridge to make a neat finished edge. Pipe the next line close to the first: the space should be the same width as a line of piping.

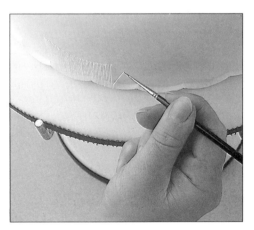

3 If the extension lines break, use a damp brush to remove them and encourage the lines to fall away from the remaining extension work to avoid damaging it. Pipe the lines straight, remove any slanting lines. Change the icing and bag frequently, working with small quantities, to prevent bursting.

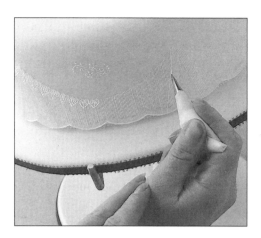

4 When over-piping curtain work, pipe a further two rows of bridge work with a no. 0 tube. Tilt the cake diagonally. Pipe the curtain threads on the right-hand side; dry. Tilt the cake the opposite way; pipe curtain threads on the left side.

CURVED FORMER

A piece of plastic which looks like a pipe cut in half lengthways. Also available with a double curve. A curved former is used to hold decorations in a curved position while they are drying. Decorations can be dried inside the former or over the back of the curve. A rolling pin, bottle or cardboard roll can be used but remember to check that the curve is not too acute and that the object is firmly supported in a stable position.

CUTTER FLOWERS

Flower Paste* Pastillage*, petal powder* or flower paste should be firm and pliable so that it can be rolled until transparent without tearing. The most life-like flowers are made from paste that is so thin that you can read through it. Finger nails need to be short for this work or they can mark the soft paste. When working with the flower paste try to keep the amount of cornflour (corn

starch) or icing (confectioners') sugar to the minimum. Cornflour (corn starch) will dry paste out quicker than icing (confectioners') sugar but it is much finer to use.

Cutters Made in metal, nickel silver and plastic. They should have sharp cutting edges and they must not buckle when pressed. Alternatively, it is possible to use cardboard templates and to cut around the edge to make petals and leaves from flower paste; however, the edge will not be as sharply defined and the paste may drag when cut with a knife.

QUICK TIP
The piece of circular plastic with some cutters is to prevent the cutter's edge from marking the hands.

Flowers on Wires The petals are cut, then modelled around a wire. If possible use fresh flowers in season as a guide or, as good substitutes, use a book of botanical flower paintings or a gardening catalogue. Keep at least one of each variety of the finished flowers for future reference.

To give large roses extra strength, use a piece of 24-gauge wire and push it up through the centre of the cone of paste. Hook the end of the wire and moisten it, then pull it back down into the paste. This ensures that the hook catches in the paste. Finish moulding the rest of the flower.

Flowers without Wires Grease a cocktail stick (toothpick) with white vegetable fat. Cut out the petals and model them around the stick. Leave until completely dry. Carefully remove the flower from the stick.

Stamens The finer the stamens, the more authentic the flowers look. The easiest way to fix the stamens is to tape them on the end of floral wire, making sure they are at slightly varying lengths, then arrange the petals around them. Or they may be placed into the centre of the flower when it has been made, before it dries.

PROFESSIONAL TIP

If the stems of the stamens are soft, dip them into confectionery glaze*, then leave to dry and harden. They will be far easier to use.

Colouring Petals may be dusted with colour when they are cut out and before modelling or once they are wired and dry.

Use a good-quality paint brush and load the powder on it from a flat surface. To highlight the petals, draw the brush just over the edge of each petal from the back of the petal forward to leave a glow of colour along the edge.

Blend silver dust in with a colour to give extra sparkle. Matt, white stamens can be coloured with food colourings.

Problem Solving — Dry Paste Rather than adding extra egg white or water which will make the paste sticky, add a small amount of white vegetable fat to lubricate the paste.

Spray Carnation Spray carnations are a very lovely, delicate flower to use on any celebration or wedding cake and they can be finished in interesting colour combinations.

Take a piece of 26-gauge mid-green wire, put a hook on one end and hook a piece of cotton or thread on to this, squash with pliers and wrap a piece of fine rose wire around the top piece. Using a thin piece of floristry tape, wrap around the top and tape down to the base of the wire.

Roll out some paste but do not roll it until it is translucent as you would for the rose: as for double frilling, it should be a fraction thicker. Cut out the carnation shape using the carnation cutter.

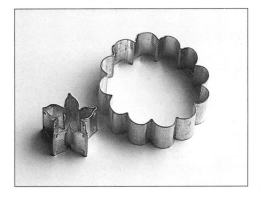

C

Using a sharp modelling knife, cut on the indentation and two or three times on the curve of each scallop. To frill the petal, take a cocktail stick (toothpick) and working with a firm rolling movement, start frilling the paste keeping it moving all the time so that it does not stick to the work surface. Continue until frilled all the way around. Turn over onto a piece of thin foam, brush egg white all over the surface up to the frilling.

Thread the wire through the centre, fold in half, remove from sponge, brush egg white over the centre third of one side and bring the left-hand side third over; repeat on the other side by turning it over and bring from the side to the centre so it is an 'S' shape if looked at from above. Squash firmly onto the wire.

Continue by rolling, cutting and frilling two further petals. These are turned over, brushed with egg white and slid onto the wire. Hang upside-down supporting between your two thumbs and first fingers.

Squash all around to get an even finish.

Make a small cone, known as a Mexican hat, rolling from the inside to the outside using a paintbrush. Cut out a calyx and then, as for pulled flowers, stick a wooden dowel down the centre to open it up. Slide this up the wire and attach to the carnation with egg white.

To make the bud, surround a yellow cone with a piece of green paste and cut through the green using a modelling knife to reveal the yellow underneath. Place onto a piece of wire. Dust the petals with a flat brush using a contrasting colour and wire with the bud into a spray.

Clematis The clematis is an attractive climber. The one illustrated is *Clematis montana*, a small four petalled species that flowers in abundance. There are many books on clematis or look in a seed catalogue as these usually include full colour pictures of clematis and other flowers.

Roll out some pink paste and cut four petals. Place on a veiner like a violet leaf, hibiscus, or any with fan-shape veining. Turn over and using a veining tool or cocktail stick, mark two curved lines then turn over so the lines are underneath and inverted on the top.

Take a small, circular piece of paste and make a hole in it. With the end of a paintbrush, squash slightly and sit inside

a wooden curtain ring. Assemble the four petals onto the tiny centre ring sticking with egg white and using the curtain ring as a support. Stick some white stamen cotton pieces around the centre – these should be dusted a mauve colour in places to produce a striped effect.

Take some yellow cotton, wrap it around tweezer ends held about 1 cm ($\frac{1}{2}$ in) apart, wind around 13 times and then twist some wire around the centre to form a figure-of-eight with the wire in the centre. Cut the two loops and trim off the excess wire. Stick the wire into the centre of the clematis to make the mass of yellow stamens in the centre. Allow to dry before finishing. Dust with a stripe of darker pink down the centre of each petal and dust a little green around the base of the petals.

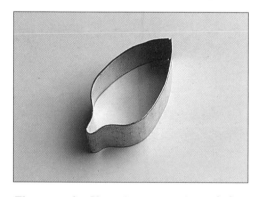

The cutter for Clematis montana is made by squashing a Christmas rose cutter. Only bend cutters if you plan to do the flowers on a regular basis, if not use a cardboard or petal template.

Petunia Petunias with their floppy flowers come in many colours, including pink, mauve, lilac, red and striped effect ones.

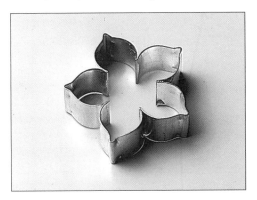

Make a cone and place the flat end on the work surface. Roll using a paintbrush until you have a central node and a refined outer area. Cut out using a petunia cutter, then place a wooden dowel into the centre and rotate it to stretch the throat open.

Holding the back of the flower, place each petal down on to a leaf veiner to vein the petals. Then holding the flower over the edge of the work surface, frill the petal edges with a cocktail stick.

Tape five white stamens together with floristry tape. Make a hole at the base of the flower and stick the stamen piece into the throat, threading it through from the back. If making an unwired petunia, trim off the excess stamen ends once the flower is dry. If wiring the petunia, slide a small hollowed cone of green onto the back and tape the stamens to a piece of wire with mid-green floristry tape.

Dust with two shades of pink for a striped effect, and add a little green in the centre.

Fuchsia Fuchsia are dramatic summer garden flowers. They come in hundreds of colours, so it is best to pick some real fuchsias to achieve naturalistic colouring. Alternatively use a gardening book with colour photographs for reference. For best effects, show them hanging out of a vase as they do naturally.

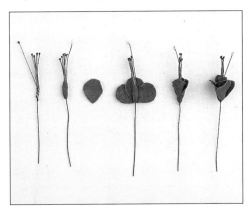

Take six stamens in dark pink with one longer than the other five. Wrap a piece of 28-gauge green wire around them. Squash a piece of paste around the wire and a piece of paste on the longer stamen.

Roll out some paste and cut six petals using a rose petal cutter. Lay three in a fan, sticking them with egg white. There are ten wrapped around the small cone of paste. Frill the further three petals slightly, then stick them in place, overlapping the joins in the first row of petals.

Roll out some more paste and, using a

pansy sepal cutter, cut out four petals. Put on to a veiner to give some detail to the petals. Roll a cocktail stick over their edges to frill them. Place the four on the outside of the fuchsia.

Make a Mexican hat shape in a second colour, rolling with a paint brush, and cut out the back piece of the flower using a fuchsia sepal cutter. Vein each petal and cup them upwards on a piece of foam. Make a cavity in the centre to hold the flower, then slide the prepared centre through the back, sticking it with egg white.

Add a calyx on to the back, and dust it according to the colour schemes; also dust the long stigma green. Tape onto a piece of 26-gauge wire for support if wiring several flowers into a spray.

Cattleya Orchid The Cattleya orchid, known as the bridal orchid in America,

comes in shades of cream, pink, mauve, lemon and white highlighted with various pastel colours.

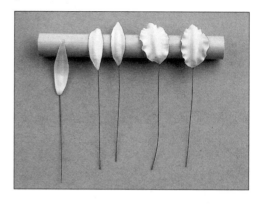

Roll out some white paste using a paintbrush, retaining a thicker part at one end. Cut three long, thin petals and two more that are slightly shorter and wider. The thin ones should have deep, wide veining on the backs of the petals; one is set-off against the tubing and the two wider petals are both frilled and veined and set-off over a curve. All of these petals go on 30-gauge green wire.

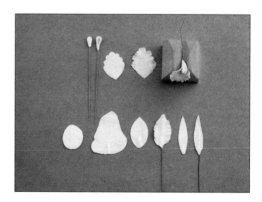

Begin the throat by making a column, which is shorter than that for the cymbidium. Vein down both sides. Make a small yellow ball and cut it in half, then place this into a small cavity on the column. Cut out the throat petal and vein it on any fan formation leaf veiner. Alternatively you can buy orchid throat veiners. Frill all the way around. Place the throat petal on a piece of sponge rubber and position the column at the base of the petal, yellow ball side downwards; bring both sides up to meet at the top, and stick with egg white. Support in an orchid throat former or over the edge of some thick foam. Dust with a pale pink and lemon petal dust.

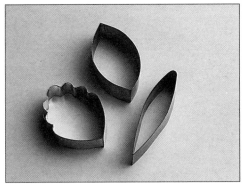

Cutters for Cattleya orchid

Miniature Cymbidium Miniature cymbidiums look very delicate on a tiny birthday cake or in a spray as a filler with larger orchids. They are fiddly and time consuming to make.

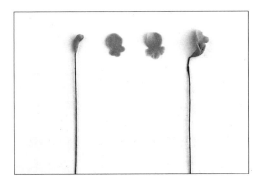

Make a tiny hook on a piece of 28-gauge wire. Place a small cone on one end, graduate its shape to form a bulbous tip. Vein on both sides, then bend the top over.

Roll out some pink paste and cut the throat petal. Frill the bottom edge and cup the two sides, then attach to the prepared column with egg white as shown. The sepals on this type of cutter are all in one; roll out some pink paste and cut out the petals. Vein each one down the centre.

Cup one petal, then turn over and cup the other four, when you turn the petal over again they will curve backwards. Slide the throat into the centre of the petal sticking with a little egg white; leave until dry.

Dust with a darker pink and paint a few delicate spots using petal dust mixed with clear spirit.

Cutters for miniature Cymbidium

Doris Pink These are a mid-summer flowers and part of the Dianthus family. Use the smaller cutter and the same method to make French marigolds.

Hook a piece of 25-gauge Nile green wire. Make a medium-sized cone of green paste, dip in egg white and insert the wire into the finer end of the cone. Make a cavity in the top of the cone for the petals.

Roll out some pink paste. Using a medium primrose cutter, cut out the petals and make a few tiny cuts around each petal. Frill the petals with a cocktail stick. Dust with dark pink powder straight away. Brush a little egg white into the cavity of the calyx, place the first petal in position and repeat with a further three or four petals until the flower is finished. The centre petal should be squashed up to fill the cavity.

Marigold Use the cutter which is the next size down to the Doris pink and use dark yellow paste with orange dust. The calyx has tweezer pinches down it and has a touch of burgundy petal dust put on when dry.

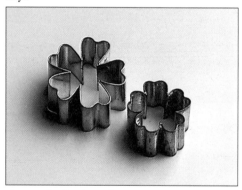

Cutters for Doris pink

D

DESIGN

The best-executed decorating techniques can be spoilt by badly planned designs. Thought should be given to the overall design before the cake, or cakes, are baked, particularly when working with tiered cakes.

Plan Draw up an accurate plan. Designs can be made larger or smaller by scaling them on graph paper; however, an easier method is to have an enlarged or reduced photocopy taken of the design. This is an inexpensive service available in local print shops or other outlets with suitable photocopiers.

Proportions Cakes should be made in proportion: small cakes should not be too deep, large cakes should not be very shallow. A band of ribbon or a deep base border can help to break the height of a cake, making it appear less deep. Wide, shallow cakes may need an upstanding border around the top edge to compensate for the lack of height.

Texture Create interest by combining smooth and textured surfaces. For example, the smoothness of a sugarpaste-covered cake combined with an area of the design piped in cornelli work*; stippling royal icing with a natural sponge will give a textured surface and this technique is both quick and easy to apply.

Spacing Decorations Allow space for all piping and decorations so that the attention is focused rather than being drawn in many different directions. An evenly spaced, repeated pattern creates harmony. A spray of flowers of numerous shapes is not as effective as one made from three or four types of blooms. For inspiration look at the arrangements in a florist's shop. A name or message on a cake should have plenty of space around to ensure it commands maximum importance.

Using Colour By repeating colour you can link up different types of decoration used on a cake. Always repeat a colour somewhere on a cake, even in a different shade, or perhaps by reflecting the colour of the icing in a ribbon.

Unless you are making a novelty cake, do not use too many colours as this can become distracting, drawing attention away from the overall design.

Cake Stand Contributes to the overall impression of the cake. The stand should repeat the shape of the cake and its depth must be in proportion to the bottom tier of the cake.
Spiral Metal Stand: A stand of this type adds space and movement to the display of a wedding cake. The metal curves can be eye catching and create a hard impression. Decorated discreetly with flowers and ribbons to complement the cake, this type of stand provides an attractive modern surround.

DOILIES

The traditional role for doilies is as a decorative plate lining. They may also be used as a base for a simple method of finishing sponge cakes.

Decorative Sugar Topping This is useful for a plain Victoria Sandwich or sponge cake. Layers should first be sandwiched with jam or jam and cream. Lay a doily on top of the cake and hold it in place with one hand. Then dredge the top with icing (confectioners') sugar. Use both hands to lift the doily off the cake, making

sure it comes away cleanly and vertically to leave an attractive pattern.

This same technique may be used on a cake which is coated in chocolate but the chocolate must be allowed to set completely first. Try coating a chocolate cake with white chocolate, then applying a decorative topping of cocoa through a doily.

DUMMIES

Used as a base on which to practise piping and designing decorations.

Wood: Available round and square, also in some other basic shapes, these are heavy and stable with a large base. May be ordered from specialist cake decorating shops. Expensive but worthwhile for serious practising. Moisten with water to remove hardened icing.

Polystyrene: These are lightweight and inexpensive. Available in a variety of shapes and sizes to use for practising piping techniques and for working out designs. Use an all-purpose craft glue or royal icing to stick the dummy on a heavy base. Without careful handling, the polystyrene can crumble away when icing is removed.

QUICK TIP
Cover a polystyrene dummy in a coat of royal icing to protect the surface.

EGGS

Should be fresh and obtained from a reputable source. Store eggs in their covered cartons in the refrigerator and take the required number out some hours before cake making. Discard any eggs with cracked shells.

> *QUICK TIP*
> *When cracking eggs, use a tea-spoon to remove any pieces of shell that may drop into the bowl.*

Whisking Egg Whites Use a perfectly clean, glazed earthenware or stainless steel bowl and scald it with boiling water. Dry well with a clean tea-towel or absorbent kitchen paper. Plastic bowls can retain grease on their surface so are not suitable.

Egg whites will not aerate if any grease is present. The smallest amount of grease breaks down the bubbles in the whites, preventing them from trapping, and holding, air. The whites become fluffy and white when whisked due to air being trapped in their structure.

Freezing Reconstituted dried egg white and fresh whites can be frozen. Allow sufficient room in the container for the liquid to expand. When required, thaw out in the refrigerator. Whites may be stored for up to 6 months.

Egg yolks may be frozen separately but they must be combined with a small amount of sugar and they do not keep as well as whites. They should be used within 1–2 months.

ELECTRIC BEATER

Also known as food mixer. A heavy-duty electric beater, of the type with an integral stand and optional attachments, is a great asset to a cake decorator. This type of machine may be used for mixing stiff batches of rich fruit cake* and for beating royal icing*. It is also useful for whisking the lightest of sponges and for making large quantities of buttercream*

A hand-held machine is suitable for many tasks but it will not cope with the heavy mixes, when the motor could be burnt out if the machine is overloaded. A hand-held beater is more suitable for whipping cream. If you do whip large quantities of cream in a larger machine, take care not to overwhip it.

Royal Icing When made in a machine this can very easily be overbeaten. Use the beater attachment rather than a whisk implement which will rapidly turn the icing into a fluffy meringue-like mass. Keep the machine on the lowest speed and add the icing (confectioners') sugar gradually until the mixture is of a soft peak consistency. The longer the icing is beaten the whiter it will be.

Remember . . . *Always check the manufacturer's instruction book to ensure that the machine is suitable for mixing the quantity which you are preparing.*

EMBOSSED SILVER OR GOLD PAPER

See Papers, coverings and wrappings.*

EMBOSSERS

Small implements with relief designs on their surfaces, used to stamp a pattern into soft sugarpaste* or pastillage*. The design may be coloured by painting with food colour or petal dust.

The process probably evolved from the embossing tools used to create designs on leather work. This is a quick and easy method of applying patterns to a sugarpaste surface. Mark the pattern while the paste is still soft. Apply only enough pressure to stamp the design and avoid making a mark with the base, or edge, of the embosser.

An easy way of embossing the top of a cake is to use a stiff plastic doily. Place it on top of the soft sugarpaste. Start in the centre of the cake and use a rolling pin to roll towards the back.

Start again in the centre and roll forward. If anyone is available, ask them to hold the doily firmly while the design is rolled on. Depending on the type of cake, a firm cake board can be placed over the doily and pressed down evenly.

QUICK TIP
Look out for buttons, badges or other firm items which have a raised pattern on their surface and are suitable for marking a shape into sugarpaste or pastillage. Thoroughly wash and dry them before use, using a new hard toothbrush to clean the tiny areas in the pattern.

EQUIPMENT

Buy as you need and gradually build up a comprehensive stock. Specially designed sugarcraft boxes have plenty of compartments to hold equipment; however, a fishing tackle box is equally efficient and often less expensive. These boxes are easy to carry and they have individual sections to hold equipment.

Ball Tools: A selection of different sizes are required, although a glass-headed pin stuck into a piece of dowelling can be used in place of a small ball tool.

Bowls: A selection of various sizes, preferably glass, all clean and free of grease.

Brushes: Use sable-hair brushes for the best effect and have several different sizes to hand.

Cake Boards: These come in a wide variety of shapes and sizes designed to correspond with the various cake tins (pans) on the market.

Cocktail Sticks (Toothpicks): Use to add colouring to icing and in modelling work. Japanese birch are the best quality sticks that are available.

Colours: Dry dusting colours, paste colours and liquid food colouring are all needed for the various techniques.

Cranked Artist's Palette Knife: Useful for sliding under runouts* or to pick up lace pieces. Make sure it is rustproof.

Crimpers and Leather Embossing Tools Used for decorating sugarpaste and marzipan.

Cutters: A wide selection of cutters is useful. Flower, pastry, sweet (candy) and biscuit (cookie) cutters are used for making plaques and cutouts, while frills and flounces are made with Garrett cutters.

Desk Lamp with Flexible Arm : For drying runouts*.

Dummies: Used for practice and competition work.

Electric Beater* or Food Mixer: Invaluable for beating large quantities of cake mixture. Also useful for the following.
- Whisking egg whites.
- Beating sponge batters.
- Making royal icing* in quantity.
- Making buttercream* in quantity.
- Blending colour into sugarpaste*.

Florist's Wire: You will need varying gauges for flower work, and modelling.

E

Icing Bag Stand: Not essential but keeps the work surface clean and stops the tubes once filled from drying out.

Icing Tubes (Tips)* Remember that different manufacturers produce different sizes. The best quality are precison made from nickel silver and they appear to be seamless. The seam in the metal is visible in icing tubes (tips) of lesser quality.

Icing Tube (Tip) Cleaner: Fine brush to clean out icing tubes (tips).

Knives: A good kitchen knife with a fine sharp blade is essential. You may also wish to use a scalpel for fine cutting and trimming work.

Long White Plastic Rolling Pin: To enable a large piece of paste to be rolled out without leaving marks. Keep wrapped in polythene especially for rolling sugarpaste.

Long Serrated Knife: To cut through gâteaux easily.

Measuring Jug: The 500 ml (1 pint) is most useful.

Metal Rule or Icing Ruler: Sometimes called a straight edge. To smooth royal icing. A plastic ruler will bend.

Modelling Tools: These may be bought from specialist suppliers although you will be able to improvise with various common household tools. The bone-shaped tool is one of the more versatile of these.

Moulds: Used in sugarcraft work and chocolate work, these come in a wide variety of shapes and sizes for many different applications.

Non-stick Board: Keep especially for flower modelling.

Paint Brushes: Use a 2.5 cm (1 in) brush to apply apricot glaze* to cakes. This is easier than using a pastry brush. You also need a good-quality fine brush.

Palette Knife: With firm blade, 10–15 cm (4–6 in) long. Make sure the blade is rustproof. A long-bladed table knife with a rounded end makes a good substitute.

Paper and Card: Greaseproof and silicone paper are used for icing bags and runouts. Card is used to make templates.

Scissors: One good pair of large scissors and a pair of sharp fine-bladed scissors are also required.

Scrapers: For smoothing royal icing or buttercream on the sides of cakes. Made of plastic or polished stainless steel, these are available with many different edges to give a variety of finishes. Plain and serrated or comb edges are the most common; however, others include scallop and dot patterns.

A plain edge with one notch may be used to mark an even, continuous ridge around a cake. This provides a useful guide for adding decoration, for example when applying loops. Triangular scrapers combine two or more different edges.

Scriber: Fine lines are scratched or scribed onto a cake using a scriber.

Sieve: Keep a small fine mesh, nylon sieve for sieving icing sugar only.

Smoothers: To achieve a smooth surface on sugarpaste and marzipan.

Spacers or Marzipan Spacers: To roll out marzipan to an equal thickness. The spacers are used underneath the rolling pin, placed on either side of the paste which is being rolled. This ensures that equal pressure is applied all over the paste. Without spacers, if unequal pressure is used the result is an uneven surface.

Spatula: Plastic or rubber for use when preparing cake and icings and wooden for mixing royal icing.

Turntable*: Must turn easily (check before buying) and be a suitable height.

Tweezers: Use fine pointed tweezers with grooved ends.

Wallpaper Brush: To brush the work surface free of icing (confectioners') sugar and cake crumbs before washing down.

Wooden Dowelling: Use for pulled flower work and modelling.

Wooden Spoons: Kept especially for beating royal icing.

Work Surface: Melamine, non-stick plastic and marble surfaces are best. Be sure that they are thoroughly clean and grease-free.

EXTENSION WORK

A built-out design consisting of bridge work* and curtain work*. The extension work usually extends from the base of a cake. This is a technique for the experienced decorator.

Bridge Work This is piped around the base of the cake, built up by overpiping line upon line, usually in a scallop design. The number of lines of piping will depend upon the size of the tube (tip) used. These lines are left to dry.

Curtain Work Fine lines piped to drop vertically from the side of the cake out to the edge of the bridge work. These lines should be spaced so closely that not another line can be piped between them; however they must not be joined together.

SECRETS OF SUCCESS

Start the first line of piping in the middle of each scallop, or section, and work out-wards on either side. This method ensures the lines follow the same angle.

Colour The base covering on the cake may be brushed with a pastel blossom tint* before the extension work is applied. This will glow through the work. Alternatively, the bridge work may be piped in a contrasting colour or the curtain work may be coloured. Tiny dots, known as hail spotting, piped on the curtain work may be worked in a contrasting colour.

SECRETS OF SUCCESS

Use blossom tint to colour the icing for piping. Most paste colours contain glycerine which would weaken the lines of curtaining or bridge work.

Designs The top edge of extension work can be shaped to create interest, rather than working from a straight edge. Several rows of extension work may be applied in tiers to the side of a cake. Extension work can be applied in small sections, it does not have to form a continuous band around the cake. For example, heart shapes, bell shapes or flower outlines, such as tulip, may be worked at intervals around the base of a cake. Make use of the various styles to create individual designs.

Fluted or Bevelled Extension The bridge work is built out with each row being slightly shorter than the last. This gives an attractive horizontal curve to the extension as it flows around the base of the cake. Alternatively, this may be worked as illustrated, by piping short rows of icing first, building out the bridge by lengthing them.

VARIOUS STYLES AND METHODS USED IN EXTENSION WORK

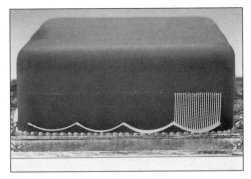

Plain Extension Work with a Straight Top. This shows rows of bridge work piped one on top of another and the vertical lines piped from the top edge, over the bridge and secured underneath.

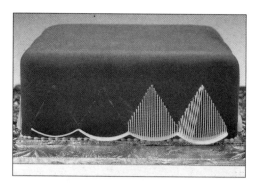

Overpiped Extension Work. Showing build up of the first bridge, the vertical drop lines and finally the second bridge with overpiped curtain effect.

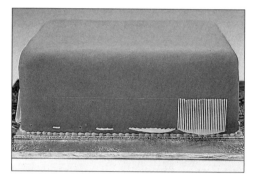

Fluted or Bevelled Extension Work. This shows each row of bridge starting in the centre with a short line; a longer line is piped on top in the next row extending the same distance each side of the first line; each row is longer until the bridge covers the whole section.

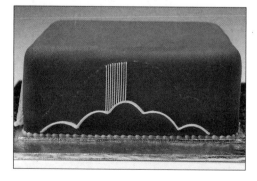

Upside-down Bridge. This is piped with the cake resting upside down on a firm, clean surface.

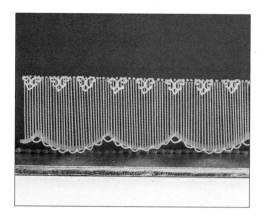

Basic Extension Work. Piped with no. 0 tube (tip) and finished with drop loops and lace pieces.

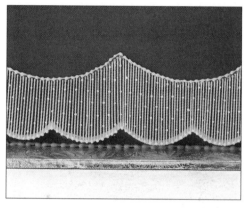

Extension Work with a Shaped Top. The template is made by marking the base scallops and cutting the large scallop at the top, the width of two base scallops. Pipe the bridge and curtain work and finish by piping hail spots evenly over the surface. This must be done with a very light touch or the threads will break. The top edge is finished with a fine snail's trail and the bottom is completed with tiny dots.

PROFESSIONAL TIP

Having icing of good consistency is vital when piping extension work. Pipe a string of icing across two fingers and you should be able to move them apart gently if the icing is of the right consistency.

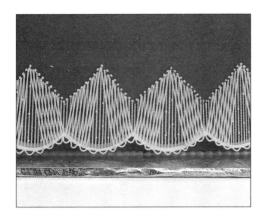

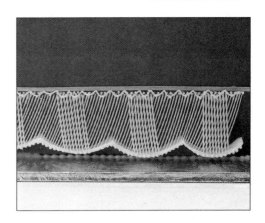

Overpiped Extension Work. The top edge is cut into points. Pipe in the usual way and allow to dry. The second bridge is piped exactly the same as the first and following the same lines. When all the rows are dry, the diagonal lines of the overpiping are done by tilting the cake to one side before piping in the direction the cake is leaning. Tilt the cake in the opposite direction to pipe the diagonal lines on the other side.

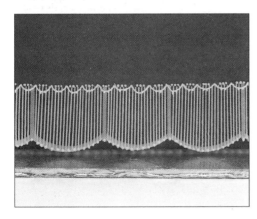

Plain Extension with Ribbon Inserts. Narrow ribbon is let in at intervals by cutting the ribbon the same length as the piped lines and attaching it with a dot of icing at the top and the bottom between each scallop. The top edge is finished with drop loops hanging away from the cake.

This is achieved by tilting the cake towards you very steeply, allowing gravity to pull the loops away from the cake. When the loops are dry, pipe tiny dots on them.

Diagonal Overpiped Extension Work. This is a little more difficult and plain extension work should be perfected before attempting it.

Pipe the bridge as before and dry. Tilt the cake towards you and at the same time, put a prop underneath one side so that it is leaning sideways. This will allow the diagonal lines to hang straight. Pull out a strand of icing from the top line and attach it to a point on the bridge moving about 5 mm ($\frac{1}{4}$ in) to the left or right. Pipe all lines close together and evenly so that the angle remains the same all round. Dry. Remove the prop. Pipe a second bridge over the top of the first one. When this is dry, place the prop the other side of the cake then overpipe with diagonal lines in the opposite direction.

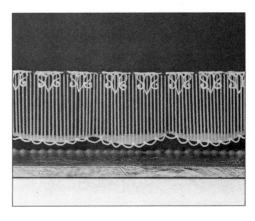

Fluted or Bevelled Extension Work. The base lines for this type of extension work are straight instead of scalloped. The first line is very short and centred between the section marks. The second row is piped on top and a little longer, extending the same distance either side of the first line. Each line of the bridge is piped a little longer and the last line extends across the whole section. The finished bridge is in the shape of a crescent.

Extension Work Bells. Make a template in the shape of a bell and mark the design on the side of the cake. The bases of the bells are piped as for bevelled extension work but are slightly arched. The cake should be turned upside-down for this. The shape of the bell is piped by running drop lines from top to base, following the line of the bridge. Pipe a large bulb of icing at the base for the clanger.

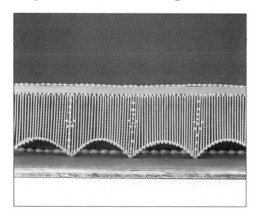

Extension Work Suspended on Points. For this type of extension work, the board should first be covered with a thin layer of paste. The covered cake is placed in position and a fine snail's trail piped around the base of the cake. The band of ribbon is attached before begining to pipe the extension work.

Using a template, mark the place where the extension will touch the board, about 8 mm ($\frac{3}{8}$ in) away from the cake and the normal width for the scallops. Mark a straight line for the top. Turn the cake upside-down and elevate it so that the board surrounding the cake can be clearly seen. With a no. 1 tube (tip) pipe dropped loops from the board, suspending them from one mark to the next. Allow to dry for several hours before turning the cake upright. Leave until next day before piping the vertical lines.

Pipe the fine threads from the top line, ending just below the arched loop which is standing on the board. Care should be taken not to knock these loops as they cannot be repaired unless the cake is turned upside-down again. When the drop threads are quite dry, pipe on decoration if required. Finish off the base of the drop threads with tiny dots. The top is also finished with dots, piped on both sides of the band of ribbon.

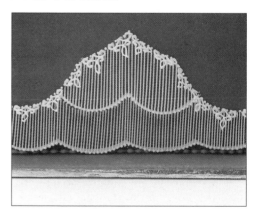

Tiered Extension Work. The illustration shows two tiers but three tiers can be used if required.

Mark the base scallops on the cake. At the same time mark another row of scallops at the required height. Here, the top of the second tier is shaped to a point but any shape may be used to suit the cake.

Pipe the first bridge and when dry pipe vertical lines all around the cake. The second bridge is made by dropping loops close to the top of the first layer of curtain lines. Pipe several rows as before. Pipe curtain lines from the top of the design to the bridge and finish off both bridges with dots.

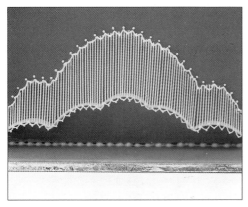

Extension Work with Arched Bridge. Mark the design using a template cut to the shape you require. To pipe the bridge, the cake must be inverted by placing a piece of perspex or a smooth board on top and turning it upside down. The cake should be iced several days in advance to avoid damaging the surface when inverting the cake. Pipe the bridge in the usual way and leave to dry, then turn the cake back with its correct side uppermost. Continue with the extension work.

Line-supported Extension Work. Ribbon or flowers may be arranged and attached to the bottom edge of the cake before the bridges are set in place. The decoration around the edge shows through the finished work and looks most attractive.

Draw a template the size of the coated cake, then divide it into sections. Use a set of compasses to draw the scallop on one section, then trace it on the other sections for accuracy. Trace the scallop several times to make the bridge pattern. Cover the bridge pattern with wax paper. Use a no. 1 tube (tip) to pipe the bridge (scallop). Care must be taken to pipe the bridge pieces accurately. Leave to dry flat.

Place 2 small squares of 2.5 mm ($\frac{1}{8}$ in) thick corrugated card on the cake board under the position of each bridge. The card must be of the right thickness to space the bridge from the cake board. Support the bridge pieces in place on the card. When all the bridge pieces are in position, secure them to the cake with dots of icing.

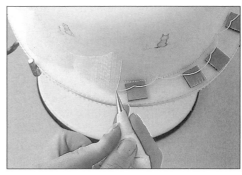

Tilt the cake towards you. Using a no. 0 or 00 tube (tip), pipe the extension lines from the cake. As the extension work is piped, carefully remove the pieces of card.

Bridgeless Extension Work. Insert sterile pin tips evenly around the cake, 5 mm ($\frac{1}{4}$ in) from the board. Brush melted white fat on pins. Using a no. 0 tube (tip) and fresh icing, pipe loops from pin to pin: they must be even in length and distance from the cake. Leave to dry.

Use a no. 00 tube (tip) to pipe the threads of extension work. Do not damage the bridge loops. Remove the support pins as you progress. To pipe a second layer of extension work, replace the pins between the extension strands while the icing is pliable. For the second layer of extension work pipe another row of loops from the greased pins. Take care to avoid touching the existing extension work with the second layer of loops.

Tilt the cake towards you and pipe the second row of extension work, removing the pins as you work around the cake. This work is mainly used on exhibition cakes.

F

FEATHER ICING

Also known as marble icing. This technique adds a professional finish.

Colours Colour the icing for piping slightly deeper than required as it tends to weaken on being dragged through the soft base icing. This is one cake decorating technique which looks good using a bright colour because the lines of colour are very thin. A design using two colours is also very attractive.

Preparation Have ready the cake brushed with apricot glaze*, the glacé icing* ready over heat or the royal icing* of a flooding consistency. Have small piping bags filled with coloured icing; scissors and a fine-bladed knife, fine metal skewer or cocktail stick (toothpick) for dragging the icing.

Icing Most usually worked in glacé icing but royal icing can be used very successfully on more sophisticated cakes. The icing for piping does not need to be as fluid as the surface coating.

Technique Flood the cake with the icing. Use a palette knife carefully to encourage the icing outwards but try to let the icing flood of its own accord. If the icing does not flood satisfactorily, place the cake on a wire rack, then tap the rack up and down to move the icing.

Cut a small hole in the piping bag filled with coloured icing and pipe lines across the flooded icing. Quickly draw the back of a knife, fine metal skewer or cocktail stick (toothpick) across the lines. Wipe the implement clean after each stroke.

QUICK TIP
Before attempting this design on a cake, have fun experimenting on biscuits (cookies). Use plain tea biscuits (cookies), that will not crumble easily. Once iced, place them in the oven on a very low heat, with the door ajar. Remove when the icing is firm and they will be crisp to eat on cooling.

Use
Use glacé icing on fatless sponges, Victoria Sandwich, Madeira-type cakes and small fancies. Use royal icing on fruit cakes.

FILIGREE

See Cornelli work.*

FLOWER NAIL

Also known as an icing nail. A circular piece of plastic or metal attached to the top of a long nail-like holder. Most flower nails have a flat top but some may be slightly domed.

Use
To support flat flowers while they are being piped. A square piece of non-stick or waxed paper is placed on the flower nail, held in place by a dab of icing. The flower is piped on top of the paper which is then removed and the flower left to dry. The flower nail is held in one hand and the flower piped with the other. The nail is rotated as the flower is piped.

Icing Tube (Tip) A petal tube (tip) is used to pipe a variety of flat-based flowers, such as daisies, violets, pansies and primroses.

QUICK TIP
As an alternative to a bought flower nail, spear a cork on top of a cocktail stick.

FLOWER PASTE

Used primarily for hand-modelled flowers, this can also be used for other decorations that are delicate or which require the strength of the paste which sets hard.

There are various recipes for making the paste, which should include gum tragacanth*. This gum strengthens the paste and enables it to be rolled out until it is translucent. Flower paste can be home made or bought from the cake decorating suppliers, either in small blocks or as petal powder*, ready to mix with water.

Home-made Flower Paste Use a heavy-duty electric beater. The stiff consistency of flower paste needs a strong beater. Liquid glucose* used in the paste is stiff when cold but once warmed it becomes fluid. Remove the glucose from the jar with a hot, wet spoon. Scrape away any excess liquid glucose that is attached to the base of the spoon. Remember that the quantity should be measured using standard measuring spoons.

When adding the egg white, keep part back and only add it if needed.

PROFESSIONAL TIP

Once the paste is made, leave it for at least 24 hours before using. This allows the gum tragacanth to swell and gives the paste its full stretching power.

Keeping Qualities Store the paste tightly wrapped in a plastic bag inside an airtight container in the bottom of the refrigerator. The paste will keep for weeks but because it contains gelatine, which is an animal product, it will eventually produce tiny spots of mould.

Freezing Can be frozen in small blocks. Wrap well in polythene, freeze, then place in an airtight container for longer storage. Allow to thaw overnight in the refrigerator before use.

RECIPE

FLOWER PASTE

Makes about 500 g (1 lb).
500 g (1 lb/3 cups) icing (confectioners')
sugar
1 sheet leaf gelatine
10 ml (2 tsp) white vegetable fat
(shortening)
10 ml (2 tsp) liquid glucose
5 ml (1 tsp) gum tragacanth
20 ml (4 tsp) CMC (carboxymethyl
cellulose)
1–1¼ medium egg whites

●

1 Put icing (confectioners') sugar in a heatproof bowl, covering surface closely with greaseproof paper to prevent formation of a crust. Warm in a 150°C (300°F/Gas 2) oven.

2 Meanwhile soak gelatine in a large bowl of water for 5 minutes until pliable. Remove gelatine from water and place in a small heatproof bowl with fat and glucose. Stand bowl over a saucepan of hot (not boiling) water and stir until dissolved.

3 Mix warmed (confectioners') sugar, gum tragacanth and CMC in warm dry bowl and add 1 egg white, with gelatine mixture. Begin mixing on slow speed. Increase mixer speed and beat until paste is white and pliable, adding more egg white if necessary.

4 Store in a clean polythene bag in an airtight container for 24 hours before use or freeze until required. Make sure the paste is double wrapped to prevent it from drying out during storage or it will harden and crack.

FLOWERS

See Blossom Cutter, Briar Roses*,*
Buttercream Roses, Chocolate Roses,*
Crystallized Flowers, Cutter Flowers*,*
Ganache, Moulded Flowers*, Piped*
Flowers and Pulled Flowers*.*

FONDANT

Available from some specialist cake decorating shops in the form of a firm white paste. Can also be bought as a powder to which either water or fruit juice is added.

True fondant, not to be confused with sugarpaste*, is softened over heat and flooded on cakes. The bought fondant is inexpensive and usually superior to any made at home.

Making Fondant Fondant is made by boiling sugar syrup to 115°C (240°F). A small amount of liquid glucose* or cream of tartar is added to stop the liquid crystallizing. Keep the inside of the pan free of sugar crystals during cooking by dampening it frequently with a cold wet pastry brush. When the correct temperature is reached the liquid is cooled quickly and agitated, or worked, to form small sugar crystals. This may be done on a marble slab using a palette knife to 'fold' the syrup. The mixture gradually thickens then it is kneaded until smooth before being stored for future use. Make fondant at least 24 hours before it is required.

Flavouring When the fondant has melted, add grated chocolate, coffee essence or essential oils – use only a drop or two as they are very strong. Essential oils are available from health food shops. Stir until the flavouring is evenly mixed: chocolate should be melted into the fondant before use.

To Use Place the fondant in a bowl over a saucepan of hot water, away from the heat, until melted. Stir until lukewarm to the touch. If overheated the fondant will lose its gloss. If the fondant is too stiff, stir in a little prepared sugar syrup. A few drops of colouring may be added.

Colouring Fondant To obtain a variety of colours from one batch of fondant, use the following method. Start off with white, then add yellow. Next add pink to obtain peach, then add green. Finally, add brown colouring or cocoa powder to obtain a brown icing. The colours may be used separately on individual cakes or to create a design, for example feather icing may be worked in fondant.

> *QUICK TIP*
> *Run water over the surface of the fondant to help it soften before melting. Literally hold the lump of fondant water under the cold tap for a few seconds.*

Preparing the Cake If the fondant is poured directly on the surface of the cake it will lose its gloss as some will be absorbed by the cake. To prevent this, apply a thin coat of marzipan* to the cake surface. Alternatively, brush the cake with hot apricot glaze* and allow it to cool before coating with fondant.

Coating a Cake Stand the cake on a wire rack placed over a baking sheet. Leave plenty of space between individual cakes. For small cakes use a wire rack with a small mesh to prevent the cakes from overturning. Pour the melted fondant into a hot wet jug and carefully pour it over the cake.

Versatility
- For a smooth, buttercream-type icing, warm fondant then beat in half its weight of unsalted butter.
- Softened fondant with added icing (confectioners') sugar and peppermint oil may be kneaded and used to make peppermint creams. Roll out to 5 mm ($\frac{1}{4}$ in) thick, cut out shapes and leave until firm. The peppermint creams may be half dipped in melted chocolate.
- Pipe melted, flavoured fondant into chocolate shells. Leave to crust over, then top with more melted chocolate to seal in the filling in home-made chocolates.
- While hot, fondant may be used to stick flowers to the side of a cake which is coated in royal icing* or sugarpaste. Dip the base of the flowers in the hot fondant, then apply them to the cake – particularly

useful when arranging cascades of flowers down the side of a wedding cake. This is the *only* way in which the fondant is used hot and it may be helpful in other situations as an 'edible glue'.

STEP-BY-STEP TO SUCCESS

FONDANT

Practice eases the process of making fondant as the sugar syrup can be difficult to work if you are a beginner. Kneading small pieces of sugar at a time is easier than trying to work the whole batch.

500 g (1 lb/2 cups) caster (superfine) sugar
15 ml (3 tsp) liquid glucose or pinch of cream of tartar
90 ml (6 tbsp) water

•

1 Make a syrup, using caster (superfine) sugar, glucose or cream of tartar and measured water. When syrup registers 115°C/240°F, the soft ball stage, pour it onto a wetted marble slab or cool grease-free surface and allow it to cool slightly.

2 Using two palette knives, scrapers or spatulas, scrape the syrup from the sides to the centre, using a figure-of-eight movement. Continue working the fondant in this fashion for about 5 minutes or until it forms a stiff white paste.

3 Break off pieces of fondant and knead firmly until smooth and supple. Finally knead all the small pieces together to form a ball. Place in a clean bowl, cover with a damp clean cloth and leave for 24 hours to mature before storing in a screw-topped jar for up to 2 months. Do not store in the refrigerator.

4 To prepare a pouring fondant icing, place fondant in a clean bowl over a saucepan of hot (not boiling) water. Stir occasionally until melted. Add 1 tbsp sugar syrup. Continue to heat mixture, adding more syrup if necessary, until it coats the back of the spoon. Add colouring and flavouring as desired.

F

FROSTED FLOWERS

See page 218.

These are used to decorate gâteaux and light cakes covered with sugarpaste. They should be added at the last minute.

GANACHE

A mixture of chocolate and cream which has a variety of uses. Single (light), whipping or double (heavy) cream may be used.

Proportions Use double the amount of chocolate to cream, for example 250 g (8 oz/8 squares) chocolate to 125 ml (4 fl oz/ $\frac{3}{8}$ cup) cream. Bring the cream to the boil in a small saucepan. Melt the chocolate and add the cream, then whisk both ingredients together. If necessary the mixture can be re-melted by warming it in a basin over hot water.

> *QUICK TIP*
> *Block chocolate may be grated into the warm cream. The higher the quality of the chocolate the better the gloss on the ganache.*

Use
- While the ganache is liquid, flood it over a gâteau*.
- Whisk while the ganache is warm and beginning to set, until lighter in colour and creamy. The ganache should hold its shape and it may be piped at this stage.
- Leave to set to a firm paste, then cut into shapes to use as centres for dipped chocolates.
- Whipped as for piping, then rolled into balls and coated in cocoa powder or grated chocolate this makes truffles – useful for arranging around the top edge of a simple chocolate gâteau.
- Ganache may be used in the same way as buttercream*.

Ganache Roses Beat the ganache until it holds its shape. Use a large petal tube (tip) and medium piping bag, then pipe roses (see piped flowers*). For a larger rose, pipe the ganache around a piece of thin dowelling which has been shaped to a point at the end. Leave the roses until firm before use.

Freezing Ganache Roses Piped and moulded roses may be frozen for up to 2 months. Place in the refrigerator the day before using.

RECIPE

WHIPPED GANACHE
A wonderfully rich mixture which whips to double its volume when chilled. Add liqueur with caution: too much may curdle the ganache. Sufficient to fill and coat an 18 cm (7 in) layer cake.

250 g (8 oz/8 squares) dark dessert chocolate, chopped
250 ml (8 fl oz/1 cup) double (heavy) cream
2.5–5 ml ($\frac{1}{2}$–1 tsp) liqueur

●

1 Mix chocolate and cream in a heavy-bottomed saucepan. Melt chocolate over low heat, stirring constantly with a wooden spoon. Still stirring, heat for 10 minutes or until smooth and thick. Do not boil.

2 Pour into a clean bowl, cool, then refrigerate for 1 hour. Stir in liqueur. Whisk until ganache is pale in colour and has doubled in volume.

GARRETT FRILL

A frill of sugarpaste*, named after a South African lady, Elaine Garrett, who introduced the idea. Frills can be applied in a straight line along the base of a cake, in scallops around the sides of the cake and in overlapping layers. The frill can also be applied around the top edge of a cake and made to stand out; it may be used to surround a plaque*, or it may even be attached upside down by inverting the cake to apply the frill. The frill should be allowed to stiffen before turning the cake the right side up.

Template It is important to make an accurate template to fit the area of the cake. Mark a fine groove into the icing on the cake along the top of the template to show where to attach the frill.

SECRETS OF SUCCESS

The cake needs to have deep sides to show off a scalloped frill to perfection. If the cake is too shallow, apply a straight frill around the base.

Cutters Special garrett frill cutters are available from cake decorating shops. A scone cutter or a straight length of paste may also be used. If the centre of the circle has to be cut out, remember that the smaller the section cut out of the middle, the deeper the frill.

Two types of garrett frill cutters
Left: one size round cutter with scalloped edge
Right: scalloped cutter with removable centre sections for making frills of different widths

Pastes Sugarpaste is most often used to make frills. However a mixture of one-third flower paste* to two-thirds sugarpaste will result in a stiffer paste which will hold its shape well. A deep frill is heavy and it may well need the strength.

Frilling the Paste Start by brushing a thin line of water along the template line on the cake. This will make the paste slightly sticky to make the frill adhere.

Use a wooden cocktail stick (toothpick) as plastic will not grip sufficiently. Roll out the paste to approximately 2.5 mm ($\frac{3}{8}$ in) thick, or slightly less. If the paste is too thick it will not frill.

The paste dries out quickly, so cut one section at a time. Roll along the edge of the frill with the cocktail stick (toothpick), using firm pressure. If the paste splits, discard the cocktail stick (toothpick) for a new one. Carefully cut the circle across and straighten it out.

SECRETS OF SUCCESS

If the paste splits along the top edge, try frilling the paste before cutting out the centre portion of the paste. This way, the edge of the paste does not dry out.

Attaching the Frill Brush a second line of water to the section of cake required. Support the frill on the palm of the hand, then gently stick it on the cake.

STEP-BY-STEP TO SUCCESS

ATTACHING THE FRILL

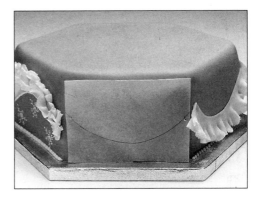

1 Make a paper template to indicate the curve of the frill; attach to the cake securely with pins.

2 Using a scriber or needle, scribe the line of the curve on the cake.

3 Attach the frill to the cake using a little egg-white or water.

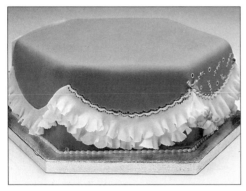

4 The second frill is attached with a crimper. Pipe tiny dots in contrasting colour following the crimped line.

Chocolate Frills Make the chocolate paste as for chocolate* roses. This paste can be rolled out thinly and cut to make garrett frills. If the paste is sticky, use a little cocoa powder when rolling out. Use the end of a paint brush to frill the edge of the paste and attach it to the cake with melted chocolate.

Decoration If the frill is applied to a freshly coated cake, crimpers can be used to join the frill to the sugarpaste on the cake (as shown). The frill is much thinner to crimp than the surface of the cake, so be sure to apply most of the crimped design to the cake surface.

Broderie Anglaise Decoration: May be added to the frill as well as to the surface of the cake. Stamp a pattern of holes before attaching the frill. Do not make too many holes or the frill will weaken. When the frill has dried, pipe outlines around the holes in royal icing* using a fine writing tube (tip).

Royal Iced Cakes Frills can be applied to royal icing. Pipe a line of icing just below the marked line on the cake, then press the frill, firmly but gently, in place.

SECRETS OF SUCCESS

Support the frill on a piece of thin card as you attach it. A quick method of decorating the top edge of the frill, and also making sure it is well applied, is to run a dressmaker's tracing wheel along the edge while the paste is still soft. The rounded end of a small paint brush may also be used to mark decorative impressions in the edge of the paste.

Flouncing the Frill One method of lifting the frill is to pipe a rope of royal icing fractionally below the marked line on the side of the cake. Apply the frill when the icing is dry and it will flow over the iced line.

While the frill is soft it may be lifted. Run a paint brush sideways under the frill to lift it slightly. Position cocktail sticks (toothpicks) at intervals into the cake to support the frill. Leave until the frill is dry, then carefully withdraw the sticks.

Alternatively, place rolls of plastic wrap under the frills and remove them with tweezers when the frill is dry.

Double Frill Apply a frill around the cake. Leave to dry. Position a second frill, overlapping the first by about half its depth. A third frill can be applied if desired. Layered frills are always applied from the base upwards.

> *QUICK TIP*
> *When applying layered frills, make each layer of frill a paler shade than the last one.*

Colouring The cut-out paste can be dusted with colouring before the frilling technique is applied. This way the blossom tint* can be brushed on directly where it is required. Frilling the paste will ensure the dust clings into the paste. This method also reduces the risk of breaking the frill, which may happen if brushed once the paste is on the cake and dry.

However, to obtain a coloured edge only on a frill, dust it with colour once it is dry. Load a paint brush with colour and apply the tint from underneath the frill. This will coat the edge of the frill with blossom tint.

GATEAUX

The French word for cakes, generally used in culinary terms for highly decorated, light cakes based on sponges and often completely covered with cream.

A base of fatless sponge, Genoese sponge or Victoria Sandwich is sliced into layers and sandwiched with one or more fillings. The layers of cake are often moistened with liqueur or a flavoured stock syrup (sugar dissolved in water, brought to the boil, cooled and used as required). The decoration may be simple – a dusting of icing (confectioners') sugar – or more elaborate with toppings such as chocolate, whipped cream, crème au beurre* or buttercream*.

Preparation Cut a small groove down the side of the cake. This will help in placing the layers of the cake back in the same position. Lay the palm of the hand flat on top of the cake and use a serrated knife to cut the layers.

Portion Control When the gâteau has been coated but before adding the decoration, mark the top into equal portions.

Torten Divider A rigid, circular plastic divider with blades radiating from the centre. Used to divide a gâteau into portions of exactly the same size.

Types of Icing for Gâteaux Lemon or orange curd, jams, whipped cream, ganache*, chocolate buttercream, fondant* and buttercream*.

Decorations Piped decorations, chopped nuts, fresh fruit, chocolate shapes, feather icing*, vermicelli and marzipan*.

> *QUICK TIP*
> *Return the gloss to dull vermicelli, by placing in a basin over hot water for a few minutes.*

G

GELATINE

A substance extracted from protein found in bones. Available in two forms, powdered, which is the most common, and leaf.

Powdered Gelatine Always add gelatine to the liquid, not the other way round. Sprinkle it over cold water, do not stir, and leave to stand for 15 minutes. By then the gelatine will have absorbed the water and swollen to a spongy consistency. This process is known as sponging. Stand the bowl over hot water, away from the heat, and leave, without stirring, until the gelatine has dissolved completely into a clear liquid. Stir before use.

Leaf Gelatine Sheets of clear, brittle gelatine, embossed with a diamond pattern, available from specialist shops.

Dissolving: Place the sheets in a bowl of cold water and leave to soak for 10 minutes. If the pieces of gelatine are too large, they can be broken into smaller sections; however, do not break them into small pieces. By this time the gelatine will be soft. Remove it from the liquid and dissolve it in the required amount of liquid, in a bowl over hot water.

Decoration Leaf gelatine may be used to make very realistic lattice windows for models. The diamond pattern, already imprinted on the gelatine, creates the authentic look. The size of the pattern may need to be reduced, in which case use the tip of a red hot wire to score extra lines on the leaf gelatine – it will not melt. Attach the windows to the model with royal icing*. A stained-glass window effect can be made either on the windows of a model or on the surface of a cake. This effect is achieved by placing a drawn design under the gelatine and tracing it, using food colour and a paint brush, straight on the gelatine. Do not have too much liquid on the paint brush when painting the sections.

RECIPE

GELATINE PASTE
Makes about 500 g (1lb 2oz) paste.

500 g (1lb 2oz/4$\frac{1}{2}$ cups) icing (confectioners') sugar
60 ml (2 fl oz/4 tbsp) cold water
5 ml (1 tsp) white vegetable fat (shortening)
5 ml (1 tsp) liquid glucose
15 ml (3 tsp) gelatine

•

1 Soak the gelatine in the cold water and place over a pan of hot water until dissolved and clear. Do not allow the gelatine to boil.

2 Add the fat and glucose to the gelatine and stir until melted. Add this mixture to the sifted sugar and knead together to form a firm paste. Add a little more water if the paste is too stiff.

3 To help the keeping quality of the paste, pat the surface all over with a little water then place in a plastic bag. Store in a cool place; it is not necessary to refrigerate this paste. Leave for 24 hours.

GLACE ICING

Quickly made and applied, this is a liquid icing for flooding over cakes and biscuits. It dries very quickly.

Ingredients Water and icing (confectioners') sugar give a semi-transparent coating. To obtain a more opaque finish replace the water with egg white. This results in a whiter icing and one which will allow time for adding decorations before it starts to dry out.

Preparation If possible coat the base of the cake as this is usually a firmer, flatter surface. Brush with hot apricot glaze* and leave to cool before coating. The glaze creates a barrier and stops the icing sinking into the cake surface.

Consistency Although this icing is quick to make it can cause trouble when it is too thin, in which case it will run off the cake, or too thick, when it will not flow. Stir the icing gently. Do not beat it or air bubbles will appear and they are difficult to remove.

Test for Consistency: Think of a puddle and raindrops. Drop just a little of the icing from a teaspoon into the bowl of icing. The impression made by the drop should disappear after a moment or two. For a large cake use slightly thinner icing than for small cakes.

Flavouring Replace the water with orange or lemon juice for tangy flavour to complement the sweetness. Add coffee essence or dissolved cocoa powder. Other flavourings may be added as wished.

Coating the Top and Side of a Cake Put the cake on a wire rack over a baking sheet. Pour all the icing over when the apricot glaze is dry. Immediately tap the rack on the work surface to tease the icing all around the side of the cake.

Remember . . . *Place any decorations on the icing before it dries or it will crack.*

RECIPE

GLACE ICING
Sufficient to top a 20 cm (8 in) cake. Orange or lemon juice may be used instead of water.

*185 g (6 oz/$1\frac{1}{4}$ cups) icing
(confectioners') sugar
10–15 ml (2–3 tsp) warm water
flavouring and/or colouring as desired*

•

1 Sift icing (confectioners') sugar into a bowl and gradually add liquid, stirring constantly until icing slackens sufficiently to coat the back of the spoon.

2 Pour the icing over the cake, smoothing the surface with a spatula which has been dipped in hot water. Apply any decorations quickly, avoiding any that might shed colour.

GLYCERINE

Sweet, colourless and odourless liquid, also known as glycerol, which attracts moisture from the atmosphere.

Use
In cakes to delay the staling process. In paste colours and piping gel* to keep them moist. Glycerine is also added to royal icing* to prevent it setting too hard.

GREASEPROOF PAPER

See Papers, coverings and wrappings*.

GUM ARABIC

A pale-coloured powder obtained from the acacia tree. Gum arabic is available from specialist cake decorating suppliers. To dissolve the gum completely, place it in a small basin. Add cold water, then stir and stand the basin over hot water until the gum dissolves.

Use
● As a hot glaze on petits fours once removed from the oven.
● As a glaze applied to dry marzipan animals or fruits.
● As an edible glue, for example to stick the petals of small pastillage* flowers together.

RECIPE

GUM ARABIC GLAZE
This glaze can be painted on any surface which requires a shine. It also makes a good adhesive. Rose water can be used instead of water but it is more expensive!

*5 ml (1 tsp) gum arabic (acacia) powder
15 ml (1 tbsp) water*

•

1 Place the gum arabic in a small bowl, then stir in the water. Heat over hot water, until completely dissolved.

2 Heating the gum arabic will make it keep better.

GUM PASTE

There are many recipes, containing either gelatine* or gum tragacanth* to make a stiff white paste. This is used for making models, such as churches, containers and decorations for the tops of cakes. The paste dries out quickly when exposed to the air and should be stored in a tightly closed plastic bag, then placed in an airtight container.

Use
Cut off a piece of paste and knead it until it is soft enough to work with. A small amount of vegetable fat can be worked into the paste if it cracks. Gum paste is not suitable for making flowers.
Models: Place the rolled-out paste on a flat-surface, preferably glass or perspex. Use a long, sharp knife to cut out pieces. Do not drag the knife or make small cuts. Cut out any other sections, without moving the paste. Leave to dry in a warm place without removing from the glass. Turn over after 24 hours.

> *QUICK TIP*
> *When making models, sand down the edges of the pieces before joining them together.*

GUM TRAGACANTH

A gum extracted from a small tree or bush found in Mediterranean countries, including Greece and Turkey, Iran and Syria. The name is derived from *traga-kantha* – *tragaos* (goat) and *akantha* (thorn).

It is available as a cream-coloured powder which expands when moistened. It is expensive but only a small amount is needed to stiffen paste.

ICINGS

This chart shows which icings to use on different cakes.

	ROYAL ICING	SUGARPASTE	GLACE ICING	BUTTERCREAM	CREME AU BEURRE	AMERICAN FROSTING	MELTED CHOCOLATE	WHIPPED CREAM
Rich Fruit Cake	•	•						
Light Fruit Cake	•	•						
Madeira Cake		•	•	•		•	•	
Victoria Sandwich		•	•	•	•	•	•	•
One-Stage Cake		•	•	•	•	•	•	•
Chocolate Cake		•	•	•	•		•	•
Genoese Sponge		•	•	•	•		•	•
Fatless Sponge			•	•	•	•	•	•

ICING TUBES (TIPS)

Buy the best quality icing tubes (tips) from specialist cake decorating suppliers. These are made from nickel silver and they have virtually invisible seams. The best icing tubes (tips) have well-defined points and sharp definition to any serrations. They should be long and narrow to fit perfectly into a paper piping bag without leaving a gap for icing to ooze out. Price is always a good guide to quality. Cheaper icing tubes (tips) are sometimes badly seamed which may result in the icing twisting as it flows.

Sizes All icing tubes (tips) have numbers stamped on them but the sizes indicated by number vary from one manufacturer to another. The cheaper quality writing tubes (tips) have larger openings.

Screw-on Tubes (Tips) These are intended for use with screw adaptors and nylon piping bags. The bags are too big and difficult to grip for fine work.

Icing Syringe Difficult to use and far too large for most work. It is not easy to control the amount of icing pushed out from these gadgets.

Savoy Tubes Made in cream-coloured plastic as well as metal, with plain or star design. Used to pipe quantities of whipped cream, these are fitted in a heavy-duty material piping bag.

Care of Icing Tubes (Tips) Soak the tubes (tips) immediately after use in a cup or basin of water. A fine brush cleaner is useful to clean the opening. Do not poke a sharp implement into the point as this could damage the edge. Always check that the hole at the end of a fine tube (tip) is clear before drying and storing.

Storing Tubes (Tips) Store separately to avoid damage. Plastic boxes can be purchased with individual compartments to house the icing tubes (tips).

Suggested Uses for Popular Icing Tubes (Tips)
No. 1 Writing: Lines, trellis*, filigree*, writing, dots and loops*.
No. 2 Writing: Lines, trellis, writing, dots and loops.
No. 8 Star: For buttercream* and royal icing* shells and stars.
No. 12 Star: For buttercream stars, shells and rosettes.

No. 43 Star: For royal icing stars and shells.
No. 44 Star: For royal icing stars, shells and scrolls.
No. 22 Basket Work: For royal icing basket work*.
No. 57, 58, 59 Petal: Different sizes of petal tubes (tips) for making a variety of flowers and frills. Also for left-handed users.
No. 59 Large petal: For piping buttercream or ganache* roses.

TUBE (TIP) SIZES AND PIPED RESULTS

The pictures below and on the following page give some indication of the different effects which can be achieved using some typical icing tubes (tips). Practise on a piece of card, using bright-coloured icing to discover the potential of each icing tube (tip).

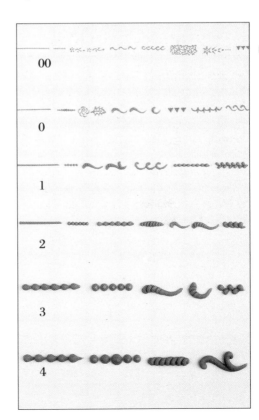

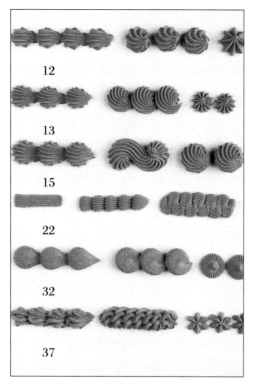

12

13

15

22

32

37

K

KNIVES

The choice and quality of knives is all important. The right knife can make all the difference between success and failure. Good quality knives will last for many years if treated well.

Cook's Knife: A heavy kitchen knife with a long, straight blade. This is used to cut a straight edge in one movement. Useful for marzipan* and sugarpaste*.

Craft Knife: A small, scalpel-like implement with a sharp, wedge-shaped blade. For making small cuts in modelling work. To slit petals on pulled flowers and other fine cutting operations.

Cranked Palette Knife: With an extra thin blade, obtainable from art shops. Some may not be rustproof, so check before buying. This thin and flexible blade is useful for sliding under runouts* and lace* sections.

Long Serrated Knife: For slicing gâteaux and levelling the tops of cakes.

Palette Knives: Stainless steel with firm blades, 15 cm (6 in) and 10 cm (4 in) blades. For spreading buttercream* and royal icing*.

Wedding Knife The bride and groom make the first cut into the wedding cake using the ceremonial knife which may have a pearl handle. A cluster of small flowers and ribbons may be tied around the handle. A regimental sword may be used in place of the knife. Once the cake is taken behind the scenes, a large, sharp, cook's knife should be used for cutting it into pieces.

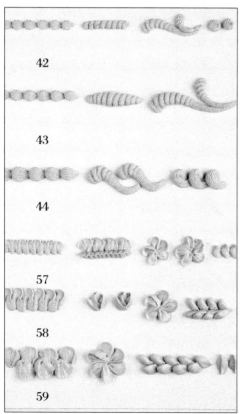

42

43

44

57

58

59

88

Merry Christmas Plaque Cake
see page 187

Christmas Bauble
see page 189

Santa's Slide
see page 191

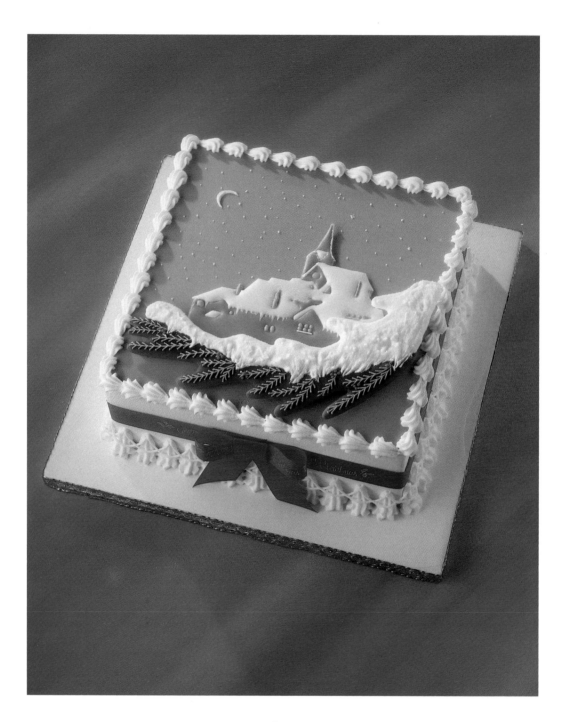

Silent Night
see page 193

L

LACE WORK

An old needlecraft skill which has been copied in icing and applied to modern cakes. The lace is piped in separate pieces using royal icing*. Once dry, the pieces of lace are attached to the iced cake with dots of icing.

Template With practice, lace may be piped freehand; until then use a template of the lace pattern. Graph paper, marked with coloured lines to denote the required depth of the lace, is a half-way alternative to a template.

> *QUICK TIP*
> *Draw a row of the lace pattern pieces, each slightly apart to allow for piping. Attach a tag of stiff card to the bottom of the sheet of paper: use this tag to slide the paper as you finish piping each row of lace pieces.*

Icing The royal icing should be made with egg white or pure albumen powder*. If the icing has been made using an electric beater, beat a small amount with a wooden spoon for a few minutes to achieve a smooth texture. The icing is best made a day ahead to allow it to settle.

SECRETS OF SUCCESS

To eliminate air bubbles, and any minute grains of hard sugar, force the icing through a piece of nylon stocking. Keep a piece of new stocking in your cake decorating kit for this purpose, scalding it before and after use to keep it perfectly clean. This is one of the finest sieves available and it is ideal for any fine work.

Piping The size of the icing tube (tip) will vary according to expertise: the more experienced you are, the finer the size. However, do not use a tube (tip) larger than no. 1. Experiment with piping on a sloping surface similar to a draughtsman's board – some cake decorators find this an easier way to work.

A design without too many joins is quicker to work and it looks neater. If the top of the lace is pointed, place the template with the point facing towards you. Pipe one side of the piece of lace, ending at the point. Then pipe the second side, bringing the line of icing to finish at the point and to complete the section of lace.

Pipe down to the point of the lace

Choice of Paper As well as wax paper, pipe the lace on teflon-coated paper, smooth roasting wrap or cellophane. When dry, the lace pieces may be removed easily from all these types.

Attaching the Lace to the Cake Pipe a small section of icing along the line on the cake. Attach the lace while the icing is still soft. Alternatively, pipe two dots of icing on a piece of lace, then apply it to the cake.

Short Cuts Lace can be tedious to make so it is worth taking a few short cuts when you are familiar with the technique.

Square Cake: Pipe a horizontal line on the paper. While the line is wet, pipe lace pieces which touch both the line and each other. Once dry, attach the lace to the cake in strips.

Bell: A quick way of attaching lace around the edge of a moulded bell – place the bell on paper and draw around the outside edge. Draw a second line 5 mm ($\frac{1}{4}$ in) inside the first line. Use the inside line as a template to make small lace pieces, all touching each other. Once dry, turn the lace over carefully. Pipe a line of royal icing around the edge of the bell and place it gently on top of the lace circle.

Alternatively, support the bell sideways and pipe hanging loops on a section of the edge. Allow to dry before moving the bell to pipe another section.

Colouring Lace Use blossom tints* to colour the icing for lace. Most paste colours contain glycerine* which attracts moisture from the atmosphere and they will soften the lace.

> *QUICK TIP*
> Attach a sheet of lace design templates on a firm board and use as a permanent fixture for immediate use.

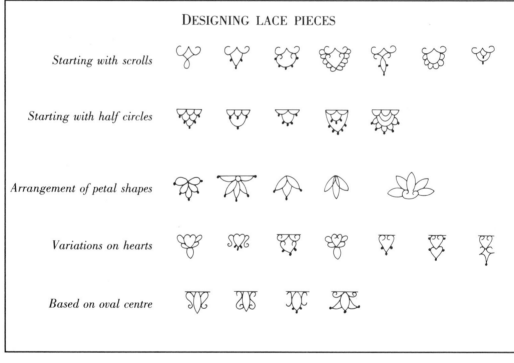

DESIGNING LACE PIECES

Starting with scrolls

Starting with half circles

Arrangement of petal shapes

Variations on hearts

Based on oval centre

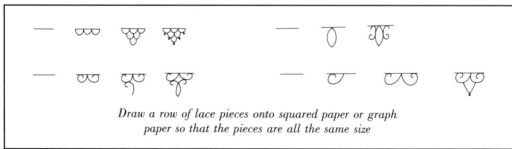

Draw a row of lace pieces onto squared paper or graph paper so that the pieces are all the same size

LATTICE

See Trellis.

LEAVES

It is important to match the leaves with the flowers for best effect on a cake. Some leaves which grow naturally with their flowers are not necessarily the best choice for use on the comparatively small cake surface – tiny lily of the valley flowers and their large leaves are a good example. Also, a contrasting leaf can look wonderful, as in the case of roses displayed with variegated ivy leaves.

PROFESSIONAL TIP

Always curve leaves as you make them so that they dry into a realistic shape.

Leaf Cutters These are available in too many shapes and sizes to list, from rose or ivy leaves to oak and holly leaves.

Marzipan* and Sugarpaste* Leaves As well as using leaf cutters, diamond shapes may be cut and marked with the back of a knife, for example to make holly leaves.

Rose Leaves Press the back of a clean rose leaf on thinly rolled paste. Use a cocktail stick (toothpick) to pull out tiny points around the edge of the leaves. Do this by making a tiny scratching movement at the edge of the paste.

Pastillage Leaves Make these using a cutter and mark them with a plastic veiner.

Wired Pastillage Leaves Burn the paper coating off the top 1 cm ($\frac{1}{2}$ in) of the wire. Moisten the end of the wire and place it in the leaf. This gives a neater result as the paper covering on the wire tends to show.

Chocolate Leaves See under Chocolate*.

Piped Leaves A leaf piping tube (tip) may be used. Alternatively place firm buttercream* or royal icing* in a strong piping bag. Push the icing down to the point of the bag. Using the thumb and forefinger, flatten the point of the bag horizontally, then cut an arrowhead shape in it. Keep both sides of the arrowhead equal in length. The buttercream or icing can then be piped directly on the surface of the cake.

Bought Leaves Available in green, gold or silver paper, with or without wires. Silk and satin leaves are sold as well as the old favourite dried fern.

Ivy Leaf Ivy leaves are particularly useful for Christmas cakes. The ones shown are variegated ivy but the principle is the same for all types.

L

Method
Take a piece of pale ivory-coloured paste and roll into a ball. Squash, and roll with a

paintbrush, retaining a thicker part at one end for the wire. Cut out the ivy leaf, positioning the base at thicker part of the paste.

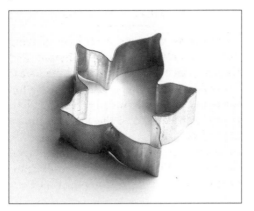

Hook a piece of 28-gauge green wire and dip the hooked end in egg white. Hold the leaf firmly between your thumb and first finger and insert the wire. Place on an ivy leaf or violet leaf veiner or use a real ivy leaf. Vein on both sides. Run a cocktail stick (toothpick) over the edge to soften slightly. Place on a sponge and vein the centre of the leaf using a veining tool or cocktail stick (toothpick). Pinch the bottom slightly and leave to dry.

When dry, dust the back green, then work the variegation by using two shades of green. Brush the lighter shade on first using a flat paintbrush and brushing from the centre to the outside of the leaf. Then using a darker shade, dust on top of the lighter colour, again working from the centre outwards.

Periwinkle The periwinkle is made in the same way as the variegated ivy but using

the same cutter as clematis. The green is painted on by mixing green colouring with spirit. Start with a very pale green for the background, then slowly build up the colour by adding two stronger shades. Dry before using.

Foliage Several varieties of foliage can be made in the same way as the ivy, using various cutters. They should be coloured in different shades of green, either by dusting with powder colour, painting or varnishing to achieve the different effects.

Ferns Make a hooked wire skeleton, as for ivy, then cut out the leaf shapes. Stick them on with softened flower paste which acts like strong glue. Dust or paint green.

LIQUID GLUCOSE

Known as corn syrup, or clear corn syrup, in America, glucose is a simple sugar. Liquid glucose has a thick, syrupy texture and it becomes runny when warmed. Obtainable from cake decorating suppliers and chemist shops.

> *QUICK TIP*
> *Chemists also sell powdered glucose – this is chemically pure glucose which is not the same as liquid glucose.*

Use
● Liquid glucose attracts moisture and it is used in a variety of pastes to keep them pliable.
● Add a small amount of liquid glucose to a sugar syrup to prevent crystallization.

LOOPS

These are a graceful addition to the side of a decorated cake. If a cake is too deep, pipe two or three layers of loops to give the impression that the cake is less high. They look very authentic on a drum novelty cake, particularly if piped in red.

Marking the Cake Mark the cake before piping the border along the top edge. Use a template to mark sections measuring about 3.5 cm (1½ in). The wider and deeper the loops are made, the more difficult it is to pipe them and to control their shape.

Piping Use a small bag with a writing tube (tip). The icing should be well beaten and it should flow easily out of the tube using a small amount of pressure. Have the cake positioned at eye level and with the top tilting slightly away from you.

Touch the icing tube (tip) to the cake surface to connect the icing. Then draw the icing away, keeping up the pressure on the bag, and let it hang before touching the icing tube (tip) back against the cake to attach the icing. Do not try to pipe against the side of the cake. Allowing the loop to hang will let it fall into a natural curve.

SECRETS of SUCCESS

Counting as you pipe each loop of icing helps to achieve an even rhythm and therefore an equal length for all the loops. To make a large loop, start from the top edge and allow the thread of icing to flow down to the centre of the loop. Start the second half of the loop from the opposite top edge then secure the thread of icing in the centre. Disguise the join in the centre of the loop with a suitable decoration.

Upturned Loops or Arches Use a firm support with a diameter smaller than the cake, for example a smaller cake tin, and cover it with a clean tea-towel. Place the cake upside down on the support. Pipe the loops hanging down and leave to dry before carefully turning the cake upright.

Piping hanging loops on a bell instead of attaching lace sections

M

MADEIRA CAKE

See also Cakes*.

A plain cake similar to American pound cake, this may be used as an alternative to Victoria Sandwich when a firm surface is required for decorating. To lighten the texture of the cake, slice through it twice and sandwich together with a filling such as flavoured buttercream*.

Madeira cake may also be used as an alternative to a rich fruit cake* for a celebration cake. Marzipan* and royal icing* or sugarpaste* can be used to cover the cake.

Plain Madeira cake should be topped with a piece of candied peel.

Crinoline Lady Cake The shape of this cake requires it to be cooked in an ovenproof basin or bowl, or a Dolly Varden tin (pan) is the name given to a tin (pan) formed in a basin shape. Because of the depth of the cake a Victoria Sandwich mixture tends to sink, therefore the firmer consistency of Madeira cake is ideal for the longer cooking time required.

PROFESSIONAL TIP

Madeira cake differs from Victoria Sandwich cake in the proportion of flour to other ingredients; it contains more flour to fat. This makes it more stable for making larger, deep cakes which may sink if made with Victoria Sandwich mixture.

MARZIPAN

Has been around for a long time – the oldest recipe said to be in existence dates from the 1400s.

Home-made Marzipan Can be made with whole egg, egg yolk or the whites alone. The last does not have as much flavour but it keeps for longer. The large amount of sugar used acts to some extent as a preservative.

SECRETS OF SUCCESS

Do not overwork the marzipan by kneading it for too long as the oil will be released from the almonds making the paste greasy. A recipe which involves making a sugar syrup, then adding ground almonds and egg will always be smoother than one made by mixing all the ingredients together.

Bought Marzipan or Almond Paste If the word marzipan or almond is used on the packet this indicates that the product is made up of about two-thirds almonds and one-third sugar.

The pale marzipan is of higher quality than the yellow variety.

Powdered Marzipan A ready-to-mix marzipan available from some specialist cake decorating suppliers. Cooled, boiled water is added and mixed to a paste. This product may then be used as for ordinary marzipan.

This powder keeps well and is useful when a small amount of marzipan is needed. It can be made up as necessary and saves having spare packets of marzipan which may harden.

Remember . . . *When adding the water, do not add the total quantity at once: too much will make the marzipan sticky and by adding additional icing (confectioners') sugar you will spoil the proportions.*

Applying Marzipan to Cakes To estimate the quantity of marzipan required to cover a cake, first weigh the cake base. The weight of the cake represents the combined weight of marzipan and sugarpaste. Divide the weight in half to calculate the quantities of marzipan and sugarpaste. For example, if the cake weighs 1.8 kg (3¾ lb), you will require 900 g (1 lb 14 oz) each of marzipan and sugarpaste. This calculation does not allow for coating the board. Prepare the cake before beginning to roll out the marzipan. Trim the top of the cake with a sharp serrated knife to make it level.

Roll out the marzipan between spacers to ensure that it is evenly thick. Use a long, sharp knife to cut a straight edge in one movement. Roll out marzipan on icing (confectioners') sugar, not flour or cornflour (corn starch) which could ferment if trapped between the cake and marzipan. When rolling marzipan keep it moving to stop it from sticking to the work surface.

Always apply marzipan to the base of the cake and use that for the top surface.

Covering the Side of the Cake When applying apricot glaze* to the side of the cake, ensure that it does not spread too near the marzipan on the top. If any glaze smudges on top of the marzipan it can cause a stain to show on royal icing*.

Roll out a long sausage shape of marzipan by hand, then flatten it. Use a rolling pin to roll the marzipan to the required thickness, then cut it to the depth and circumference of the cake. Roll up the paste like a bandage and wrap it around the side of the cake, overlapping the cut edges.

PROFESSIONAL TIP

To obtain a neat join, make a clean vertical cut through the two layers of overlapping marzipan and remove the surplus.

Applying Marzipan for Sugarpaste* Covering If the cake is deep it can be difficult to remove the pleats that form in the marzipan. Therefore apply the marzipan separately to the top and sides and use the palm of the hand or a plastic smoother to blend the top edge of the cake into a soft curve. Leave to dry for 3–4 days, covered loosely with greaseproof paper.

Keeping Qualities Marzipan will dry out if exposed to the air. Wrap it well in a plastic bag to keep it soft and pliable, then store in a cool, dry place. If the marzipan has become hard, warm it for a few minutes to make it softer by placing in a bowl over hot water.

MARZIPAN CHART

Cake Size	13 cm (5 in) square 15.5 cm (6 in) round	15.5 cm (6 in) square 17.5 cm (7 in) round	17.5 cm (7 in) square 20 cm (8 in) round	20 cm (8 in) square 22.5 cm (9 in) round
Marzipan	375 g (12 oz)	750 g (1½ lb)	875 g (1¾ lb)	1 kg (2 lb)

Cake Size	22.5 cm (9 in) square 25 cm (10 in) round	25 cm (10 in) square 27.5 cm (11 in) round	27.5 cm (11 in) square 30 cm (12 in) round
Marzipan	1.25 kg (2½ lb)	1.5 kg (3 lb)	1.75 kg (3½ lb)

RECIPE

BOILED MARZIPAN
Makes 900 g (2 lb) marzipan.

450 g (1 lb/2 cups) granulated sugar
155 ml (5 fl oz/$\frac{2}{3}$ cup) plus 60 ml (4 tbsp)
water
large pinch of cream of tartar
350 g (12 oz/3$\frac{1}{2}$ cups) ground almonds
2 egg whites
icing (confectioners') sugar
almond essence (extract)

●

1 Place the sugar and water in a large saucepan and heat very gently, stirring with a metal spoon. Do not allow the syrup to boil until every grain of sugar has dissolved.

2 Add the cream of tartar and bring the syrup to the boil, then boil rapidly without stirring until it reaches the soft ball stage – 115°C (240°F) on a sugar thermometer. Do not overboil, or the icing will thicken and be crumbly to handle. To test for soft ball, drop a small teaspoonful of the syrup into a cup of cold water – it should form a soft ball when rubbed between the fingers.

3 Stop the syrup boiling by placing the base of the saucepan in cold water, then immediately stir in the ground almonds and unbeaten egg whites. Return the pan to a low heat and stir until the mixture thickens slightly.

4 Turn the mixture out onto a marble slab or a plastic laminated surface and work it until it cools and thickens. When it is cold enough, knead the mixture with your hands until it is smooth, using a light dusting of sifted icing (confectioners') sugar.

5 It will take up to half its weight in icing sugar, but if a lot of sugar is kneaded in, you must add some almond essence to flavour the mixture as well. Store in an airtight jar or thick polythene bag until the marzipan is ready to use. If it dries out, it can be moistened with a little egg white.

6 The recipe can be doubled in quantity; however, if you want to increase the quantities still further, you must use a very large saucepan and work surface.

STEP-BY-STEP TO SUCCESS

APPLYING MARZIPAN COATING

1 Place the cake on a thin cake board cut to its exact size. Pack any uneven areas or holes in the cake with marzipan – this gives a smooth surface when coated. Place the cake on a clean piece of greaseproof paper so that it may be moved easily.

2 Use good quality marzipan at room temperature and knead it until it is pliable on a clean work surface. Spread a thin layer of apricot jam over the cake. Lightly dust the work surface with icing (confectioners') sugar, then roll out the marzipan to 1 cm ($\frac{1}{2}$ in) thick.

3 Check the size of the marzipan against the dimensions of the cake. Using the hands and forearms, lift the marzipan over the cake. Polish the top with a smoother to remove air bubbles.

4 Smooth the side of the marzipan into place with the palm of your hand. If pleats form, gently lift the marzipan slightly away from the cake, then tuck your hand down firmly into the base of the cake and smooth the paste upwards.

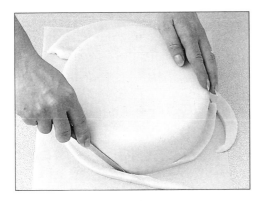

5 Trim the marzipan to about 3 cm (1¼ in) larger than required. Use a knife to tuck the marzipan into the board around the base of the cake, then trim off the excess to ensure a neat bottom edge.

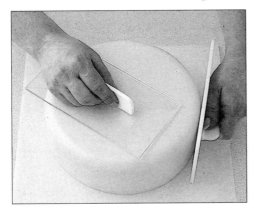

6 Using smoothers, polish the marzipan until it is completely even. Any flaws in the surface of a marzipan coating will show through the sugarpaste covering. Leave the cake to dry on the paper.

MARZIPAN FLOWERS

See also Moulded flowers*

Marzipan is an excellent medium for modelling flowers. It is pliable, easily coloured, soft enough to model yet stiff enough to hold its shape. A variety of flowers can be modelled by hand, including roses, daffodils, fuschias and carnations.

Storing Leave the flowers to dry in the air. Store in a cardboard box, supported by tissue paper.

METAL RULE

Also known as a ruler, royal icing blade or straight edge. A metal rule will hold its shape when smoothing the icing across a cake surface. The edge should be fine and smooth, without any indents or flaws that may mark the icing.

A ruler, rather than a knife, will obtain a smooth, flat coat of royal icing. The edge of a wooden ruler is too thick and a plastic ruler will bend with the weight of the royal icing.

MEXICAN PASTE

Traditional Mexican celebration cakes are often decorated with models of figures. The paste used for the models and their clothes is made from a combination of icing (confectioners') sugar, gum tragacanth*, liquid glucose* and water. Once made, the paste should be stored for a few days to allow the gum to expand, then it may be rolled out until transparent, cut to shape and used to 'dress' the models.

SECRETS OF SUCCESS

If the paste dries out, add a small amount of white vegetable fat or mix in some sugarpaste*.

MEXICAN PASTE
Makes about 250 g (8 oz) paste.

*220 g (7 oz/1¼ cups) icing
(confectioners') sugar
15 ml (1 tbsp) gum tragacanth
5 ml (1 tsp) liquid glucose
30 ml (2 tbsp) cold water*

●

1 Sift the icing (confectioners') sugar and gum tragacanth on a clean work surface and make a well in the middle. Add the liquid glucose and 25 ml (5 tsp) of the water.

2 Gradually mix the ingredients to a paste, adding the extra water if the mixture is too firm. Knead briefly until smooth. Then wrap the paste in a polythene bag and place it in an airtight container.

3 Excess paste may be wrapped tightly and frozen in an airtight container.

MODELLING

Pre-formed moulds are readily available and will produce competent figures but the poses and sizes available are restricted. Far more original and lifelike results can be attained by building up the figure freely with the use of an armature (wire support).

If the figure or animal is to be dressed, the body itself can be a fairly rough shape as it will be hidden and the areas that will be visible, such as the arms and head, can be modelled in greater detail. One important point to remember is that the addition of clothes will enlarge the figure, so the body needs to be thinner and it must be thoroughly dry before adding clothing or it will crack.

Proportions are very important when modelling human figures. The head should measure one-sixth of the body size. When modelling a child, this proportion is different. The head is much larger and will measure roughly a quarter of the body size. When the arms are held at the side of the body, the fingers should reach mid-thigh. Many people tend to make the arms far too short and this will spoil the balance of the figure. Ask someone to pose if possible so that a natural position can be achieved.

The Face This is the most important area as it tends to be the focal point of the figure and the whole effect can be spoiled if, for instance, a flower fairy, Goldilocks or baby has a cracked or lined face with a crooked nose. A mould can be made from plaster using a doll's head cut in half. The head can be formed by pushing a small ball of paste into the mould so that the features are formed on one side and the back part of the ball forms the back of the head.

When painting on the features, the eyes should focus on an area within the modelled scene, so that they don't appear vacant or staring. Paint the iris (the coloured area of the eye). When dry, paint the black pupil and again, when dry, highlight with a dot of white. This should bring some life to the eyes. Blush the cheeks with dusting powder, lightly add freckles, if desired, with minute dots of paprika paste colour. Paint lips also with paprika, not bright red or bright pink.

Hair can be piped with royal icing or it can be made by pushing soft paste through a garlic press or a clay gun. It could also be rolled with the fingers into fine strands. It can be applied to form tight curls or, by using the gun, plaits or ringlets.

Modelling Animals When modelling animals, try to work from photographs, real life or illustrations so that the pose is correct and most important, the colour and markings of the fur and formation of paws and features are correct and a realistic likeness is achieved. The body shape and pose are important if the model is to bear any resemblance to the particular creature, even if an animal is used as a fantasy animal.

Paste For the rough body shapes or anything that will be hidden with royal icing or clothes, use gelatine paste. For finer detailed work, clothes, face, hands, for instance, use fine pastillage, flower paste or modelling paste.

Breakages It is advisable to make spares of fragile items in case of breakages because of time involved in the drying process.

Use of Wire and Plaster Moulds A warning must be given if wire, plaster moulds or cocktail sticks have been used to support the modelling in case it is eaten by a child.

BABY WRAPPED IN QUILT

Head Make baby's head by pushing a large ball of skin-coloured paste into a plaster mould (made from cutting a small doll's head in half and making the impression). Place on a cocktail stick and leave to dry.

Body Make a large cone, bend the cone slightly backwards to give an exaggerated shape to the abdomen. Create a curve between the back and bottom using forefinger. Make indentations with a large ball tool where head, arms and legs are to be placed. The quilt disguises the body shape.

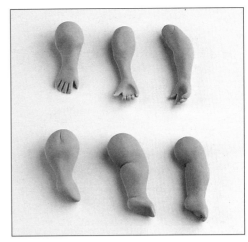

Hands and Arms Tap one end of a sausage and flatten to form a spade shape. Cut out a small 'V' for the thumb then cut fingers. Separate each finger, smooth and round tips. Place onto a piece of foam and curve fingers by drawing a ball tool over them towards the palm, indent palm with ball tool. Form wrist, elbow and upper arm by rolling paste with fingers. Place in a natural pose to dry.

Legs Taper one end of a sausage and flatten to form a spade shape as for arms. Make 4 cuts for toes, round ends. Form heel and ankle using thumb and forefinger. Shape knee and thigh. Indent bottom of foot to create arch. Place in a natural position and dry.

To Assemble Attach head to body, and legs to torso. Make a nappy by rolling a piece of white paste to medium thickness and wrap around body. Texture nappy by pinching paste with fine pointed tweezers to create a towelling-like effect. Attach arms. Pipe on hair using royal icing. Paint facial features and dust cheeks.

Quilt Position baby on a tissue paper template and practise wrapping baby in tissue until satisfied with folds. Shape and lay the quilt so that when the baby is wrapped in the actual paste it can be handled as little as possible, as over handling and re-wrapping will cause the paste to crack and tear. When satisfied, mark on template the position of the baby's bottom. When the quilt is completely dry, paint in the patchwork pattern with a fine brush using clear paste colours. If working with more than one colour on each pattern, allow each colour to dry thoroughly or streaking will occur. Keep the brush as dry as possible, over-wetting of the paste will cause it to disintegrate.

SECRETS OF SUCCESS

Use a baby doll with movable limbs as a model. Note the way in which arms and legs curve. Practise by making several babies, then use the best for the cake. If you are likely to make several models exactly the same in the future, it is worth keeping one example, unassembled, for reference.

CLOWN JACK-IN-THE-BOX

Illustrated on page 271
Templates on pages 243–244

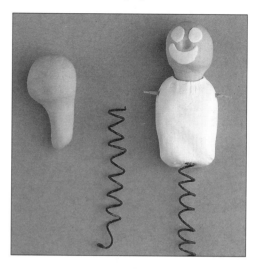

Spring Make a spring by wrapping a heavy gauge wire around a round pencil, remove and screw into body shape. Push a perspex tube up through the spring and push into the body, dry.

Face Make a ball of skin-coloured paste. Roll to form neck, roll and push finger into paste to form a chin.

Cut out two white ovals for the eyes and curved half moon for the mouth. Indent with a ball tool for nose. Paint on features with black and red paint, add a red ball of paste to nose indentation. Glaze nose with gum arabic glue or confectionery glaze.

Clothes Make a fairly rough body. Using pattern cut out T-shirt. Place on the body, create creases and folds in the paste. When dry, paint on the stripes. Cut a long strip of red paste, wrap around the waist area for the trousers. To create a baggy effect, pull down and stretch edge with finger and thumb. Cut two thin strips for braces. Make two buttons by rolling two small balls of cream paste, flatten and indent a circle with a large icing tube, make two holes to create a shank with a large needle.

Cut out jacket-fronts. Smooth cut edge with a large ball tool. Shape bottom edge to create a natural effect. Cut out back of jacket and glue in place. Cut two lapels. Ball to slightly frill cut edge. Roll and form lapels, again to create a natural effect.

shape, make a cone of skin-coloured paste, push a cocktail stick into the paste and taper the end; leave to dry. Push the wrist shape into the arm, leave to dry.

To Assemble Pipe royal icing on edges of square, butt edges together. Support until dry. Assemble three sides. Push clown on perspex rod into cake. Place three box sides around clown, attach fourth side and lid. Make beach ball from gelatine paste and paint when dry. Make a small rag doll or teddy, prop against ball. Attach ribbons to cake in colours to match clown.

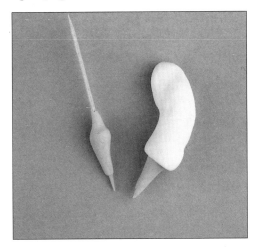

M

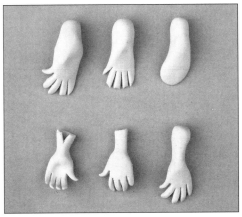

Arms Make a long sausage for the arm, bend and leave to dry. To make a wrist

CHRISTMAS TREE

Shaping the Tree Make a tall cone. Using a sharp, fine-bladed pair of scissors, cut paste into points. Start at the base and

work upwards. The points become smaller towards the top of the tree. Make sure there are no gaps between them.

Decorating the Tree If the tree is made of green paste it can be decorated with coloured baubles of icing, parcels, and a star attached to the top point. Dredge with icing (confectioners') sugar for a snowy effect. If the paste has not been coloured, dust with silver snowflake dusting powder.

SIMPLE CHOIR BOY

Body Shape a white cone for the surplice. Make a red sausage for the underskirt and flatten to the correct size. Attach underskirt to cone with egg white or gum arabic.

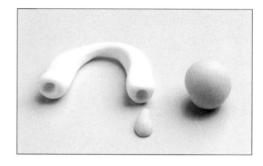

Head and Arms Make a long white sausage for arms. Measure against figure to obtain the correct length. Thin down the sausage where it crosses neck. Make indentations at the end of each arm. Make hands by rolling two small flesh-coloured sausages. Flatten and curve with ball tool; place into indentations. Roll a flesh coloured ball for the head.

Collar and Features Make a frilled collar with a small carnation cutter. Frill edge with a cocktail stick. Place on body. Attach head. Make hair by cutting out a piece of yellow paste with a medium blossom cutter. Paint in eyes, nose and mouth. Roll out a thin white rectangle for the songsheet.

SIMPLE FAIRY OR ANGEL

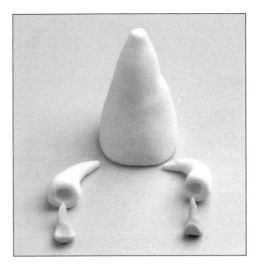

Body Make white cone for body. For arms, make two sausages from white paste, taper one end for shoulder. Indent sleeve end for hands. Model hands; completely curl one hand to hold the wand, which is made of florist's wire with a tiny cut out sugarpaste star stuck on the end. Assemble the fairy, taking care to keep the shape as modelled. Remember that even though the figure is very simple it should not be roughly made. The simple shape allows for a better finish.

M

Head and Hair Head is a small ball of flesh coloured paste. Hair and features are as for choir boy: make the hair by cutting out a piece of yellow paste with a medium blossom cutter. Attach the hair with egg white or gum arabic, then carefully paint in the eyes, nose and mouth.

Wings Cut wings from white paste using a large rose petal cutter. Attach to back of cone with royal icing. Decorate edges of dress with piped dots of royal icing.

Body Make a red cone for body. Make two red balls and flatten for legs. For boots make a black sausage, indent in middle with little finger and flatten bottom edge of sole to give shape. Assemble body, legs and boots. Make arms from sausage-shaped paste, indented at one end to take mitts. Make mitts and place on arms.

Sack For sack, make a large fat sausage of brown paste. Indent with finger. Rotate sack while pinching with fingers to open up. Pinch two corners at base and flatten sack so that it will stand. Model presents and toys to fill.

Head Attach small ball of flesh coloured paste for head. Make cone of red paste for hat. Pinch top to give shape. Paint features. Pipe in beard and fur edging. Add a small ball of red paste for nose.

Chimney Make large sausage in pale brick coloured paste for chimney. Flatten each side to form a square. With a scalpel remove a section of paste from inside chimney top. Leave chimney to dry. Paint in bricks with paste colour. Insert logs and boots or arm. Pipe snow with soft royal icing.

MODELLING PASTE

See Flower Paste*, Mexican Paste* and Pastillage*.

MODELLING TOOLS

Invaluable help for modelling flowers, for marzipan* work and for many other uses, these may be purchased singly or in sets.
Pointed Piece of Wooden Dowelling: For making pulled flowers*.
Bone-shaped Tool: This has two sizes of ball for marking eye sockets, curving petals, making open mouths or thinning petals of small flowers.
Large Ball-shaped Tool: For thinning edges and cupping large petals.
Shell-shaped Tool: Used to mark feet or to press a design on sugarpaste*.
Thin-bladed Tool: Used to cut small sections of marzipan or sugarpaste and to make creases in marzipan fruits.
Cone-shaped Tool: Used for modelling trumpet-shaped flowers.
Serrated Cone-shaped Tool: Used for marking flower petals and marzipan fruits.

MONOGRAMS

Two or three letters linked together. This type of decoration is suitable for a wedding cake, using the initials of the bride and groom. It may also be used for highlighting an individual's initials, or those of a company, on a wide variety of cakes.

Spacing If the monogram is to be placed on the side of the cake, ensure there is also sufficient space for the top and bottom decorations. The monogram needs to have space above, below and around it to give it impact.

Use clear, simply curved lettering for monograms. Intricate detail can be hard to decipher.

Linking Initials If possible, the initials should be interwoven two or three times, such as: under, over, then under again. Some letters are more difficult to link, noticeably those composed of straight lines.

Trace the chosen letters on separate pieces of greaseproof paper or tracing paper. Place one tracing on top of the other and adjust the position of the letters until a well-balanced design is achieved. Allow space between the sections of the letters to ensure each one is readable. Trace this design on one piece of paper. For a clear guide when piping, colour the letters individually in bright colours.

Piping The flooding consistency icing should be put in a bag and set aside. A small hole is cut in its tip just before use. Use a no. 0 or 1 writing tube (tip). Outline the monogram, then flood alternate sections. Leave each section to dry until the top surface of the icing has crusted over. Flood in the empty sections of the letters and leave to dry in a warm place.

Secrets of Success

A desk lamp with a flexible arm can be used to dry the sections of icing. Position the lamp approximately 15 cm (6 in) away from the icing.

Colouring Monograms The icing may be coloured before piping or colour may be painted on once the monogram is dry. Gold or silver is often used for monograms but, although non-toxic, it is not edible.

Round Cakes A monogram placed on the side of a round cake needs to follow the curve of the cake. Use a cake tin the same diameter as the cake and secure the template in position on it with dots of icing on the side of the tin. Support the tin on its side and pipe the monogram. A desk lamp with a flexible arm should be positioned immediately above the monogram to dry the top surface of the icing before it has a chance to move on the curved surface.

MOULDED FLOWERS

Roses are the most popular moulded flowers; others include carnations, daffodils and fuschias. Once you have mastered the technique of moulding roses you can progress to others.

Marzipan Roses Marzipan is pliable and easy to mould so these are the easiest to make. Always keep the marzipan covered when working to prevent it drying and cracking.

Use the best-quality marzipan for modelling as cheap marzipan will crack when moulded. White marzipan is obtainable from cake decorating suppliers and some supermarkets.

Tips on Technique
● Make the petals about the same size in depth as in width – if they are too deep they will flop over.
● To create a curve at the base of the rose, thin the top half of the petal but keep the base thicker.
● Only make sufficient petals for each layer, then add them to the flower. Freshly moulded petals should stick to each other; if necessary apply a spot of water to the base of the petals.
● Curl back the petals as each layer is applied. A few cracks along the top edge can look quite authentic but not too many.
● As each petal is placed in position, press the base firmly together but leave the top free to curl back.

Colouring Roses Colour is generally worked into the marzipan before modelling. Paste colours will not make the marzipan sticky. The easiest way is to thoroughly knead the colour into the marzipan on the work surface. If the paste is streaky the roses will be variegated.

Often, real roses are a deeper colour in the centre than on the tip of the petals. Colour a portion of paste dark for moulding the central petals, then gradually knead in extra uncoloured paste to mould outer layers of paler petals.

In nature, roses, like other flowers, tend to show different shades of one colour and they are often tinged with a different colour. Brushing a hint of blossom tint* on the moulded rose gives a realistic result.

Sugarpaste Roses Sugarpaste* is soft and experience is needed to model flowers from it successfully. The paste may be stiffened by adding 2.5 ml ($\frac{1}{2}$ tsp) gum tragacanth* to 125 g (4 oz/$\frac{1}{4}$ lb) of sugarpaste. Leave the paste overnight, well wrapped, for the gum to expand. Use the same technique as for moulding marzipan.

SECRETS OF SUCCESS

If the paste becomes sticky, thin the petals inside a smooth plastic bag, then leave the flowers to dry with some support to keep their shape.

Attach the roses to the cake with royal icing* or use a little sugarpaste mixed with water.

STEP-BY-STEP TO SUCCESS

MOULDING ROSES
The roses can be made in any size from sugarpaste or marzipan. The principle is the same. If you are using sugarpaste, knead in a little white vegetable fat (shortening). You can leave the rose at any of the first three stages, making it into a

bud, medium or a larger rose. The size of the cone and ball of paste for the petals will determine the size of the finished rose.

1 Mould a cone of paste.

2 Take a piece of paste, roll into a ball and then place between a folded piece of polythene. Flatten the paste to make the petals and thin out the edges.

3 Remove the petals from the polythene and wrap around the cone, enclosing the cone completely. Form a 'waist' in cone to establish the shape of the flower.

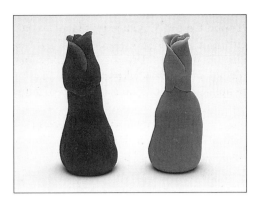

4 Place two more petals, made in the same way, around the cone. Keep the edges of the petals thin and maintain the 'waist' as you build up the flower.

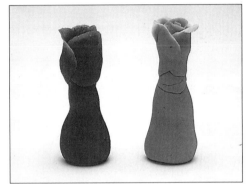

M

5 The third row has three petals, making a total of six petals. At this stage you may like to introduce a paler shade of paste for this and the final layer of petals.

6 The finished rose with an outer layer of four petals has a total of ten petals. The rose is cut cleanly off the cone.

N

NON-STICK PAPER

See Papers, coverings and wrappings.*

NOVELTY CAKES

Tins (pans) can be bought or hired for many designs, alternatively shapes may be cut out of a slab of cake; however, this quite often results in a lot of leftover cake. Work out the quantity of mixture required for tins (pans) following the guidelines given for baking tins*.

Choice of Icing Most novelty cakes are made from Victoria Sandwich or Madeira cake and eaten within a few days.
Sugarpaste: The usual covering for unusual-shaped cakes; however, the paste can be too sweet for some tastes. Roll out the paste just thick enough to make a smooth surface but not excessively thick.
Buttercream Coating*: Spread the surface of the cake with a thin layer of buttercream, then leave this to firm up in the refrigerator. Apply a second coat and decorate.

Covering Unusual-shaped Cakes with Sugarpaste Follow the instructions under the entry on sugarpaste for covering the side of the cake with a sharp top edge. To cover the top of a cake, dust a cake board slightly larger than the cake with icing (confectioners') sugar. Roll out the sugarpaste for the top of the cake and place it on the cake board, top surface down. Place the cake, upside down, on the sugarpaste. Cut away the surplus paste around the shape of the cake and place a board on the base of the cake. Holding both boards together, turn the cake the right way up. Remove the top board and neaten the edge of the paste.
Horseshoe Cakes: If the cake is coated in royal icing*, it can be difficult to ice within the curve of the horseshoe. Coat this area with a layer of sugarpaste in a matching colour, using a straight-sided jar to smooth the paste in place.
Character Cakes: Outline the facial details with piped lines of a deep colour. Fill in the remaining surface with piped stars of buttercream or royal icing.

MAKING AND PREPARING MINIATURE NOVELTY CAKES

These may be plain sponge, chocolate cake or rich fruit cake, all of which are made using the normal method, but using smaller quantities. Simply halve the amounts of all the ingredients used in the standard recipe, or quarter the amounts to make a really small cake.

Baking times will be reduced, especially for rich fruit cakes. The small cakes described below made in 7.5 cm (3 in) hoops take about 20 minutes for a Victoria sponge-type mixture, and about 1½ hours for a rich fruit cake.

The main difference between baking ordinary and miniature cakes is in the selection of small tins (pans).

Choice of Cake Tins (Pans) There are a number of different small cake tins (pans) that can be used to bake miniature cakes.

Depending on the the size of the cakes and the number required, you could bake a sheet of cake and cut out the required shapes. This method is obviously better suited to straight sided units that will not create waste cake. If you do find that you have cake trimmings, try making trifles, country cakes, frangipan tartlets with the sponge cake waste and rum truffles with the fruited cake crumbs.

Crumpet or muffin hoops, available from cookshops and department stores measure approximately 7.5 cm (3 in) in diameter and are 3 cm ($1\frac{1}{4}$ in) deep, and are ideal for baking small round cakes.

Yorkshire pudding tins (pans) are also a useful size. Build up the sides to make deeper cakes by adding a band of thin card, then line the tin (pan) as usual.

Pudding basins or foil containers make a good shape for domed miniature cakes. Once baked and cooled the upside-down pudding shape can be cut, layered and trimmed as required.

Conventional cake tins (pans) are probably best for square and oblong shaped cakes. Sheets or slabs of cake can be baked in these and used for cutting out unusual shapes, or shapes that are unavailable as tins (pans). Using a rectangular tin (pan), for instance, you can bake a full cake and cut it into two smaller square shapes. If you do not require two cakes, freeze or store one for later use.

Lining Hoops and Tins (Pans) Use double thick greaseproof paper for all tin lining. To line the small hoops, fold along one edge of the greaseproof paper about 1–1.5 cm ($\frac{1}{2}$–$\frac{3}{4}$ in) wide. Position the hoop on its side with one edge of the hoop on the fold. Mark the depth of the hoop as shown, and draw a line along the length of the paper, then cut along the line.

To measure the length of paper required to line the sides of the hoop, position the seam or join of the metal hoop at one end of the paper strip and carefully roll the hoop along the length of the paper. Where the seam of the hoop next touches the paper will indicate the required length, then allow about 1 cm ($\frac{1}{2}$ in) overlap and cut to size.

N

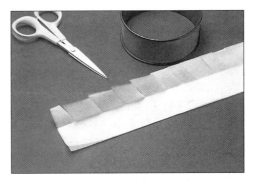

Snip along the smallest side of the fold using scissors. Make the cuts at an angle so that they overlap when positioned in the hoop.

QUICK TIP
Cut several lengths and rounds of paper ready to line the hoops or tins on another occasion. Store them in a polythene bag.

For the base lining, place the hoop on a double thickness of greaseproof paper and draw around the inside of the hoop as shown. Cut out the circles just inside the line to allow for the thickness of the tin, and ensure a good fit.

The prepared greaseproof paper liners are then positioned neatly in the hoops; remember to place the hoop onto a cardboard and greaseproof paper-lined baking sheet or Swiss (jelly) roll tray before lining and depositing filling into them.

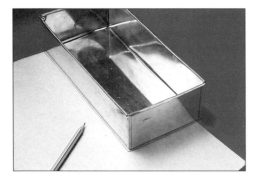

To line square or rectangular tins, place the tin (pan) on a double thickness of greaseproof paper and draw around the base shape as shown. Position the tin so as to overlap the paper by about 5 mm ($\frac{1}{4}$ in) on two edges; this will allow for the thickness of the tin when the paper is cut out.

For the sides, fold 1–1.5 cm ($\frac{1}{2}$–$\frac{3}{4}$ in) along the longest edge of the paper sheet. Place the tin (pan) on its side with one edge on the paper fold. Mark the depth of the tin (pan) and draw a line; then cut along it.

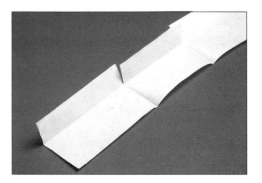

Take the inside measurements of the sides of the tin (pan), either using a ruler or by placing the tin (pan) on the paper and marking off, and fold the paper as shown to correspond with the dimensions. Cut along the shortest folds on two opposite sides.

Position the side and base liners.

SECRETS OF SUCCESS

Cardboard is used as a base for hoops to give added protection during baking.

PREPARATION OF MINIATURE CAKES FOR DECORATION

Leave the greaseproof lining paper on the baked cake until the last minute before decoration. This helps to keep the cake fresh and to retain a good shape while also reducing the risk of damage to the cake

After baking, the cakes should be allowed to cool slightly, then transferred to a cooling wire. The cake bases should be stored for at least 12 hours (but no more than 24 hours) before use. This allows the crumb to close a little and the cake to firm up, thus enabling easier handling.

Baked cakes which have been made in muffin hoops as described earlier

Chocolate cake made in a rectangular-shaped tin (pan). The depth of the baked cake is about 3 cm (1¼ in)

Sheets of cake that are baked level to the top of the tray are best left in the sheet trays and stored one on top of the other, the top sheet being reversed and separated from the other with a sheet of greaseproof paper. If only one sheet of cake is being stored, a lightly weighted tray can be placed on top to give a close texture.

Before cutting, layering or covering the cake, remove the crust by drawing the back edge of a long knife across the cake. This way the thin crust is removed without damaging the cake. With smaller units, such as sandwich-type bases, use a sharp serrated knife. Depending upon the type of cake and sometimes the bake, a loose crust can be removed by gently rubbing and peeling it off with the fingers.

Crust can be used like normal cake crumbs in truffles or trifles.

SECRETS OF SUCCESS

During preparation, always keep the bases covered to prevent the cake drying out. Never leave cakes exposed to the atmosphere, especially when they are cut.

Cutting and Slicing To achieve even and accurate slicing, which helps with good

layering, use special cutting boards. These are pieces of wood or polypropylene cut to various thicknesses. Place a board at each side of the cake, then use a sharp knife, resting it on the boards.

Cut through the cake, using the boards as a guide to create accurate layers.

Once the crust has been removed, the cakes can be layered and shaped. It is important to trim the edges to remove dark crust and create flat, straight sides.

Filling and Layering Use a palette knife to spread an even layer of cream or jam on the cake. Work the filling to just short of the edge of the cake. Replace the layers of cake in the order that they were cut, unless you are dealing with an unevenly shaped cake. A slanted cake, for instance, may be rectified by replacing the cake layers in a different position.

Trimming and Shaping The cooled cake should be cut and layered with filling.

Before shaping the cake, chill it for 30 to 60 minutes to firm both cake and filling. This chilling makes shaping easier. Use a good, sharp knife to trim and shape the cake. Wiping the blade on a clean cloth and dipping the blade into warm water before each cut helps to achieve a clean, neat appearance. Trim off a little at a time until the desired shape is created. Remove all excess crumbs before decorating.

SECRETS OF SUCCESS

When cutting and decorating an intricate novelty cake, part freeze before cutting, then freeze before decorating.

Preparing Fruit Cakes Allow the cakes to cool for about 15 minutes after baking, then liberally brush with a mixture of equal parts sugar syrup and rum. There should not be any need to prick the surface of the cake, simply brush the liquor on top, allowing it to penetrate slowly into the cake, leaving the lining paper in position. This addition of syrup will close the crumb a little and make a firmer, yet moister eating cake. When the cake has cooled completely, wrap it in greaseproof paper and store in a cool, dry place until required.

Coating Use this conventional method as for large cakes: roll out the marzipan using a little icing (confectioners') sugar. Brush the top of the cake with apricot glaze and place the cake centrally on the marzipan. Trim off any excess with a knife. Brush the sides with apricot glaze.

Roll out a long, narrow strip of marzipan slightly larger than the depth and circumference of the cake. Roll-up the marzipan, then unroll it around the sides of the cake. Trim and seal at the join.

For slabs of fruit cake, use your normal square or rectangular cake tins (pans) but reduce the amount of cake mixture by approximately half to produce a shallow cake. Baking times for smaller cakes will be considerably reduced. Allow to mature then cut to the required size.

Remember... *Never wrap fruit cake directly in cooking foil: the acid from the fruit causes the foil to disintegrate*

Trim off any excess marzipan around the top edge. Cut towards the centre of the cake top so as not to peel back the marzipan on the side of the cake.

For the sides of a square or oblong cake, roll out a rectangle of marzipan slightly wider than the width of the cake and as long as the depth of four cake sides. Position the cake coated with apricot glaze on its side and trim round neatly.

Turn the cake over to the next side and again place on the marzipan and trim round; repeat on the remaining two sides.

Neaten the marzipan on the sides using plastic smoothers.

NUMBER CAKES

A base of Madeira cake* or rich fruit cake* will give a firm foundation for decorating, in either a formal or comparatively simple style. Number-shaped tins (pans) or frames may be purchased or hired. Alternatively, a standard-shaped cake may be trimmed to represent numerals.

Number Templates to Cut Cakes Measure the size of the tin (pan) in which the cake was baked and use graph paper to work out the measurements for the numerals. Transfer the design to thin card. To avoid unnecessary waste, make round cakes for round numerals, for example 0, 3 and 8; and square or slab cake for the remaining numbers.

Cutting the Cake Use a knife with a long, straight edge to make a straight cut in one movement. A sharp, long but fine-bladed knife is best for cutting curves. If the cut edges of the cake crumble, apply hot apricot glaze* to set the crumbs or soft buttercream*. Place the cake in the refrigerator to firm the coating before applying the top coat.

Double Number Cakes These need a large board of approximately 41 cm (16 in) to give sufficient space for displaying both cakes. Transfer iced cakes to the board one at a time: place the left hand cake on the board, then decorate its side and base. Sift icing (confectioners') sugar on a piece of non-stick paper. Place the second cake on the paper and proceed to pipe the left hand bottom border and any side decoration on that side. Carefully lift the cake from the paper and slide it gently on the board. Continue with the rest of the decoration.

ORCHIDS

There are many varieties to copy as there are literally thousands of species. Flower paste* may be rolled out until transparent to model the petals. What appears to be a flower head made up of petals, in an orchid also includes sepals. Cutters can be bought for making some of the popular orchids. Here are a few of the better known types; consult a specialist, well-illustrated book for details.

Cattleya Orchid: A pretty flower with frilled petals.

Cymbidium Orchid: A large bloom with smooth petals and a well-marked tongue.

Philaenopsis Orchid: Also known as a moth orchid due to its flat petals on either side.

Singapore Orchid: A small orchid often used in bridal bouquets.

Slipper Orchid: A name derived from the large pouch in front of the orchid.

Orchids can be made in two ways. Firstly, by cutting out petals and sticking them together immediately, in which case place small pieces of plastic wrap between the petals until they are dry to help give the flower movement.

Alternatively, wired orchids take longer to make but they are very realistic and the flower can be arranged once the petals are made. Each shaped petal has a wire threaded through the middle. Once the petals are dry the orchid is taped together.

Colour A quick and effective way of colouring the mottled tongue is to use a toothbrush dipped into liquid food colouring. Use the forefinger to gently pull back the bristles and release a fine spray of colour. The colour may be applied when the tongue is cut out and before shaping.

The bitter lemon colour gives a fluorescent glow to orchids.

SECRETS OF SUCCESS

Have a bowl of sifted cornflour (corn starch) ready. To curve the 'tongue', partly wrap it around a wide piece of dowelling. Place the tongue into the cornflour (corn starch), then carefully withdraw the dowelling, leaving the tongue upright and allow the front to curve down slightly.

OVERPIPING

This is a technique that needs a steady hand and considerable practice using fine tubes (tips). The lines of icing are built up one upon another, each line thinner than the last. The light and shade effect created gives a sculptured look. This is known as the English look or Nirvana style, which translates as 'the highest state of perfection'.

The technique of overpiping may be used in various other ways. For example an overpiped line may be applied to writing, usually in a contrasting colour. Overpiping white writing with a fine red line adds a festive touch to Christmas cakes.

Overpiping Template Used for patterns on the side or top of cakes. The precisely cut template has the first line of piping placed very close to it. The template is then carefully removed and the remaining lines piped.

Overpiping on Shells The shell shape must be piped with a finely grooved tube to allow the lines of icing which are to be overpiped, to lay upon a smooth, even surface.

Three, Two, One A common term is 3, 2, 1, used to describe step-like overpiping. The work starts with a line piped using a no. 3 tube (tip), then it is overpiped using a no. 2 tube (tip). Next, using the same nozzle, a line is piped alongside, very close to, the overpiped line. Then a no. 1 tube (tip) is used to pipe a line on top of the first overpiped lines and the second single line. Lastly a single line is piped using the no. 1 tube (tip) to complete the graduated decoration.

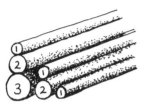

Above: a cross-section through 3, 2, 1 overpiping. The numbers indicate the size of the tube (tip) used to pipe the work.
Below: finished 3, 2, 1 piping has a 'step-like' appearance.

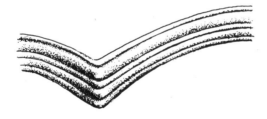

SECRETS OF SUCCESS

Each line must be dry before starting to pipe over it as there is a danger of the lines collapsing from the weight of the icing. Touch the surface of the iced cake with the tube (tip) to attach the thread of icing, lift the tube up to allow the icing to hang as it is guided along the row below. To finish the line, touch the tube (tip) down and the icing will break off.

P

PAINTING

Painting is not as difficult as it may at first appear to be, particularly if the design is traced. The original picture can then be copied to reproduce the way in which the colours have been applied.

Brushes The best quality brushes are sable which have soft bristles. They can be used to paint a fine point or used to cover a large area, depending on the size of brush. A nylon brush is useful for fine lines.

To clean brushes, soak them in water and check that colour is not lurking in the base of the bristles. Smooth the hairs to a point and leave to dry facing upwards.

Mapping Pen A nib with a very fine point, slotted into a holder. When not in use the nib can be reversed for storage in the holder. This gives greater control than a brush when drawing fine lines. Use with food colours, diluted with water if necessary. Often a picture can be given impact by outlining it with a fine dark line drawn in this way.

Surface The iced surface should be smooth and dry. As the coverings are mainly sugar, the liquid used must be kept to a minimum, otherwise the surface will dissolve. Food colourings can be painted on pastillage*, sugarpaste*, runouts* and royal icing*. The last icing is the most difficult on which to paint as it is very absorbent and any mistakes cannot be erased without leaving a mark.

Technique Lightly trace the picture on the surface. Hold the tracing paper firmly so that the design does not slip. Trace in the main details and outlines. Smaller parts can be painted in freehand. Paint in the light colours first as they can always be made darker, if required, at a later stage. Shadows give a painting a three-dimensional appearance. There must be a distinct difference between light and shade, perhaps in the way a flower petal turns.

When painting a scene with the sky in the background, make the colour of the sky on the horizon paler than it is at the top of the picture. This will give depth to the picture. Similarly, paint the smaller, farther-away lines of the painting in softer, hazy colours. Anything in the foreground will look sharper.

Remember . . . *If the base colour of the cake or plaque is a pastel shade, this can alter the shades of the colours applied to the picture.*

Choice of Colours Keep the colour scheme simple. On the comparatively small surface of a cake, a clear painting with few colours will create more impact than a multi-coloured painting.

For example, use three colours and paint these in various shades. Alternatively, use two colours in the same colour range and the opposite colour in small quantities. For instance, pale and deep pink with a touch of violet.

Stir gold and silver non-toxic paint well as it tends to settle in the base of the jar. Metal paints are not edible.

QUICK TIP
Some colours take a long time to dry. Food colouring diluted with clear alcohol dries out quicker than that diluted with water.

Painting Flowers Keep the colours light, adding slightly deeper shadows. If lines have to be painted on the petals, start the line from the centre of the flower and gradually ease the pressure on the brush so the line ends in a fine point.

Portraits Are for the professional or highly experienced, and artistic, cake decorator. Most figures applied to cakes are positioned facing sideways – this eliminates the need to obtain a life-like expression.

PAPERS, COVERINGS AND WRAPPINGS

See also Teflon-coated paper*.

An ever-increasing variety is available. Here is a brief guide to some of the most useful types.

Acetate: Firm, clear plastic sheeting, usually associated with use on overhead projectors. Acetate makes an ideal surface on which to make runouts*.

Cellophane: Transparent plastic wrapping, sold by the roll at cake decorating shops or stationers. Useful as a base for making runouts, also for making a see-through lid to cover delicate work which is placed in a box, particularly work which is prepared for exhibiting.

Cooking Foil: Use to wrap rich fruit cakes* for storage only as an outer wrapping over greaseproof paper. Can only be used successfully as a covering for cake boards if thoroughly glued down; not recommended for special cakes.

Embossed Silver, Gold and Red Papers: Obtainable from cake decorating shops and specialist stationers. Used to cover cake boards*.

Greaseproof Paper: Depending on the brand and where you buy it, greaseproof paper varies in strength. Look out for the strong variety for making piping bags*. Bags made of thinner paper may well burst during use.

Use for lining tins and for wrapping rich fruit cakes.

Non-stick Paper: Also known as baking parchment or non-stick cooking parchment. Use to line tins (pans), make strong piping bags or for making small runouts. Do not use for making large runouts as it tends to wrinkle.

Rice Paper: Two thicknesses are available, the thicker type is usually available from cake decorating shops. Use as a base for making pictures in piping gel*. Liquid food colour and food colouring pens may also be used with care to paint on rice paper. Water will soften rice paper, so use a thin coat of piping gel or royal icing to attach it to a cake.

Roasting Film: This is easily peeled off dried runouts and lace* sections. Make sure the film is free of creases as they will weaken the runout.

Tracing Paper: Available from art shops. Use to make lasting templates and as a strong surface for tracing designs.

Waxed Paper: Traditional surface used as a base for piping runouts; however, the excellent range of alternative papers has overtaken this in popularity. There is no reason why waxed paper should not be used but some other types do allow for easier removal of the runout pieces.

Plastic Wrap: Dampen a piece and place it directly on royal icing* before replacing the airtight lid on the container to help retain moisture.

PASTILLAGE

Pastillage is a stiff white paste used for making flowers and models. Recipes vary but most include icing (confectioners') sugar, white vegetable fat, water, gelatine*, liquid glucose*, gum tragacanth* and egg white. When cold, the paste sets hard but it will quickly become pliable once warmed and kneaded by hand. It can be rolled out extremely thinly, until it is transparent, when it can be cut and modelled into flowers. Once dry the paste resembles thin china – firm, yet brittle and easily broken.

Making Models Roll the paste out, moving it occasionally to make sure it is not sticking to the work surface, and keep any dusting of icing (confectioners') sugar

or cornflour (corn starch) to a minimum. Excess powder will dry the pastillage.

Position the pastillage on a piece of glass or perspex, cut away any sections from inside the model and only then cut around the edge. This will stop the paste from distorting. Wipe the blade of the knife with a damp cloth occasionally, to prevent a build up of sugar. Leave on the glass or perspex to dry out in a warm room. After two days turn the pieces over to allow the base to dry.

QUICK TIP
Glass and perspex retain heat. If they are slightly raised up, this will allow the warm air to circulate and speed up the drying process.

Colour Can be added to the water in the recipe, but allow for the fact that the large amount of icing (confectioners') sugar used, will reduce the depth of the colour.

Adding liquid colours will make the paste sticky. Paste colours are strong and only a little will be required. Use a cocktail stick (toothpick) to add colour. Many colours deepen on standing, therefore add the colour gradually and allow the paste to stand for a while before assessing the colour.

When dry, pastillage may be dusted with blossom tints* or it may be painted with food colouring.

Remember . . . *Keep the paste covered at all times. It will dry out quickly if left open to the air. Break off only as much as needed at each time.*

Keeping Qualities Well wrapped in a plastic bag, inside an airtight container in the refrigerator, the paste will keep for at least 2 weeks. However, as the paste contains gelatine, small spots of mould can appear on the surface if the paste is old.

Freezing Cut up, wrap well and freeze in an airtight container.

Pastillage Moulds Pastillage can be used to make a variety of moulds. These will set hard and they can be re-used many times. For example, a firm object stamped into the paste will make an impression which can be left to harden. Decorations can be created by pressing paste dusted with cornflour (corn starch) into this mould.

PETAL POWDER

A white powder available from cake decorating suppliers. Add water as directed to make petal paste which can be rolled out or hand modelled. Sift the powder into a bowl. Add the water and blend with the tip of a round-ended knife. When the paste is made, use your fingertips to knead it into a smooth, firm ball. The paste is used mainly for making flowers.

SECRETS OF SUCCESS

Reserve some of the water suggested and add it later if needed. Adding icing (confectioners') sugar to overcome the problem of having a sticky paste can reduce the stretching power of the paste. Always keep the paste covered. It will dry out very quickly if exposed to the air. Add a little white vegetable fat (shortening) if the paste is dry.

Colour This can be added while making the paste. Once the paste is dry, colour or blossom tints* can be painted on.

Freezing Any made up paste can be frozen in small blocks. They should be thoroughly wrapped and stored in an airtight container.

PHOTOGRAPHY

A camera with a zoom lens will produce close up photographs of cakes to show fine detail. A telephoto lens may also be used. Photographs taken with an ordinary camera do not show details of the decoration.

Daylight gives the best results – if possible take the cake outside. On a sunny day place the cake in the shade. Alternatively, place the cake near a window and stand to one side to take the photograph. If possible use a tripod or position the camera on a firm surface.

The side of the cake away from the window will be in shadow. To reflect the light back on this side, position a white surface (thin white card or polystyrene) just out of camera view.

Choice of Background Having a background means that the cake will show up without the distraction of room details around. The choice of background colour depends on the colour of the cake. If possible, extend the background to cover the table area and drape it behind the cake.

Try not to take a photograph while the cake is on a silver stand, which is reflective and will blur the details.

QUICK TIP
The wedding cake stand can be dulled for a photograph by applying a thin coat of window cleaning fluid.

PILLARS

Tiered cakes can be assembled on numerous types of support. Pillars are made of plaster, plastic or acrylic.
Hollow Plastic Pillars: For use when the cakes are iced with sugarpaste* and the soft surface will not take the weight of the heavy cakes above. These pillars disguise wooden skewers that run down their middle and it is these that take the weight of the upper cakes.
Clear Acrylic Pillars: Give a light, airy look to a cake and they blend in with any colour scheme.

P

Acrylic Separators: In various shapes to complement the design of the cake. These are clear stands which come complete with acrylic pillars to support and to spread the weight of the upper cakes.

Silver and Gold Pillars: The metallic colour should be repeated elsewhere on the cake or the shiny surface of the pillars can be too eye catching.

Plaster Pillars: Plaster will absorb water so they can be tinted to match a colour scheme by dipping them into diluted food colouring.

QUICK TIP
Plaster pillars need careful storage to avoid breakages.

Using Hollow Pillars Place the pillars carefully on the cake. Insert the wooden skewers, point down, through each pillar and the cake until they touch the cake board. Mark a line on each skewer level with the top of the pillar. Remove each skewer separately and cut level at the mark before replacing.

Remember . . . . *Each skewer should retain its original position once cut as the depth of the cake may vary from place to place.*

Glasses: For use on royal iced cakes instead of pillars. Small, sherry-type glasses can be used and they make an unusual talking point. They should be placed upside down, perhaps with a flower inside.

Tall Pillars: These are needed for large, deep cakes. Plaster pillars are obtainable up to 13 cm (5 in) tall. These give an imposing look to large cakes.

Tapered Pillars: Should be placed with the width at the base, allowing the narrow end to point upwards to the apex of the cake.

Royal Iced Cakes The surface of royal icing* should be firm enough to allow any type of pillar to be used. It is sometimes the custom to attach the pillars to the cake with dabs of royal icing. However, the pillars can easily get knocked over and shatter the cake decoration. It also makes transportation difficult. Place the pillars in a separate box and position them carefully on the cake when it is being erected.

Placing the Pillars Pillars should blend in well with other decorations and follow the shape of the cake. A small top cake will only need three pillars to support it. Place two towards the front of the cake and one in the centre back. The pillars must be the correct height to balance the depth and width of the cakes. Tall pillars, which are in proportion with large, deep cakes, look silly on smaller cakes. Always practise arranging the cakes before the big day.

DESIGN IDEA
Narrow bands of ribbon or tiny sprays of flowers make an attractive decoration when wound around the pillars.

STEP BY STEP TO SUCCESS

MAKING PASTILLAGE CAKE PILLARS

These pillars can be made to match the colour of the cake perfectly. The weight of each tier must be supported on wooden dowel. Make several extra pillars and select the best match for the cake. The .finished pillars may be decorated with piping, lace or ribbon.

1 Roll out flower paste on a lightly greased board. Trim the paste to the same

Poinsettia Cake
see page 194

Lantern Cake
see page 201

Saint Nicholas Bas Relief
see page 203

Basket Cake
see page 205

length as a piece of perspex tube, then dampen the tube with egg white. Roll the paste around the tube.

2 Cut off the excess paste, ensuring that the ends fit together without overlapping. Use a smoother to gently roll the pillar until the paste is smooth. Trim both ends level before leaving to dry.

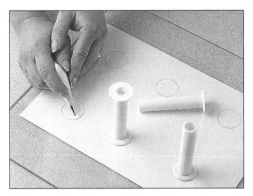

3 Trace the shape of the pillar ends and cover securely with cellophane. Outline the circle using a no. 1 tube, then flood the outside edge (not the centre). Stand the pillar in the soft icing. When dry, repeat for the other end.

PIPED FLOWERS

These can be made well in advance and placed on the iced cake when required. Many different varieties of flowers can be piped, using the one petal tube (tip) and they will last indefinitely if stored in dry conditions. Warmth will not affect them but moisture could do so.

Use a small piping bag and ensure that the narrow end of the petal tube (tip) opening is facing upwards. The end of the paper piping bag must sit above the hollow at the base of the petal tube (tip) or the icing will creep through.

Use royal icing* which is well beaten and firm. Half a teacup of royal icing is sufficient to make many flowers. The icing should be stiff enough for the flower petals

to hold their shape and for those of roses to stand upright. If the icing is too soft for piping roses, it may be the correct consistency for flat flowers which do not require the same stiffness to give the petals their shape.

SECRETS OF SUCCESS

Add 2.5 ml ($\frac{1}{2}$ tsp) albumen powder* to a small amount of icing (about half a teacup). Beat well, place in an airtight container and leave to stand for a few hours before using.

SIMPLE PIPED FLOWERS

P

Hold the paper piping bag at an angle so it is almost flat with the surface. Pipe the petals flat in a circular movement, bringing the end inwards. Pipe 6 petals in a circle. Use contrasting icing to pipe beads in the centre.

Drop Flowers Are the easiest to pipe. Work on non-stick paper. Make sure the paper is secured down, then hold the tube (tip) vertical and very near the paper before starting to pipe.

Flat-surface Flowers For example daisies, these are piped on a flower nail. The last petal is always the most difficult to pipe – hold the icing tube (tip) angled away from the first petal so as not to smudge the icing.

Rose Buds Using a petal tube with the thick end on the base, pipe a cone. Add more petals around the outside to the required size.

Open Roses Pipe as for the rose bud, adding more petals as required but holding the tube flatter to create more open petals.

Violets Holding the petal tube flat, pipe the petal shape in a circle. Pipe another 2 petals on each side. Pipe the fourth petal to join up the circle. Pipe the last petal the opposite way round in a circle. Pipe yellow dots of icing in the centre.

Roses These can be made in two ways, either around a cocktail stick or piped on a flower nail. A third type of wired rose is made by the same piping technique used for cocktail stick (toothpick) roses.
Cocktail Stick Method: Use a wooden cocktail stick (toothpick) and make a small, tight coil of icing around the tip of the stick. Build up the petals on this base, overlapping them as you begin to pipe each one. Remove the rose from the stick by pushing a square of non-stick paper up the stick until the rose rests on the paper.
Flower Nail Method: Use a star tube (tip) to pipe a cone-shaped mound of icing on the nail and leave to dry. Pipe the petals on this base – these roses can be quite large.

SECRETS OF SUCCESS

Pipe a quantity of dome-shaped bases, leave them to dry, then pipe the petals around them when they are firm.

Wired Roses: Make a small hook at the top of a piece of medium gauge floral wire. Pipe a small coil of icing around the hook and leave to dry. Proceed to pipe the petals around the icing base, as for the cocktail stick (toothpick) method.

Colouring White roses may be left to dry, then airbrushed* with different colours. Alternatively, flowers may be dusted with blossom tints* when dry. Two colours of icing may be placed in the piping bag to make variegated flowers.

PROFESSIONAL TIP

When making a batch of flowers to arrange as a centrepiece for a cake, remember to make them in different sizes. There should be a few small closed buds as well as half-open flowers and full blooms.

STEP BY STEP TO SUCCESS

PIPED ROSES USING A FLOWER NAIL

The knack of piping well-shaped, even roses on a flower nail is one which is mastered with practice. Many cake decorators, particularly beginners, prefer to use the cocktail stick (toothpick) technique. However, the cocktail stick (toothpick) method is best for small blooms.

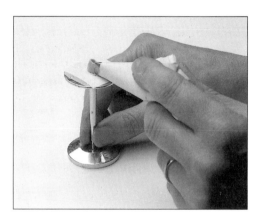

1 Secure a piece of greaseproof or waxed paper to the rose nail with a bead of icing. Pipe the centre using a petal tube (tip) on the paper and turning the nail at the same time to form a cone shape. Keep the piping tube (tip) upright and the thick end of the tube (tip) at the base.

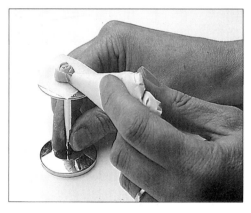

2 Pipe the third petal around the centre petals turning the nail at the same time as pressing the bag.

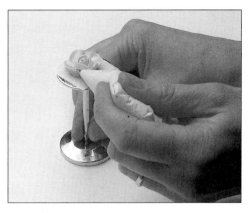

3 Hold the piping bag at an angle to pipe the final petals. To pipe a rose bud, start with the centre cone, then pipe around more petals to the required size.

PIPING ROSES AROUND A COCKTAIL STICK (TOOTHPICK)

For this, the piping bag is held so that the tube (tip) is standing up, with the wide end of the tube at the base and the curved thin end pointing outwards to assist in forming the correct shape of the petals. Pipe a rose on a cocktail stick (toothpick), removing the stick before using. Have ready a piece of thick, clean white card with holes pierced at intervals of about 2.5 cm (1 in) all over it. This will be used to hold the finished roses.

1 Start with a central cone, rotating the cocktail stick as you pipe. Allow to dry, making subsequent piping easier and the flower will retain a better shape; however, drying is not essential.

2 Next pipe two vertical petals tucking the second one into the first, allow to dry.

3 Finally pipe three petals to form a full rose, each one being tucked into the previous one. Pipe the larger outer petals in a lightly frilled horseshoe shape. For buds, simply pipe the central cone and pipe on a calyx using green icing.

4 To remove the flower from the stick, slide the stick down through one of the holes in the prepared card and the bloom will slip off to rest on the card, where it should be allowed to dry hard.

PIPING

Begin by practising piping techniques using buttercream*. It is easy to use and you will soon become confident about filling the bag correctly and being able to control the buttercream as you pipe.

Royal Icing This should be well beaten and of the correct consistency. The smaller the icing tube (tip), the softer the icing so that it flows evenly.

Piping Bags The size of the icing tube (tip) will dictate the size of the bag. For example, a tube (tip) with a fine point, which is used to pipe delicate embroidery, should be placed in a small bag.

Filling the Bag First fit the icing tube (tip) into the bag. If too much paper is cut away from the end of the bag the tube may push out as you are piping. To avoid this, measure the point of the tube against the end of the bag and only cut away sufficient to clear the opening in the point.

Use a palette knife to put the icing into the bag. Place the tip of your thumb and forefinger together to form a circle. Gently drop the bag into the circle made by your finger and thumb. Place a dollop of icing on the end of the knife, then push it into the base of the bag. Withdraw the knife, using the pressure of your thumb to remove the icing from it as you do so. Do not overfill the bag. Fold the two sides of the opening into the middle, then fold the top edge over.

Remember... *Place the icing tube (tip) in the bag and make sure it fits neatly before filling with icing.*

Piping Practice
● Use a dark, laminated board or place a piece of coloured paper inside a plastic folder as a practice sheet that can be wiped clean.
● Always try to work so that you are piping towards yourself.

• Begin all piping very near to the surface of the cake to ensure that the icing makes firm contact.

• Piping lines and dots provides useful practice: try to make the lines all the same length.

• Straight lines are easiest, so gain confidence by practising these first. The trick is to first make the icing grip the surface, then to continue squeezing the bag, at the same time raising the icing from the surface and moving along towards the required end of the line. To finish piping the line, lower the icing tube (tip) to touch the surface again. This way you will find that the icing falls in a straight line.

• Keep the opening of the icing tube (tip) free from excess icing which can blur the design.

SECRETS OF SUCCESS

If the line breaks, you may be using too little pressure as you pipe. If the piped line is wiggly, you may have used too much pressure.

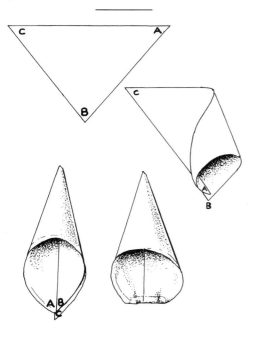

Making a piping bag

Shells, Rosettes, Stars and Scrolls For success these need well-beaten icing. Always re-beat machine-made icing by hand for a few minutes. Use strong non-stick or greaseproof paper for making bags as you have to apply some pressure to form the iced shapes. Always ensure that the edge of the paper is clear of the opening in the icing tube (tip) to allow a free flow of icing, otherwise the paper may obliterate, or at least smudge, the design.

If the point of piped stars is too peaked, immediately push it down slightly with a dampened finger or the point of a dampened paint brush by lightly touching the surface of the icing.

Shells should have a curved outline when viewed from the side.

> *QUICK TIP*
> *If the bag bursts just as you are nearing the end of piping a decoration, cut away the point of a new bag and place the torn bag inside it to finish the work.*

P

SIMPLE PIPING

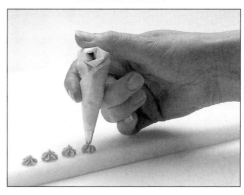

Stars. Hold the piping bag vertically and pipe a simple star of icing. Stop pressing the bag to stop the flow of icing and lift up sharply.

> *QUICK TIP*
> *If there is air in the piping bag the flow of icing will break. Do not jerk the bag away but hold it steady and continue piping.*

Shells: Hold the bag at an angle and pipe a row of shells. Stop pressing the bag to finish each shell, before piping the next one.

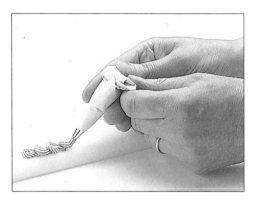

Scrolls: Hold the piping bag at an angle and pipe reverse scrolls as a border. Pipe one scroll towards the edge and the second scroll away from the edge.

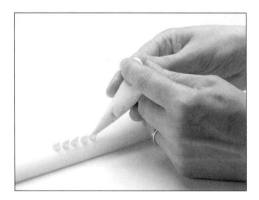

Leaf Border: Use a greaseproof paper piping bag snipped into a V shape and pipe leaf shapes as a border.

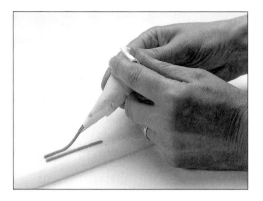

Lines: Use a plain writing tube (tip) to pipe lines of icing. Secure the end of the icing to the surface, then pipe allowing the thread to fall in position. Break off the thread by sharply lifting the tube upwards.

SCROLLS

Hold a paper piping bag fitted with a star tube (tip) at an angle to pipe individual scrolls. Stop pressing the bag and pull off sharply to finish each scroll.

Piping a line of joined-up scrolls.

Hold the paper piping bag fitted with a star tube (tip) at an angle and pipe a continuous line of icing in a rope design.

TRELLIS

Use a paper piping bag fitted with a plain writing tube (tip) to pipe a lattice or trellis design. Pipe evenly spaced lines of icing, allowing the thread of icing to fall straight.

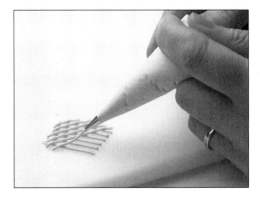

Overpipe threads of icing in the opposite direction to form a lattice or trellis design.

PIPING GEL

A clear, sticky gel which becomes fluid when warmed. When coloured it may be used for piping on firm royal icing* or sugarpaste*. Since it is not absorbed, the gel may also be used on rice paper.

Brush Embroidery* A small amount of piping gel added to royal icing gives it a smooth, elastic consistency. The icing does not dry as quickly, allowing longer for brushing it.

Creating Pictures Pipe a fine dark outline in royal icing or chocolate* and flood it in with coloured piping gel.

A beautiful stained glass window design can be piped by outlining diamond shapes with royal icing or a thin line of chocolate and flooding in the sections with coloured piping gel. The surface of the gel dries and remains sparkling but it is soft to eat.

Pipe the outline of a champagne glass in icing and make the contents and bubbles using piping gel.

Icing Tubes (Tips) These are only needed for piping an outline. To fill in with gel, place it in a small piping bag and cut a hole in the pointed end.

Colour Piping gel can be coloured with paste or blossom tints*. Stir the colour in well to prevent streaks; however, do not beat the gel or air bubbles will form in it.

PIPING STAND

Available from good cake decorating shops and suppliers, this is a metal stand with six holes to support piping bags. When using several bags fitted with different icing tubes (tips), or filled with different coloured icing, for piping intricate designs, the bags may be rested in the stand when not in use. A piece of sponge at the base of the stand is moistened and the points of the tubes (tips) rest on it to prevent them drying out.

PLAQUES

The plaque may be made well in advance and stored ready to be placed on the cake. It can be made of pastillage*, gum paste*, sugarpaste* or by making a runout*.

Several plaques can be made and the best one chosen for the cake. A plaque can be removed from a celebration cake and kept by the owner as a prized possession long after the cake has been consumed.

Runout Plaques: These may be made in any shape or style and they have a slight sheen which looks very attractive.

Paste Plaques: Roll out the paste thinly. A cardboard template can be used to cut around with a sharp knife; however, a sharper edge is achieved by using a cutter, for example a pastry cutter or special plaque cutters. Leave the paste to dry in a warm place, turning it over after 24 hours.

DESIGN IDEA

Raise a plaque on top of a cake to give it more impact. Pipe a few dots of royal icing on the cake, leave them to harden, then pipe on top of them again and carefully position the plaque. A plaque can be tilted forward slightly to display its content to best advantage.*

Writing on Plaques To avoid writing on a cake, make two or three extra plaques to give yourself plenty of opportunity for perfecting the message. Any unused plaques may be stored for future use.

Remember . . . *When writing initials or a monogram on a plaque, have sufficient room on all sides so that the lettering is not cramped.*

STEP BY STEP TO SUCCESS

PLAQUES

Plaques provide the ideal introduction to basic runout technique; it is worth spending a little time mastering the skill before moving on to more complicated designs.

1 Trace chosen design and fix it to a drying board with masking tape or drawing pins. Cut a piece of wax paper slightly larger than drawing; fix it in place with masking tape or drawing pins. Make sure wax surface is uppermost and that pieces of paper are flat.

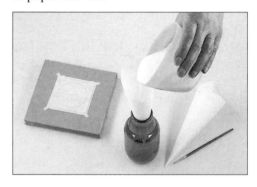

2 Select a medium bag with or without a no. 2 tube (tip) and support it in a wide-necked bottle or jar. Prepare a batch of runout icing. Pour the icing into bag until half full. Fold down top tightly. If no tube (tip) was used, cut end of bag to the size of a no. 2 tube (tip).

3 Have ready a small paper piping bag fitted with a no. 1 tube (tip) and filled with royal icing. Use this to outline design. Make sure any joins are neat; touching each other but not overlapping.

4 Pipe a line of runout as close as possible to the outline. If there are any gaps, tease the icing in place with a paint brush. Continue to flood remaining area, maintaining a steady pressure on the bag so that the icing is gently forced through the tip, rather than allowed to flow out. Keep end of bag in icing.

5 Gently tap drying board on surface to level run-icing. Any air bubbles rising to the surface can be burst with the tip of a paintbrush. Place plaque under an angled desk lamp to dry.

6 When you are ready to use the plaque, place it face down on a piece of foam and carefully peel off wax paper. Pipe a line or some dots of royal icing on reverse and position piece right-way-up on cake.

FLOWER PLAQUES
Illustrated on page 272
Templates on page 245

Appliqué plaques are highly effective as a form of decoration. Easier to work on than cakes, they have the added advantage that they can be angled on the cake for clear

visibility – and removed before the cake is cut as a tangible reminder of the occasion.

The flowers displayed on the plaques are all variations on appliqué, whereas leaves are painted directly onto the coating surface. Melt a small amount of vegetable fat (shortening) in a small bowl. Create a palette by placing small mounds of green, brown, yellow and skin-tone dusting powder (petal powder*/blossom tint*) on a dinner plate set over a bowl of warm water. Mix dusting powder with a drop of hot fat. When required depth of colour has been reached, paint leaves on plaque, mixing colours if liked to create natural-looking foliage. The advantage of this method is that delicate colours can be created. Liquid colours are often very bright and may run if the surface is absorbent.

Anemones Trace design on page 245, scribe it on plaque and paint leaves. Cut out card templates of each flower silhouette. Begin with flower that appears to be furthest away. Roll out pink paste as thinly as possible on a lightly greased board. Using template and scalpel, cut out flower shape. Mark petals with wide end of veining tool, working from outer edge of each petal towards centre. Dampen plaque lightly and position flower silhouette. Make card templates for petals that are raised from the background. Cut out petals, texture them by marking several lines with narrow end of veining tool; attach to flower. Make all flowers in the same way. For each centre, flatten a small ball of black paste and texture with veining tool. Pipe small dots of yellow icing round each flower centre to represent stamens. Pipe or paint card and inscription.

Daffodils Scribe design on page 245 on plaque and paint leaves. Cut out card templates of flower sections. Roll out yellow paste and cut out the three back petals, using template and scalpel. Mark lines on petals with veining tool. Dampen plaque lightly and attach back petals. Repeat for two side petals. Cut out trumpet

P

in two pieces, frilling edge of oval shape with a cocktail stick (toothpick). Build up flower shape by placing the petals directly on top of each other.

Using the same technique as for leaves, make up yellow and orange blossom tint or dusting powder colour and paint the daffodils – the added fat will give them a realistic waxy appearance.

Pansies These are made in much the same way as the anemones, but instead of building up shape by adding extra petals, detail is provided by brush embroidery. Scribe design on page 245 on plaque; paint leaves.

Pipe the curve, using a no. 1 tube (tip) and white royal icing. Cut around card templates of the pansies from blue paste and attach to plaque. Using a no. 2 piping tube (tip) and white royal icing, outline the edge of the petal which appears furthest away.

Make up dilute solutions of food colouring in several toning shades. Dip the brush in food colouring, then brush icing over petal. Continue to outline one petal at a time until both flowers are complete. Paint a little black colour on the bottom petal of each flower. Pipe centres, using white royal icing.

Roses Each rose is made up of three layers of petals. After scribing design on page 245 and making card templates for petals, paint leaves on plaque. Cut back petals from pink paste. Attach to lightly dampened plaque. Cut out two more layers of petals; leave on a board to dry.

Using white royal icing, brush embroider around the edge of all petals, including those on plaque, then leave to dry.

When icing is completely dry, assemble roses, securing each layer of petals with royal icing. Pipe a small bulb of yellow icing in the centre of each and surround with tiny dots for stamens.

Complete the picture by adding small white paste flowers cut out using a primrose cutter, then pipe or paint card and required inscription. Allow to dry.

PULLED FLOWERS

A wide variety of small flowers can be made using this method with flower paste*, pastillage* or petal powder*. The paste must be firm to withstand the pulling technique that is used to shape the petals.

Although many flowers have five petals, they can look quite different. It is the shape of the petals, the movement they are given and the colour applied that makes pulled flowers look individual and realistic.

Proportions The size of the piece of paste used determines the size of the flower. A pea-sized piece of paste will make a flower the size of a primrose.

Shape the smoothed paste into a cone and skewer the wide end on a piece of pointed dowelling. Use your forefinger and thumb to thin the wide end of the paste by gently pressing against the dowelling.

Make a number of cuts into the paste. The number of cuts equals the number of petals, for example five cuts will make a five-petal flower. The depth of the cuts dictates the eventual shape of the petals. Deep cuts will produce long petals which can be widened by rolling them sideways. When the cuts are made, remove the paste from the dowelling and model the petals.

Pulling the Petals Practise by making a flower with four petals first. Five-petal flowers are more difficult as it is harder to judge the cuts. The paste can always be removed from the dowelling and the cuts made using a sharp pair of scissors.

The action used to pull the petals can be compared with snapping your fingers. Hold the petal between the forefinger and thumb, then flick the thumb and finger together, at the same time applying pressure to the petal.

SECRETS OF SUCCESS

To make accurately spaced cuts, mark five dots on the piece of dowelling.

Stamens and Calyx These can be taped to floral wire and threaded through the flower when it is made, or the centre of the flower can be moistened and cut stamens placed in position. Stamens with stiff threads are easier to use individually.

The calyx can be painted on at the base of the flower. Start applying paint from the base of the flower and flick the brush up to obtain fine points at the end of the calyx.

STEP-BY-STEP TO SUCCESS

BASIC BLOSSOM

1 Take a pea-sized piece of flower-paste, this should be thoroughly kneaded so that it is soft and warm.

2 Mould into a small cone shape. Dip the pointed end of your dowel into cornflour (corn starch) and insert into the thick end of the cone.

3 Taking a sharp modelling knife make five equal cuts for the five petals. The cuts should be one-quarter to one-third of the total length of the cone.

4 Remove the dowel and open up the flower by pushing your finger into it.

5 Taking each petal in turn process by squashing, pinching and pulling.

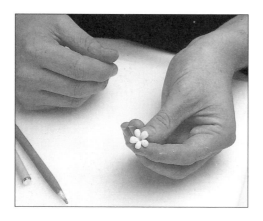

6 You should, with practice, end up with a flower with five equal petals.

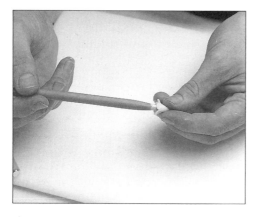

7 Place your wooden stick back into the throat of the flower and pull the petals up slightly to produce a nice shaped flower. Remove the stick.

8 Take a piece of 28 or 30-gauge covered wire. The wire usually comes in long

strands, so cut each one into four to give lengths of wire suitable for most flowers and sufficient to wire the flowers into sprays without being wasteful. Bend the wire to make a small hook on one end, dip the hooked end into a little fresh egg white and thread through the throat of the flower, as shown.

9 Pull the wire through until it sits into the soft paste at the back of the flower. Squash the flower back around the wire. You now have a finished blossom on wire.

WINTER JASMINE

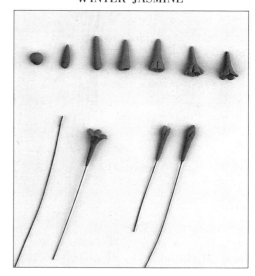

1 Colour some flower paste golden yellow, roll into a ball then into a long thin cone. Stick your dowel into the thicker end of the cone. Cut six petals and remove from dowel. Squash, pinch and pull each petal. Take a piece of 30-gauge, dark green wire, make a hook and slide down the throat. Place a single white stamen into the throat (refer to picture for positioning). To make the buds, roll a thin cone, stick the hooked wire into the thin end, cut approximately one-third of the way down with scissors and then twist the two pieces together like a spiral.

2 Dilute some dark green, paste food colouring with clear spirit and paint calyxes on each of the flowers and buds using a small, fine paint brush and leave to dry. Tape the flowers and buds in clumps on to a piece of 26-gauge wire which then acts as the main stem.

Winter jasmine is a most attractive flower to use in winter sprays and it contrasts well with the usual red and green Christmas cake spray.

VIOLET

Colour some paste violet and roll into a ball. Mould into a cone and stick a dowel into the thicker end of the cone. Cut one petal to a quarter of the total circumference of the paste and four petals from the remaining three-quarters. Open up the flower and run a cocktail stick (toothpick) over each petal in turn. Make a hook in a piece of 28-gauge green wire then bend a hook at right angles, as shown, and dip the hook in egg white. Thread the wire through the throat and push so that the wire pierces the top of the back of the cone behind the top two petals, making sure that the larger single petal is at the bottom. Cut off any excess paste and then bend back the wire. Roll out some green paste, cut a diamond shape and then cut each side almost in half to make the calyx. Place over the violet as shown. Make an orange stamen and insert into the centre of the violet. Mark a vein down the centre of the large petal.

Dust with dark violet petal dust. Mix a little white petal dust with some clear spirit and paint a few lines into the centre of the violet.

BLUEBELL

Colour some paste bluish-mauve and roll into a ball. Mould into a dumbell shape, stick a dowel into one end and cut six petals. Place each petal onto a piece of sponge and cup using a ball tool stick, then insert a ball tool up into the centre of the flower to make a bulbous cavity. Using tweezers, pinch the flower as shown to

P

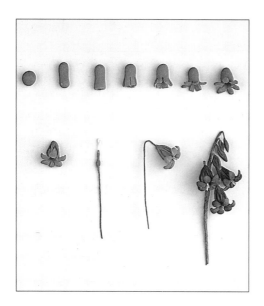

REGAL ICE

One manufacturer's trade name for sugarpaste.*

RIBBON INSERTION

produce a ribbed effect on the side. Tape two white stamen ends onto a piece of wire, and wrap round extra tape to stop the wire coming back through the flower. Thread the wire and stamens through the flower. The buds are made by making a small cone, pinched with tweezers.

Brush with a mixture of blue and violet dusting powder. Tape the buds and flowers onto a main stem as shown starting with a bud in the centre then setting another to the left then the next to the right and so on. You can make a long spray by using five to seven buds and five to seven flowers. Bluebells look attractive bunched together with other spring flowers.

A pretty technique which has admirers of finished cakes debating over how the ribbon is slotted in place. This technique is often combined with crimper* work or brush embroidery* designs. The ribbon is usually slotted around the sides of cakes but it can look attractive as part of a top decoration. Ribbon insertion can only be applied on a coating of soft icing. Allow the sugarpaste to dry for a day before decorating with ribbon insertion.

Marking the Decoration Measure the position where the ribbon insertion is required. Slightly below this point wrap either a ribbon or an even band of greaseproof paper* around the cake. Use this as a guide when making the cuts into the paste, to keep them in a straight line. Remove the paper or ribbon when the cuts are made. Ribbon insertion can also be applied in a curved design.

Ribbon Insertion Tool Ribbon insertion tools or knives have a straight end on the blade to make cuts of an equal depth.

QUICK TIP
A pair of square-ended tweezers may be used to make two slots at a time in the paste. Wrap an elastic band around the tweezers to regulate the extent of opening.

Choice of Ribbon Stiff ribbon is easier to slot into the cuts. Floristry ribbon and double-sided satin ribbon are both stiff. Make sure that the ribbon and cuts are the same depth.

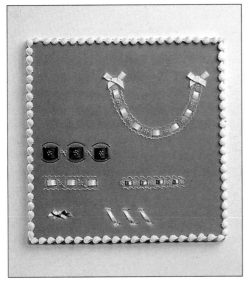

Ribbon Insertion *The sugarpaste should be skinned, (it should have dried to form a thin crust, but not be set hard). Plan the design on paper first, then use pins or a scriber to transfer it to the cake. Choose ribbon of the required width, and cut as many pieces as necessary to make the design. The pieces should be slightly longer than the spaces, leaving enough at each end to tuck in. Finish off the ribbon insertion with miniature bows and piped embroidery designs, if wished. If the ribbon is wide enough, tiny flowers can be piped on each piece.*

RICH FRUIT CAKES

These can – and should – be made and stored for months before use. However, in an emergency they can be made shortly before a celebration without too much difference in taste.

Ingredients

Fat: Use only butter for a good flavour.
Sugar: Muscovado sugar is dark and moist with a soft, fine grain. It is ideal to give colour and flavour to rich fruit cakes.

Eggs: Use fresh eggs, preferably free range.
Flour: Use sifted plain flour with a small percentage of wholemeal flour to add texture and flavour. Using all wholemeal flour can make a cake crumble when cut.
Fruit: Currants will make the cake a deeper colour while raisins make it juicy.

> ### QUICK TIP
> *Gravy browning is sometimes included in recipes to deepen the colour of a cake. It can be rather salty and with the right ingredients it is not necessary to add browning. For example, treacle adds colour and flavour. Warm the tin of treacle in a saucepan of hot water to make the contents easier to spoon out.*

Making Rich Fruit Cake Warm the bowl and beater. Beat the butter until soft before adding the sugar. The butter and sugar must be beaten to a soft, light consistency. The charts and method provide detailed instructions for making rich fruit cakes to suit any size and shape of tin (pan), as well as for standard square and round tins (pans).

To smooth the mixture in the tin (pan), repeatedly moisten the back of a metal spoon and smooth it over the surface of the cake. This will also prevent the surface of the cake from drying out.

Before baking rich fruit cake, lay a large sheet of greaseproof or non-stick paper over the top of the tin (pan), allowing it to rest on the lining paper. Carefully tuck the ends of the paper into the string around the tin (pan). This cap of paper will trap steam and give the cake greater volume and a soft crust.

> ### QUICK TIP
> *When mixing a rich fruit cake, if the mixture is too firm, dip the base of the mixing bowl in hot water for a moment, then remove and continue to beat.*

R

143

SECRETS OF SUCCESS

While the baked cake is still slightly warm pour alcohol, such as brandy, over its base and allow it to soak into the porous surface. This contributes more flavour than by adding the alcohol to the raw mixture.

Storing Rich Fruit Cake When the cake is completely cold, wrap it well in greaseproof paper, then in cooking foil and store it in a cool, dry place.

Remember . . . *Do not place cooking foil straight on a fruit cake. The acid from the fruit reacts with foil which will disintegrate on the surface of the cake.*

RICH FRUIT CAKE CHARTS

Preparing rich fruit cake mixture for tins (pans) of unusual shapes or sizes. There is a wide selection of baking tins (pans) available in different shapes and sizes. Many are not standard, so the quantity of cake mixture required has to be calculated individually for each tin. Use the following simple method, remembering that the weight of mixture may vary according to the depth of cake required.

Fill the baking tin with water to about 1 cm ($\frac{1}{2}$ in) below the rim. Weigh the water in the tin (pan): this is more or less equal to the weight of mixture required.

Follow the chart to select the quantities of ingredients which give the weight nearest to your calculated result.

Method

Sort and wash the fruit, then leave to dry. Mix the lemon rind and juice with the fruit. Stir in the brandy and rum and cover the bowl, then leave overnight. Line the tin (pan) with greaseproof paper and grease it well.

Cream the butter and sugar. Slowly add the egg, beating the mixture well. Mix in the caramel and glycerine, then fold in the flour, ground almonds and spices. Do not beat the mixture.

Stir the fruit through the cake mixture, then turn it into the prepared tin and spread it out. Wash, then wet one hand and pat the top of the mixture level.

Bake the cakes at 140°C (275°F/Gas 1). The cooking time depends on size and shape. Test by inserting a clean metal skewer in the middle of the cake – if it comes out free of mixture, the cake is cooked. Any mixture on the skewer indicates that the centre of the cake requires longer cooking.

VARYING RICH FRUIT CAKES

Although the traditional rich fruit cake is the most popular and practical for major celebrations, not least because of its excellent keeping qualities, there are times when a slightly different cake makes a change. For birthdays or anniversaries, a cake rich in the use of glacé (candied) fruits is an excellent alternative to the standard recipe.

The important point to remember when varying a rich fruit cake is that the proportion of total fruit to other ingredients must remain the same. Retain the base of currants, sultanas (white raisins) and raisins but replace part of their weight with other fruits. For example, try adding a selection of crystallised (candied) fruits, such as pineapple, pawpaw, citron peel and ginger, and increase the proportion of glacé (candied) cherries.

Dried apricots, peaches, pears and figs may all be chopped and used to replace a small portion of the standard fruit mixture. Chopped nuts, such as walnuts or brazils, may be added to contribute their own distinctive flavour, or a mixture of nuts may be used.

Instead of applying the usual marzipan and icing, consider a topping of fruit and/ or nuts, baked in neat rows on the cake. Cover with foil to prevent overbrowning during cooking.

RICH FRUIT CAKE CHART
By Weight of Mixture

Total Mixture Weight	470 g (15 oz/ scant 1 lb)	1.4 kg (3 lb)	1.9 kg (3¾ lb)	3.3 kg (7¼ lb)	4.7 kg (10¼ lb)
Currants	100 g (3½ oz/ ⅔ cup)	310 g (10 oz/2 cups)	375 g (12 oz/2½ cups)	670 g (1 lb 5½ oz/6⅓ cups)	970 g (1 lb 15 oz/7¾ cups)
Sultanas (White Raisins)	45 g (1½ oz/ 3 tbsp)	125 g (4 oz/ ¾ cup)	155 g (5 oz/ 1 cup)	280 g (9 oz/ 1½ cups)	400 g (12½ oz/ 2½ cups)
Raisins	45 g (1½ oz/ 3 tbsp)	125 g (4 oz/ ¾ cup)	155 g (5 oz/ 1 cup)	280 g (9 oz/ 1½ cups)	400 g (12½ oz/ 2½ cups)
Chopped Mixed Peel	15 g (½ oz/ 1 tbsp)	60 g (2 oz/ ⅓ cup)	75 g (2½ oz/ ⅓ cup plus 1 tbsp)	125 g (4 oz/ ¾ cup)	170 g (5½ oz/ 1 cup)
Glacé (Candied) Cherries	30 g (1 oz/ 2 tbsp)	75 g (2½ oz/ ⅓ cup plus 1 tbsp)	100 g (3½ oz/ ½ cup plus 1 tbsp)	200 g (6½ oz/ 1 cup plus 1 tbsp)	280 g (9 oz/ 1⅓ cups plus 2 tbsp)
Butter or Margarine	60 g (2 oz/ ¼ cup)	170 g (5½ oz/⅔ cup)	220 g (7 oz/ 1 cup)	400 g (12½ oz/1½ cups)	575 g (1 lb 2½ oz/ 2¼ cups)
Dark Brown Sugar	60 g (2 oz/ ⅓ cup)	170 g (5½ oz/1 cup)	220 g (7 oz/ 1⅓ cups)	400 g (12½ oz/ 2¼ cups)	575 g (1 lb 2½ oz/ 3⅓ cups)
Eggs	60 g (2 oz/ ¼ cup)	170 g (5½ oz/ ⅔ cup)	220 g (7 oz/ 1 cup)	400 g (12½ oz/ 1½ cups)	575 g (1 lb 2½ oz/2¼ cups)
Ground Almonds	15 g (½ oz/ 2 tbsp)	60 g (2 oz/ ½ cup)	75 g (2½ oz/ ½ cup plus 2 tbsp)	125 g (4 oz/ 1¼ cups)	170 g (5½ oz/ 1⅓ cups plus 2 tbsp)
Plain (All-purpose) Flour	60 g (2 oz/ ½ cup)	185 g (6 oz/1½ cups)	250 g (8 oz/ 2 cups)	440 g (14 oz/3½ cups)	625 g (1¼ lb/ 5 cups)
Glycerine	drop	1.25 ml (¼ tsp)	3.75 ml (¾ tsp)	5 ml (1 tsp)	7.5 ml (1½ tsp)
Caramel	drop	1.25 ml (¼ tsp)	3.75 ml (¾ tsp)	5 ml (1 tsp)	7.5 ml (1½ tsp)
Mixed Spice	pinch	1.25 ml (¼ tsp)	2.5 ml (½ tsp)	3.75 ml (¾ tsp)	5 ml (1 tsp)
Cinnamon	pinch	1.25 ml (¼ tsp)	3.75 ml (¾ tsp)	5 ml (1 tsp)	7.5 ml (1½ tsp)

Grated lemon rind and juice, and brandy or rum to taste. For example, use 1 lemon and 60 ml/4 tbsp brandy or rum for the largest cake.

Rich fruit cake chart
By Tin (Pan) Size

Cake Tin (Pan) Size	13 cm (5 in) square 15 cm (6 in) round	15 cm (6 in) square 17.7 cm (7 in) round	17.5 cm (7 in) square 20 cm (8 in) round
Raisins	125 g (4 oz/$\frac{2}{3}$ cup)	185 g (6 oz/1 cup)	250 g (8 oz/1$\frac{1}{2}$ cups)
Sultanas	125 g (4 oz/$\frac{2}{3}$ cup)	185 g (6 oz/1 cup)	250 g (8 oz/1$\frac{1}{2}$ cups)
Currants	125 g (4 oz/$\frac{2}{3}$ cup)	125 g (4 oz/$\frac{2}{3}$ cup)	155 g (5 oz/1 cup)
Dried Apricots, Chopped	60 g (2 oz/$\frac{1}{3}$ cup)	90 g (3 oz/$\frac{1}{2}$ cup)	125 g (4 oz/$\frac{3}{4}$ cup)
Glacé (Candied) Cherries, Quartered	90 g (3 oz/$\frac{3}{4}$ cup)	90 g (3 oz/$\frac{3}{4}$ cup)	150 g (5 oz/$\frac{3}{4}$ cup)
Cut Mixed Peel	30 g (1 oz/3 tbsp)	45 g (1$\frac{1}{2}$ oz/3$\frac{1}{2}$ tbsp)	60 g (2 oz/$\frac{1}{3}$ cup)
Mixed Chopped Nuts	30 g (1 oz/$\frac{1}{4}$ cup)	45 g (1$\frac{1}{2}$ oz/$\frac{1}{3}$ cup)	60 g (2 oz/$\frac{1}{2}$ cup)
Lemon Rind, Coarsely Grated	5 ml (1 tsp)	7.5 ml (1$\frac{1}{2}$ tsp)	10 ml (2 tsp)
Lemon Juice	15 ml (1 tbsp)	22.5 ml (1$\frac{1}{2}$ tbsp)	30 ml (2 tbsp)
Brandy, Whisky, Sherry	15 ml (1 tbsp)	30 ml (2 tbsp)	45 ml (3 tbsp)
Plain (All-purpose) Flour	185 g (6 oz/1$\frac{1}{2}$ cups)	220 g (7 oz/1$\frac{3}{4}$ cups)	280 g (9 oz/2$\frac{1}{4}$ cups)
Ground Mixed Spice	5 ml (1 tsp)	10 ml (2 tsp)	15 ml (3 tsp)
Ground Almonds	30 g (1 oz/$\frac{1}{4}$ cup)	45 g (1$\frac{1}{2}$ oz/$\frac{1}{3}$ cup)	60 g (2 oz/$\frac{1}{2}$ cup)
Soft Dark Brown Sugar	125 g (4 oz/$\frac{1}{2}$ cup)	155 g (5 oz/$\frac{1}{2}$ cup + 2 tbsp)	220 g (7 oz/$\frac{3}{4}$ cup)
Butter or Margarine, Softened	125 g (4oz/$\frac{1}{2}$ cup)	155 g (5 oz/$\frac{1}{2}$ cup + 2 tbsp)	220 g (7 oz/1 cup)
Black Treacle (Molasses)	7.5 ml ($\frac{1}{2}$ tbsp)	15 ml (1 tbsp)	22.5 ml (1$\frac{1}{2}$ tbsp)
Medium Eggs	2	3	4
Approximate Cooking Time	2 to 2$\frac{1}{4}$ hours	2$\frac{1}{4}$ to 2$\frac{1}{2}$ hours	2$\frac{1}{2}$ to 2$\frac{3}{4}$ hours

Cake Tin (Pan) Size	20 cm (8 in) square 22.5 cm (9 in) round	22.5 cm (9 in) square 25 cm (10 in) round	25 cm (10 in) square 27.5 cm (11 in) round	27.5 cm (11 in) square 30 cm (12 in) round
Raisins	280 g (9 oz/1$\frac{2}{3}$ cups)	375 g (12 oz/2$\frac{1}{4}$ cups)	500 g (1 lb/3 cups)	560 g (1lb 2oz/3$\frac{1}{4}$ cups)
Sultanas	280 g (9 oz/1$\frac{2}{3}$ cups)	375 g (12 oz/2$\frac{1}{4}$ cups)	500 g (1lb/3 cups)	560 g (1lb 2oz/3$\frac{1}{4}$ cups)
Currants	250 g (8 oz/1$\frac{1}{2}$ cups)	350 g (10 oz/2 cups)	375 g (12 oz/2$\frac{1}{4}$ cups)	440 g (14 oz/2$\frac{3}{4}$ cups)
Dried Apricots, Chopped	155 g (5 oz/1 cup)	185 g (6 oz/1 cup)	220 g (7 oz/1$\frac{1}{4}$ cups)	250 g (8 oz/1$\frac{1}{3}$ cups)
Glacé (Candied) Cherries, Quartered	175 g (6 oz/$\frac{3}{4}$ cup)	220 g (7 oz/$\frac{3}{4}$ cup)	225 g (8 oz/1 cup)	280 g (9 oz/1 cup)
Cut Mixed Peel	90 g (3 oz/$\frac{1}{2}$ cup)	125 g (4 oz/$\frac{1}{3}$ cup)	185 g (6 oz/1 cup)	250 g (8 oz/1$\frac{1}{4}$ cups)
Mixed Chopped Nuts	90 g (3 oz/$\frac{3}{4}$ cup)	125 g (4 oz/1 cup)	185 g (6 oz/1 cup)	250 g (8 oz/2 cups)
Lemon Rind, Coarsely Grated	12.5 ml (2$\frac{1}{2}$ tsp)	15 ml (1 tbsp)	15 ml (1 tbsp)	22.5 ml (1$\frac{1}{2}$ tbsp)
Lemon Juice	37.5 ml (2$\frac{1}{2}$ tbsp)	45 ml (3 tbsp)	60 ml (4 tbsp)	75 ml (5 tbsp)
Brandy, Whisky, Sherry	60 ml (4 tbsp)	75 ml (5 tbsp)	90 ml (6 tbsp)	105 ml (7 tbsp)
Plain (All-purpose) Flour	345 g (11 oz/2$\frac{3}{4}$ cups)	470 g (15 oz/3$\frac{3}{4}$ cups)	575 g (1 lb 3 oz/4$\frac{3}{4}$ cups)	685 g (1 lb 6 oz/5$\frac{1}{4}$ cups)
Ground Mixed Spice	15 ml (1 tbsp)	22.5 ml (1$\frac{1}{2}$ tbsp)	30 ml (2 tbsp)	45 ml (3 tbsp)
Ground Almonds	75 g (2$\frac{1}{2}$ oz/$\frac{2}{3}$ cup)	90 g (3 oz/$\frac{3}{4}$ cup)	100 g (3$\frac{1}{2}$ oz/$\frac{2}{3}$ cup)	155 g (5 oz/1$\frac{1}{4}$ cups)
Soft Dark Brown Sugar	280 g (9 oz/1 cup + 2 tbsp)	410 g (13 oz/1$\frac{2}{3}$ cups)	530 g (1 lb 1 oz/2 cups + 2 tbsp)	625 g (1 lb 4 oz/2$\frac{1}{2}$ cups)
Butter or Margarine, Softened	280 g (9 oz/1 cup + 2 tbsp)	410 g (13 oz/1$\frac{2}{3}$ cups)	530 g (1 lb 1 oz/2 cups + 2 tbsp)	625 g (1 lb 4 oz/2$\frac{1}{2}$ cups)
Black Treacle (Molasses)	30 ml (2 tbsp)	37.5 ml (2$\frac{1}{2}$ tbsp)	45 ml (3 tbsp)	60 ml (4 tbsp)
Medium Eggs	5	7	8	9
Approximate Cooking Time	3 to 3$\frac{1}{4}$ hours	3$\frac{1}{2}$ to 3$\frac{3}{4}$ hours	3$\frac{3}{4}$ to 4 hours	4$\frac{3}{4}$ to 5 hours

GUIDE TO TIN (PAN) SIZES, COOKING TIMES AND PORTIONS

Weight of mixture	Approx. cooking in hours	Cake tin (pan) size	No. portions
700 g (1 lb 8 oz)	3	round 12.5 cm (5 in) square 10 cm (4 in)	8–12
950 g (2 lb 2 oz)	3¾	round 15 cm (6 in) square 12.5 cm (5 in)	15–20
1.1 kg (2 lb 8 oz)	4	round 17.5 cm (7 in) square 15 cm (6 in)	20–25
1.8 kg (4 lb)	4½	round 20 cm (8 in) square 17.5 cm (7 in)	30–35
2.8 kg (6 lb)	5	round 22.5 cm (9 in) square 20 cm (8 in)	45–50
3.6 kg (8 lb)	5	round 25 cm (10 in) square 22.5 cm (9 in)	65–70
4.5 kg (10 lb)	5½	round 27.5 cm (11 in) square 25 cm (10 in)	80–85
5.6 kg (12 lb 8 oz)	5½	round 30 cm (12 in) square 27.5 cm (11 in)	100–110
7.2 kg (16 lb)	6	round 32.5 cm (13 in) square 30 cm (12 in)	120–130
8.5 kg (19 lb)	7	round 35 cm (14 in) square 32.5 cm (13 in)	140–150

You will see, when referring to the chart, that a comparatively small increase in the size of cake tin (pan) requires a fairly significant increase in the amount of rich fruit cake mixture. This is because it is the volume of the tin (the height, length and width) that is important, not just the horizontal area. It is also for this reason that at first glance you appear to do far better when cutting up a 25 cm (10 in) square cake (80–85 portions) than a 20 cm (8 in) square cake (45–50 portions), for example.

To find how many portions you will obtain after allowing a little for wastage, follow the chart to the right-hand column. Use this information when planning a wedding cake, to help you decide whether a single-tier or a multi-tiered cake is required. You will be able to calculate quite accurately the minimum amounts you will need to cater for all your wedding guests and the absent friends who wish to have some cake saved for them.

Any small omissions or substitutions of ingredients that you make to suit your own taste won't ruin the results, but it is very important to follow the method and sequence of mixing and baking the cake.

ROLLED-OUT ICING

See Sugarpaste.*

ROYAL ICING

The prefix 'royal' is said to have been bestowed after this icing was used on Queen Victoria's wedding cake. This type of icing was used long before that date. In 1609 a small cookery book included a recipe for making icing which used 24 eggs. After being beaten for hours it was applied to the cake with, 'a thick board, or a bunch of feathers'.

Making Royal Icing The icing can be made with fresh egg whites or pasteurized dried powder, albumen powder*. The powder is easy to store and use, and it does not result in a surplus of egg yolks. Icing made with albumen powder will be whiter than that made with fresh whites.

You may come across an instruction to leave fresh egg whites exposed to the air for a number of hours before using. This is because egg whites are composed of a large percentage of water, on standing some of the water evaporates leaving a stronger solution.

Lemon juice and cream of tartar are acids. When added to fresh egg whites they help to stabilize the egg foam and prevent it from collapsing. Many older books and professional reference books state that whites should be beaten in a copper bowl. The surface of the copper produces a stable foam.

Glycerine* attracts moisture from the atmosphere and when a little is added to royal icing it prevents it from becoming too hard to cut. However, properly made, royal icing will not dry rock hard. If it is beaten sufficiently it will be light when applied without being aerated.

Utensils Any grease on the surface of a bowl or utensil will cause the whites to collapse. No matter how much beating is applied the icing will not be the correct consistency.

QUICK TIP

Before making royal icing, rinse the bowls and beater with boiling water. Keep a few wooden spoons and a 13 cm (5 in) nylon sieve especially to use for making icing.

Making Icing in a Machine Royal icing can be made using a heavy duty electric beater. The beater attachment must be used, not the whisk. This avoids the hard work involved in beating by hand, particularly if a large amount of icing is required. The drawback to this method is that the icing can be overbeaten. Keep the machine on the lowest speed. If the icing is to be used for coating a cake, make it two days

before it is required so that excess air bubbles surface and are eliminated.

PROFESSIONAL TIP

Always beat the icing with a wooden spoon for a few minutes after it has been made by machine. Also, whenever the icing has been left to stand, even if only for half an hour, give it another beating before using.

Making Icing by Hand This can be of equal quality to machine-made icing but it must be very well beaten. Whisk up the whites first and gradually add the sifted icing (confectioners') sugar, beating well between each addition. The final consistency should be similar to whipped cream, white and soft in texture. Icing which is thick and leaden can be the result of repeatedly adding sugar without sufficient beating. Depending on the amount of icing being made, a few hundred separate beating actions may be required.

Royal Icing Mix Packets of royal icing mix combine icing (confectioners') sugar with albumen powder* and they are ready to mix with water. This is a convenient way of making up a small amount of icing. However, the icing does still require plenty of beating. For example, one manufacturer's instructions recommend beating by hand for 15 minutes – this is not an exaggeration and it is necessary for good results.

Consistency For coating a cake, a softer consistency is required than that used when piping shells and stars. The icing should be similar to softly whipped cream. If it is too stiff add a little egg white or water. To stiffen the icing, beat in icing (confectioners') sugar. Before adding extra sugar, always beat the icing, as this will stiffen it up slightly.

Blue Colouring Icing made with fresh egg whites is not a pure white, therefore a small amount of edible blue colouring may be added to give the optical impression of whiteness.

Traditionally a blue bag was used for this. Obtained from a good ironmonger, a blue bag is a small cloth bag containing a blue substance which is intended for making laundry look white. Useful before the variety of soap powders now available was developed. However, edible blue colouring is more appropriate for use in royal icing.

> ## QUICK TIP
> *When checking the consistency of the icing, if only a small amount of liquid is needed, drip tap water on the surface of the icing. Pour off the excess before beating. This method is preferable to adding teaspoons of liquid.*

Using Royal Icing To pipe stars, shells, rosettes, scrolls and flowers the icing should be firm enough to stand in a point. Dip the wooden spoon into the icing, then lift it to make a point or peak of icing. Hold the spoon with the icing standing up. If the peak stays upright, or droops only very slightly, it is stiff enough. If the peak of icing flops over quickly it is too soft for borders or for piping flowers.

With experience you will know whether the icing is just right. Test a small amount on a cake board, either for spreading or piping.

Coating the Cake Coat the top of the cake first. Use a stiff palette knife to spread the icing over the surface. Adopt a wave-like motion when using the knife. Push the icing with one side of the blade, then push the icing in the opposite direction with the other side. This action helps to break any air bubbles in the icing.

Wipe a metal icing rule with a damp tea cloth. Start at the far side of the cake and draw the rule across the icing at a 45° angle. Don't hurry. Correct any excess pressure on the rule that may result in the marzipan showing through. Remove any surplus icing from the edge of the cake.

ROYAL ICING QUANTITY GUIDE

It is difficult to estimate how much royal icing will be used to ice a cake as the quantity varies according to how the icing is applied and to the thickness of layers. The design also has to be taken into account, whether it is just piping, or runouts and sugar pieces.

The chart is a guide to quantities for covering each cake with two or three thin layers of flat royal icing.

Cake Size	Quantity of Royal Icing
13 cm (5 inch) square	500 g (1lb/3½ cups)
15.5 cm (6 in) round 15 cm (6 in) square	750 g (1½ lb/4¾ cups)
17.5 cm (7 in) round 17.5 cm (7 in) square	1 kg (2 lb/7 cups)
20 cm (8 in) round 20 cm (8 in) square	1.25 kg (2½ lb/8¾ cups)
22.5 cm (9 in) round	1.5 kg (3 lb/10½ cups)
22.5 cm (9 in) square 25 cm (10 in) round 25 cm (10 in) square 27.5 cm (11 in) round	1.75 g (3½ lb/12¼ cups)

Keeping Qualities Place the icing in a clean bowl. Moisten plastic wrap under the tap and place it over the surface of the icing before replacing the lid. Store in the refrigerator for 1–2 weeks.

Icing Unusual Shapes
Horseshoe and Nought: It is difficult to apply royal icing to the inside curve of these shapes. Instead cover with a layer of sugarpaste*.
Hexagonal: To ensure that the angles on each corner are sharp, coat three alternate sides and leave to dry, then coat the remaining three.
Petal: On the inside curve of the petal shape, release pressure on the scraper to prevent the marzipan from showing through.

150

SECRETS OF SUCCESS

Most cakes are given three coats of royal icing. Each covering will be smoother. When applying icing to the side of a round cake, it is helpful to use a turntable and to complete smoothing the coating in one movement.

When using the icing, keep the bowl covered with a damp cloth to prevent the air from crusting the surface.

RECIPE

ROYAL ICING

All equipment must be thoroughly clean and free of grease, otherwise the icing will not hold the air which is beaten into it, making it heavy in consistency and unable to hold its shape.

The ratio of ingredients for royal icing are 6:1 of icing sugar to egg white.

Egg White	Icing (Confectioners') Sugar
30 g (1 oz/6 tsp)	185 g (6 oz/1 cup)
90 g (3 oz/⅓ cup plus 3 tsp)	545 g (1 lb 2oz/ 3⅓ cups)
155 g (5 oz/⅔ cup)	875 g (1¾ lb)
500 g (1 lb/2 cups)	3 kg (6 lb)

The egg whites should be at room temperature. Place them in a bowl with three-quarters of the icing sugar. Beat on slow speed for 2 minutes using an electric beater. Adjust the consistency by adding the remaining icing sugar and continue to beat on slow for a further 3 minutes.

Cover the icing with a polythene bag and a damp cloth to prevent the surface from drying and forming a crust.

QUICK TIP
Drape a clean tea-towel over the food mixer to avoid making a mess.

ROYAL ICING COATING

The techniques described here are for cakes and dummies. Make the royal icing a day in advance.

Gently stir the royal icing but do not beat it. Adding 5 ml (1 tsp) glycerine to every 500 g (1 lb) royal icing produces a softer texture to the coating.

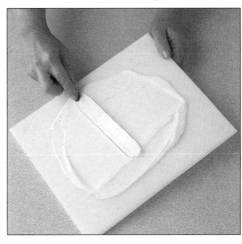

1 Place some icing on a grease-free board and work it with a palette knife to remove the large air bubbles. Place the cake on a piece of foam rubber to prevent it from slipping.

2 Spread the prepared icing on the cake top. Position the straight edge (or knife) on the far edge of the cake, then pull it across the surface. If the coating has noticeable flaws, clean the blade and draw it across the cake a second time. If the surface is still badly ridged, then apply another layer of icing and use the clean blade to repeat the process. However, do not repeat with fresh icing more than once.

5 Place the board on a piece of foam rubber. Coat with royal icing as for the cake top and remove the excess icing from the board edge using a knife. Apply thin layers of icing to obtain a good surface.

3 Remove the excess icing from the side of the cake with a palette knife. Allow the icing to dry completely before continuing.

6 When the icing is dry, remove the scraper 'take off' mark and any excess icing by gently scraping the coating with a sharp knife. Apply two or three coats of icing to the cake to achieve an even, smooth surface.

4 Position the cake on a weight on the turntable. Place another heavy weight on top of the cake. Spread the icing on the side of the cake. Hold the scraper against the cake and rotate the turntable. Remove the excess icing from the edges.

Remember . . . *Always use equipment which is spotlessly clean for applying royal icing. The smallest speck of dirt will show.*

FLAT ICING A SQUARE CAKE

The principle is very much the same as for a round cake. Generally, it is best to ice the top of the cake first so that a firm edge is formed for coating the sides and scraping off excess icing. However, this is not essential, as shown below. The method you use will depend on your experience and personal preference.

1 Flat ice the top as for a rounded cake. Use a small palette knife to smoothly spread the side of the dry cake with icing.

2 Remove the excess icing from the dry icing on the top edge of the cake.

3 Pull the side scraper across the side of the cake. Trim away the excess icing from the top edge and corners of the cake to neaten before drying.

4 The cake covered with one coat of royal icing. Dry before coating again.

SECRETS OF SUCCESS

Use bridal icing (confectioners') sugar for the final coat, as the small sugar particles will help to give a smooth surface.

The final coat of icing should be thinned with softened icing.

Do not coat the cake on the board, as the side scraper will catch on the paper and prevent the coating from being perfect.

FINISHING THE BOARD EDGE

This is important as it gives the completed cake a professional look. There are various ways in which the board edge may be finished; however applying a coat of icing gives the cake a complete look. Sometimes the cake board is allowed to show, perhaps with a piped border or runout pieces applied, or with decoration added to reflect the design on the cake.

If the board is iced, there are two options, either to coat with spreading icing or with runout icing.

1 Spread a thin layer of icing evenly all over the exposed board edge, then smooth it with a palette knife or scraper.

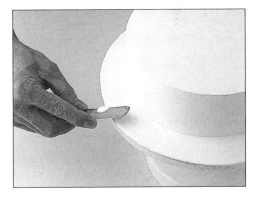

2 Here a bevelled edge is applied to the iced cake board by holding the knife at a slight angle and resting on the board, then rotating the turntable.

R

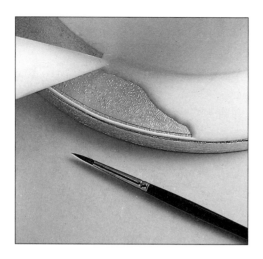

3 To coat the board edge with runout icing, first use a no. 2 tube (tip) to pipe a line of icing around the outer edge of the board, then fill with icing as shown.

RUNOUTS

Also known as runins, floodwork and colour flow. This technique can be used in many areas of cake decorating, for designs both large and small. Anything from a badge or a swan to a three-dimensional picture can be created in runouts.

A basic runout consists of an outline of royal icing* which is piped around a tracing of the required design. Then the inside area is flooded with icing which is thinned to flow smoothly. The icing will dry with an attractive sheen on the surface. Once the icing has dried the runout can be used to decorate a cake or plaque*. Try a simple runout first, such as a heart, or perhaps a butterfly. Don't attempt anything too intricate or a design with narrow areas.

Stages in Making Runouts

The Design: Prepare a clear drawing. Cover this with paper that will peel off easily once the icing is dry – non-stick paper or wax paper. Cut the paper only slightly bigger than the drawing. Unnecessarily large paper can be a hindrance as a quick movement can catch the excess paper and break the run out. Stick the paper over the drawing with dots of icing or masking tape. Adhesive tape can be awkward to use. Place the drawing on a completely flat surface, preferably a piece of glass or perspex which will attract warmth and allow the icing to dry quickly.

The Outline: Use a small bag with a fine writing tube (tip). Keep the joins in the piping neat – they should lie against each other, not overlap. Flood in the area immediately. If the outline is left to dry it can break.

Flooding: Place the flooding icing in a small or medium bag. Cut a small hole in the tip of the bag to regulate the amount of icing flowing out and break any air bubbles in the icing. Air bubbles weaken the runout. Keep the tip of the bag down in the flooding icing to ensure a smooth finish and to fill all corners. If necessary, use a fine paint brush to gently ease the icing into difficult corners.

Drying: To obtain a glossy runout, dry it under the heat of a desk lamp with a flexible arm, in the sun or in a warm area. Stand the piece of glass up on small blocks to allow the air to circulate around the work. The drying time depends on the thickness of the runout and the consistency of the icing as well as the temperature of the room. Allow two days for the work to dry.

> *QUICK TIP*
> *A stronger runout can be made by outlining and flooding the icing on a base of dry pastillage*.*

Making Stand-up Runouts Once dry, turn the runout over on its flooded side, pipe the outline and flood in the reverse side. Both sides will then be smooth and curved. If the piping bag used for outlining is made of silicone paper, simply place the whole bag in a polythene bag, seal and keep overnight.

Direct Runouts With some practice runouts can be outlined and flooded directly on the surface of a cake. This is a quick method which avoids breakages.

Curved Runouts You may want curved runouts to place on the side of a round cake. They can be made by securing the runout on a curved surface immediately it has been flooded. Apply overhead heat at once to crust the icing over before it starts to run outside the lines.

STEP-BY-STEP TO SUCCESS

CURVED RUNOUTS

Flat figures and plaques are ideal for square, hexagonal and other angled shapes, but they can look incongruous on curved surfaces. Once mastered, the ability to create curved runouts can lead the cake decorator into the area of developing runout petals for waterlilies and fantasy flowers, and into creating more adventurous models.

For curved runouts on cakes, what is needed is a drying surface which replicates the curve on the coated cake. For ornaments, the required curve, whether concave or convex, will be dictated by the design. Many items may be used as curved drying surfaces. Examples include polystyrene dummies or sections, plastic tubing or guttering, cardboard tubes and cake tins (pans). The consistency of the icing should be fractionally thicker than that required for normal runouts. If the icing is too thin, it will run down the curve before it dries. Speed is essential both while running out the plaque and when drying it.

SECRETS OF SUCCESS

When making curved runouts for use on the side of a cake, be wary of using the tin (pan) in which the cake was baked as a drying surface; remember that the marzipan (almond paste) and sugarpaste or royal icing will have altered the dimensions of the cake.

1 Prepare icing of the correct consistency. Trace selected design. Fix wax paper over drawing with a few bulbs of icing. Pipe outline in royal icing, then flood in. When working with two or more colours, fix drawing and wax paper to curved drying surface and work directly on that.

R

2 Free wax paper by sliding a palette knife between it and the drawing. Position runout on curved drying surface. Dry quickly. Take care that identical pieces are all dried at the same angle on the curve.

Figures, Crests and Pictures To obtain a three-dimensional effect this type of runout is flooded in sections. Colour and thickness combine to give an impression of depth or to highlight separate areas. Leave the icing in each section to dry on the surface before attempting to flood an adjacent area. Figures can be made to look realistic by making the icing thicker in parts which would be nearer the onlooker, such as an arm or front leg which would be thicker than a back leg. These areas can be overpiped and flooded a second time once dry.

Lettering Making runout letters takes away the worry of having to pipe them directly on the cake. Large, clear letters are ideal for children's cakes. The dry letters are attached to the cake with small dots of icing.

<hr>

RECIPE

ROYAL ICING FOR RUNOUTS
Use the icing of the consistency given below to pipe the outlines, then thin it down very slightly to run in the spaces. Makes about 1.75 kg ($3\frac{1}{2}$ lb).

60 g (2 oz/$\frac{1}{4}$ cup) powdered albumen reconstituted in
280 ml (10 fl oz/$1\frac{1}{4}$ cups) water
1.75 kg ($3\frac{1}{2}$ lb/$10\frac{1}{2}$ cups) icing (confectioners') sugar

•

1 Make up the albumen solution in a grease-free bowl. Add three quarters of the icing (confectioners') sugar and beat with an electric mixer for 2 minutes on slow speed.

2 Adjust consistency with remaining sugar and beat for 3 minutes more on slow speed until icing peaks.

3 For a small quantity, mix 20 ml (4 tsp) powdered albumen with 35 ml (7 tsp) water and add 220 g (7 oz/$1\frac{1}{3}$ cups) icing (confectioners') sugar.

Piping Gel A piped chocolate or royal icing outline worked on the cake can be flooded with softened piping gel.

Chocolate Runouts Chocolate can be thickened (see piping chocolate*) and

piped from a small bag. Use dark chocolate for the outline and flood in with a contrasting milk chocolate.

<hr>

SECRETS OF SUCCESS

<hr>

Flood the chocolate on paper with a shiny surface and it will set with a sheen. If set on matt paper the chocolate runout will be dull.

<hr>

Simple, yet sophisticated, runouts can be made by flooding with dark chocolate and immediately flooding in light chocolate. Swirl or feather the two types of chocolate with a cocktail stick or the tip of a knife.

Designs for Runouts The technique can be used for a wide variety of designs, from jolly figures to stylized flower heads or curved shapes and forms. The final chapter of this book includes many patterns that are ideal for working up as runouts. Other sources of ideas include greetings cards, books or patterns on fabric or wallpaper – simply trace or copy the required design, then make it smaller or larger to fit in with the decoration on the cake.

S

SEPARATORS

See Pillars*

SMOCKING

Does not require a lot of skill to achieve a professional result. This technique is worked on soft sugarpaste*. Fine lines are embossed in the paste using a ridged rolling pin. The lines are pinched into patterns using a pair of plastic tweezers.

> ### QUICK TIP
> *If you want to practise before investing in the proper equipment, use a section of ribbed garden or plumber's hose, strengthened with a piece of dowelling.*

Making Sections of Smocking Pieces of paste are embossed with the lines, then cut to size with a template. Moisten the surface of the iced cake and apply the section of smocking. Then pinch in the design, using tweezers, in various patterns based on embroidery.

Piping A fine writing tube (tip) and royal icing* are used to decorate the paste with tiny 'stitches'.

SECRETS OF SUCCESS

For effective results keep the lines of pinching close together. Have a fine, damp paint brush ready to eliminate any unwanted ends of icing.

STAGES IN SMOCKING

1 Mark the honeycomb pattern into the ribbed paste by pinching the folds into shape while still soft.

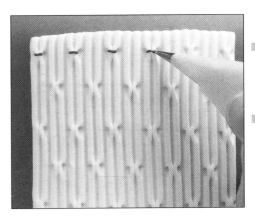

2 With a no. 0 tube (tip) pipe embroidery where marked in the honeycomb pattern.

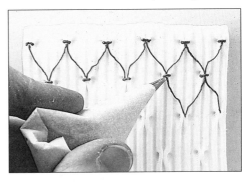

3 Continue piping, building up the embroidery pattern following the design pinched into the paste.

S

157

SMOOTHER

Flat plastic utensil for rubbing over the surface of freshly sugarpasted cakes or plaques* to obtain a smooth surface. Available in a large flexible sheet or as a firm tool complete with handle. Working with two smoothers, on opposite sides of the cake, gives a good, even finish.

SPACERS

See Equipment.*

STAMENS

Can be bought in a wide variety of colours and sizes, from black stamens for the centres of anemones to glittery stamens.

Stamens with stiff threads can be placed into the throat of a flower without difficulty. Those with soft threads can be stiffened by dipping them into confectionery glaze* and leaving to harden. Alternatively, they can be taped on wires before being placed in the flower.

Japanese Stamens These are expensive, extremely fine and difficult to handle. However, they do give a very realistic appearance to small flowers.

STANDS

A wedding cake needs a special stand to enhance it and to add extra height. For an informal family wedding a large silver tray, perhaps with a deckled edge, will show off the cake.

Mirror: A mirror the same shape as the cake makes an unusual reflective base.

Silver Stand: Either embossed with rows of beading or engraved with floral designs. They can usually be hired from a caterer or baker together with a matching knife.

Silver and Gold Plastic Stands: Are light in weight and attractive. However, they cannot compare with a real silver stand for quality.

Modern Stands: Can be bought or hired to support the tiers of the cake without the need for pillars. They are made from metal or acrylic in a variety of shapes. A popular form is the 'S' shape with either two or three platforms to hold the cakes. Other shapes and designs have staggered platforms.

STENCILS

The simplest form of stencil is a paper doiley through which icing sugar is sprinkled on the surface of a sponge cake. The following are all types of stencils which are useful for cake decorating.

Home-made Stencils: Use oiled parchment* or acetate* to make stencils, cutting them out with a sharp craft knife*. Study a book on the subject to decide where to place the 'ties'. These are the tiny sections which remain once the design is cut to enable the various parts to hold together.

Bought Stencils: Can be purchased from cake decorating shops or craft shops. Stainless steel stencils are long lasting, washable and flexible enough to remove easily.

Greetings Stencils: Offer an easy way of displaying a message on a cake. They save the trauma of worrying about spacing,

writing style and the consistency of icing for piping. Stencils for greetings such as 'Happy Birthday', 'Congratulations' and 'Merry Christmas' can all be purchased.
Picture Stencils: Depicting flowers and a variety of shapes. Use to add a quick decoration to a plaque* or cake top.

Using Stencils Place the stencil on a dry iced surface. Use a palette knife to spread the chosen icing in a thin, smooth layer over the stencil. Carefully peel or lift away the stencil.

Colour can be dabbed through the stencil by using a small piece of natural sponge.

SECRETS OF SUCCESS

The stencil must be kept perfectly still when applying the icing or the design will be blurred. A small, cranked palette knife makes the job easier.

STRAIGHT EDGE

See Metal rule.*

SUGAR

Sugar is produced from either sugar cane or sugar beet.

In the reign of Queen Elizabeth I, sugar was sold in 6.4 kg (14 lb) loaves and pieces were broken off by using a small chopper. Today there are many forms of sugar, which enables it to be used to best advantage for cooking and icing.
Granulated Sugar: Ideal for general use and for boiling syrups. Granulated sugar does not dissolve easily in cakes and its use can result in white spots on the surface of cooked cakes.
Caster (Superfine) Sugar: A soft, fine sugar which dissolves easily to give an even texture to sponges and fruit cakes.

Demerara Sugar: With large, golden crystals, this contains about 2% molasses.
Dark Soft Brown Sugar: Use to give colour and flavour to fruit cakes.
Dark Brown Muscovado Sugar: This contains about 13% molasses. It has a soft, fine texture and it provides colour and flavour when making rich fruit cakes.
Icing (Confectioners') Sugar: Made by milling and sifting white sugar until the fine powder is obtained. An anti-caking ingredient is added to keep the sugar flowing freely.
Golden Icing Sugar: A raw cane sugar which retains some natural molasses. This makes delicately flavoured, fawn-coloured icing. This is useful for buttercream but the colour is too strong for most royal icing.

> *QUICK TIP*
> *Beware of wasps! They are attracted to sugar and will quickly eat a hole into the surface of an iced cake.*

STEP-BY-STEP TO SUCCESS

SUGAR SYRUP
This syrup may be stored in a clean screw-top jar for several weeks, but will crystallize if refrigerated.

250 g (8 oz/1 cup) granulated sugar
pinch of cream of tartar
60 ml (4 tbsp) water

1 Place sugar and cream of tartar in a small heavy-bottomed saucepan. Add measured water and stir over moderate heat until sugar has melted. Try not to splash the syrup around the pan and do not boil until the sugar has completely dissolved. Continue to heat, without stirring, until syrup begins to bubble gently.

2 Boil without stirring until syrup measures 105°C/220°F on a sugar (candy) thermometer. Alternatively, test by dipping a teaspoon in the syrup and then pressing another teaspoon onto the back of it. Gently separate the spoons. If a fine thread forms, the syrup is ready.

3 Remove pan from heat immediately and plunge the bottom of it into ice cold water. This will arrest the cooking process and prevent syrup from caramelizing. When cool, pour syrup into a clean warm glass jar with a screw top. If syrup thickens on standing, warm it gently by standing jar in a bowl of warm water.

SUGARPASTE

The original name, dating back to the 1600s. This is a soft, pliable paste which is rolled out and used to form a smooth coating on a cake or plaque*. Generally white, sugarpaste is easily coloured and it can be purchased in champagne and pastel shades. The champagne shade is a soft ivory which complements ivory-coloured wedding dresses when used on wedding cakes.

There is considerable confusion over the various names which are used for sugarpaste. Sugarpaste is particularly versatile and it can be used for covering cakes, making plaques*, modelling flowers or animals and making frills. The paste can also be flavoured to make cut out sweets or centres for chocolates. It is particularly useful for making mints or orange creams which may be coated, or part-dipped, in chocolate.

Various Names Fondant icing, rolled fondant, covering fondant, plastic icing, roll-out icing, moulding icing, satin icing, gelatine icing, mallow paste and pastello. Trade names include Regalice and Renice.

Home-made Sugarpaste The paste can also be made at home but this scarcely seems worthwhile when you consider the time involved compared with the low cost and high standard of the bought varieties. If you do want to make sugarpaste, use a recipe that includes liquid glucose* and gelatine*. The glucose will give a soft, pliable paste and the gelatine will ensure that the paste will roll and stretch without cracking.

Applying Sugarpaste to Cakes Only roll out the paste slightly larger than the cake. Excess hanging paste is heavy and it can cause splits to appear along the top edge of the paste.

Apply sugarpaste on the surface of the cake slowly and carefully to avoid trapping air bubbles underneath. Support the paste

Rustic Wedding
see page 208

Summer Roses
see page 209

Roses All the Way
see page 210

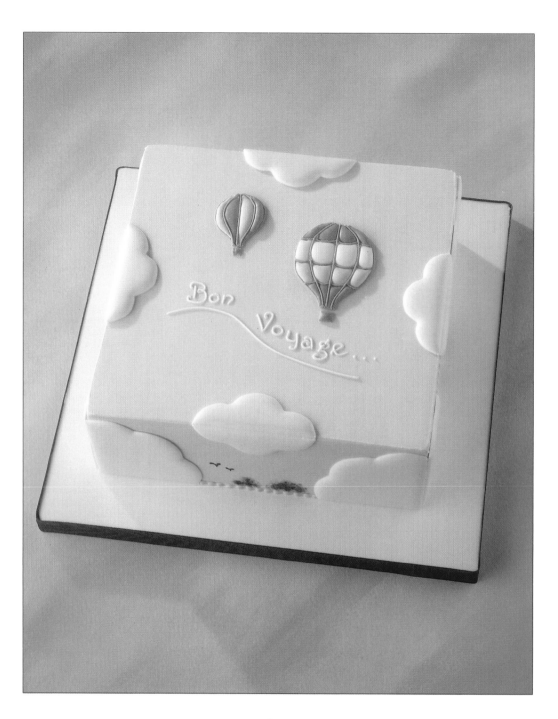

Bon Voyage
see page 211

on a rolling pin or the back of your hands and allow it to lie gently over the cake. Follow these guidelines for success.

● Remove any large rings from your fingers.

● Use an extra-long, non-stick rolling pin. The smooth surface will not mark the paste and the extra length enables large areas of paste to be rolled.

● When covering Victoria Sandwich cake, use buttercream rather than jam to cover the surface of the cake thinly before applying the sugarpaste. The buttercream will fill any uneven areas of cake to give a smooth coating.

● A thin layer of marzipan* under sugarpaste ensures a smooth finish. Brush a little alcohol over the marzipan before applying the sugarpaste so that the paste sticks down.

> ### QUICK TIP
>
> *If cracks appear in the paste, polish it gently with the palm of your hand and the warmth should make the cracks disappear. If not, leave until the surface is firm, then blend in a small amount of soft royal icing* with the tip of a finger. Softened-down sugarpaste can also be used instead of royal icing.*

Colouring Sugarpaste Use a cocktail stick (toothpick) to apply small amounts of colour. Liquid colours tend to make the paste sticky. Paste colours are strong and easy to use. Knead the colour into the paste. If a deep colour is required it is better to paint either paste or liquid on the surface of dry sugarpaste.

SECRETS OF SUCCESS

To make sure that the colour is evenly distributed, cut the paste in half and check that there are no streaks of colour remaining. Home-made sugarpaste can be coloured by adding the colour to the liquid gelatine mixture.

Storing Sugarpaste Wrap the paste tightly in a polythene bag and store it in a cool, dry place.

Freezing Sugarpaste-covered cakes may be frozen if necessary. Pack them in a large rigid container or box. Remove from the freezer 24–48 hours before required and place, still in the box, in the refrigerator. This allows the paste to thaw slowly and prevents a warm atmosphere from producing condensation on the surface.

Achieving a Sharp Top Edge Roll out a length of paste, the same depth and circumference as the cake. Cover the paste with a strip of plastic of equal size, then roll both up together like a bandage. Unroll the paste around the side of the cake, using the strip of plastic to support it. The plastic also prevents the paste from sticking when it is rolled up.

Although it is possible to achieve a fairly square edge, the finish will never be as sharp with sugarpaste as an edge on a royal-iced cake. Remember to take this into account when planning the decoration for the top border and sides of the cake.

Estimating Quantity to Cover Cake To estimate the quantity of sugarpaste required to cover a cake, first weigh the cake base. The weight of the cake represents the combined weight of marzipan and sugarpaste. Divide the weight in half to calculate the quantities of marzipan and sugarpaste. For example, if the cake weighs 1.8 kg (3¾ lb), you will require 900 g (1lb 14 oz) each of marzipan and sugarpaste. This calculation does not allow for coating the board.

Covering a Board or Plaque with Sugarpaste To coat the board or a plaque, first dampen it with stock syrup. Roll out the sugarpaste to about 1 cm (½ in) thick. Lift over the board, smoothing out any air bubbles, and trim to size. Smooth the edge by gently rubbing it with your hand or a smoother. Leave to dry.

SUGARPASTE COATING

The more experienced you are at handling sugarpaste, the quicker you work and the better the result. Paste which is over-worked, rolled out using too much sugar or dry tends to crack.

1 Dampen the marzipan with alcohol. Roll out the sugarpaste on icing sugar to 1 cm ($\frac{1}{2}$ in) thick. Using the hands and forearms, lift the paste over the cake.

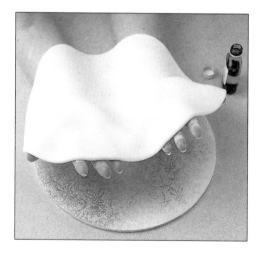

2 Polish the top with a smoother to remove air bubbles. Smooth the sides, trim off excess paste, then polish to a smooth surface. Coat the board with sugarpaste.

3 Place a little royal icing on the board, then remove the cake from the greaseproof paper and position it on the board. This method ensures that the cake has a neat base and the board is attractive when the cake is cut.

SUGAR SYRUP

See Sugar*.

The main use for sugar syrup in cake decorating is to thin fondant icing when it is reheated ready for use.

Syrup may also be diluted with spirit, wine, liqueur or fruit juice and used to soak sponge cakes when making gâteaux. This gives a cake with an excellent flavour and moist eating quality.

T

TEFLON-COATED PAPER

A shiny surfaced, glass fibre material, which is washable and reusable. Obtainable from specialist sugarcraft shops and some kitchen shops or suppliers. This material is sold in sheets.

Uses

Lining Tins (pans): When used to line cake tins it does not need greasing.

Making Runouts: Made on this material the runouts detach very easily, avoiding breakages that can occur when releasing them from paper.

Piping Lace: It is a marvellous surface on which to pipe tiny lace pieces. A gentle movement of the paper is all that is needed to loosen them.

Flooding Chocolate: The shiny surface gives the set chocolate a sheen on the base.

> *QUICK TIP*
> The paper is expensive but well worth the price. Remember not to cut it into small pieces, then find you require a large area, for example, for making a large runout. Two types of the paper are available, one darker than the other. Make sure you can see the outline of the design for the runout through the paper.

TEMPLATES

Use to mark patterns accurately on cakes. Greaseproof can be used to make a one-use-only template. For a re-usable template, use cartridge or tracing paper.

Top Designs Cut out the paper to the same size as the cake. Fold the paper into two, then into thirds: this will open out into six sections. To construct an eight-section template, fold the paper in half, three times. Cut the top of the paper into various shapes through all the thickness of paper.

MAKING A HEXAGONAL TEMPLATE

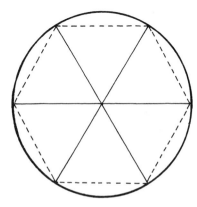

1 *Fold a circle of paper in half, then fold it into three equal wedges.*

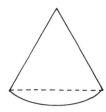

2 *Mark a straight line across the curved end of the wedge. Cut off the curve along the marked line.*

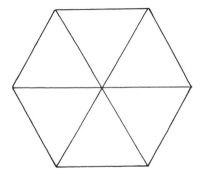

3 *Open out the paper and use as a template for cutting a hexagonal shape from a slab of cake.*

Cut a cross in the centre of the template and turn back the tiny sections of paper. This provides something to hold and to remove the template with when a line of icing has been piped around the perimeter.

Side Templates Encircle the iced cake with a band of paper, then cut to size so that the ends meet. Remove and fold into the number of divisions required. Cut to shape and unfold.

Remember... *Measure the template after the cake has been iced. It will not be accurate if measured over the marzipan coating.*

Hexagonal Shape A round cake can be accurately cut into a hexagonal shape by using a template. Use a circle of paper the same size as the cake. Fold it into two, then fold the half circle into thirds, making six layers of paper. Draw a straight line across the top section of paper, across the curve. Cut off the curve using sharp scissors.

Before marking out template designs on the top of wedding cakes, work out the position of the pillars and allow sufficient space around them for the piped design.

TRANSPORTING CAKES

Travelling with cakes can be a nightmare. Most cakes travel well provided a few rules are followed.

Packing the Cake A deep box with a separate lid is best for wedding cakes. Remind anyone who is lifting the box not to apply pressure to the sides but to take the weight on their hands under the box.

Placing a thin, folded paper under the cake board to raise it slightly provides room to grip the board when removing the cake from the box.

Obtain a wide, shallow and strong box from a supermarket for additional protection. Slit down both front corners, slide the cake box in and tape the sides together.

Small polystyrene blocks placed on either side of the board will stop the cake moving from side to side in the box. If the cake is too fragile to be placed down into the depth of a box, place the cake on the upturned lid and cover it with the base of the box.

Pack any delicate centrepiece decoration separate from the cake. Always pack extra decorations in case of damage, particularly lace. Also, remember to include a piping bag, suitable pipe and icing for repairs.

Remember... *Hexagonal boards will require larger boxes because of the angles. Measure across the widest point from corner to corner. This distance is about 3.5 cm ($1\frac{1}{2}$ in) more than if measured from the straight edges. It is easy to forget such detail, only to find that on 'the day' the cake will not fit in the box.*

Travelling by Car Holding a cake box on the knee while travelling is not a good idea. If the car jerks, the cake may get damaged. Instead make room in the boot or baggage compartment of the car which is spacious and flat. A sheet of foam or 'plastic bubble wrap' underneath the box will help to counteract any bumps and a slightly damp tea-towel placed under the box will prevent it sliding.

QUICK TIP
Sugarpaste* and royal icing* do not melt in hot travelling conditions but a drop of moisture will dissolve the surface and leave a mark. Always keep cakes covered when travelling.

TRELLIS

See also Piping*.

Fine lines piped in royal icing*. The lines can be piped straight on the top surface of a cake, over the top edge or as runouts to be applied once dry. Trellis technique can also be used to make baskets and raised domes.

Technique A no. 2 icing tube (tip) is the largest to use and a no. 1 is preferable. The tube must always touch the surface of the icing to make a connection before starting to pipe a line. Always pipe the lines towards you, even if this means constantly turning the cake. Allow the icing to hang from the tube as you pipe so that it will fall in a straight line.

Trellis piped diagonally looks more attractive than straight down and across. Start in the centre of the design, work outwards to one side, then start again in the centre and work in the opposite direction. This method ensures that the lines are all at the same angle. The closer together the lines, the more effective the trellis.

Leave the first set of lines to dry before piping over them. If you make a mistake, remove the icing using a fine, damp, paint brush.

Overpiping By decreasing the size of the icing tubes (tips), a second row – or more – of lines can be overpiped to give the trellis a 3-D effect. This can be enhanced by piping in colour, with each successive set of lines piped in a paler shade.

Trellis Around the Top Edge Scribe two lines on the cake: one on the top surface of the cake and the second just below the top edge on the side, both an equal depth from the edge. Use these lines as a guide to help keep the trellis work straight.

Trellis Baskets or Domes Trellis can be piped on a metal or plastic mould lightly greased with white cooking fat. Once dry, warm the mould. The fat will melt and release the trellis work.

PROFESSIONAL TIP

Start by piping diagonal lines at 7.5 cm (3 in) intervals around the top edge. These lines will help to keep the piped lines at a consistent angle.

TURNTABLE

A must for any serious cake decorator. Buy the best you can afford. Using a turntable enables a decorator to reach any part of the cake quickly. It is invaluable when applying royal icing* around the side of a round cake.

Tying ribbon around the cake is made easier on a turntable. With a flick of the finger you can see if the ribbon is level. *Plastic Turntable*: Light and suitable for lightweight cakes. Will not turn easily if a heavy cake is on it. *Metal Turntable*: Heavy and long lasting, turns easily and is worth the cost. Keep out on the work top for easy access. *Tilting Turntable*: Particularly useful when decorating the sides of cakes. Extending prongs clamp on the sides of the cake board. Then the turntable can be angled to show the chosen side of the cake.

Alternatives It is best to avoid some of the recommended alternatives, such as an upturned bowl. They can be a hazard if the cake slips. *Floristry Turntable*: A good second choice. *Folded Plastic Bags*: Place cakes, on boards, on folded plastic bags. This will make the board easy to swivel.

QUICK TIP
A packet of icing sugar, laid on its side, can be placed under the front of a cake board. This tilts the cake to allow easy piping on the side.

WEDDING CAKES

The ultimate goal for any cake decorator. So many people will view the cake, which follows the bride and her dress as the centre of attention.

Timing Make the cake a few months before the wedding to give it a chance to mature and allow time to work out a design. Aim to have the decoration finished about four days before the wedding. This will allow time for final adjustments and for the bride to collect the cake in good time.

Work backwards when planning the timing:
● Finish cake at least 4 days before the wedding day
● 2–3 days for decorating
● 3 days for the sugarpaste* surface to dry
● 3 days for 3 layers of royal icing* to dry base coat
● 1 day to apply a layer of sugarpaste
● 4 days for marzipan* to dry out
● 1 day to apply marzipan
● 2–3 days to make decorations, such as piped flowers, runouts, plaques or models.

This makes a total of nineteen days. Of course, experienced decorators can reduce this time, but it is useful to have some idea of how long the procedure can take.

QUICK TIP
Allow at least three to four weeks when making sugar flower bouquets.

Size of Cakes Cakes normally have a difference in size of 5 cm (2 in) between

each tier. Up to 7.5 cm (3 in) between the size of the cakes is also acceptable, particularly if the cakes are deep. A two-tier cake looks balanced if the top cake is 7.5 cm (3 in) smaller than the base cake.

The bottom cake should always be deeper than the upper cakes. If the middle or upper cakes are as deep, or deeper than, the bottom cake, slice some of the depth away.

One-tier Wedding Cakes Can be given extra height by placing on two boards, stuck together with dabs of icing. One board to be 7.5 cm (3 in) larger than the cake and the second board larger again by the same measurement. Ice and decorate both boards, making a feature of the stepped effect.

DESIGN IDEA
A large round cake with a centre hole may have a bottle of champagne placed in the middle to make an eye-catching design for a one-tier wedding cake.

Boards If the cake boards are iced this allows the eye to flow from cake to edge of board without interruption and so gives the impression that the cake is larger. It also looks more professional.

Boards under tiered cakes should not be larger than the size of the iced cake below. This rule excludes cakes with runout collars, which should stand on larger than average boards because of the risk of damaging the fragile collar. In this case, the measurement of the board for the cake standing above should be the measurement from one side of the collar to the other.

Texture Vary the texture of the iced decoration as a smooth overall finish can look very uninteresting. One way to achieve texture on wedding cakes is to add a fine pattern to the iced cake board by using a piece of natural sponge. Alternatively pipe a pattern of cornelli* work over part or all of it.

Design *See also Pillars*.* Graduate the size of piped flowers and other decorations on each tier of the cake. Repeat shapes and colours to give a feeling of harmony to the design. The wedding cake is often seen only from a distance so the decoration on the side will be more noticeable than piping on the top surface.

The space left between the pillars on large cakes can often look bare. Remedy this by placing an upstanding model such as a pastillage* half-open ring box, complete with ring, a posy of flowers or a butterfly.

The top decoration should not be too wide and it should have some height to balance the appearance of the tiered cakes by bringing them to a point. Do not place flowers in a very tall, thin vase. They look insubstantial against the weight of the cake and, at worst, can topple over. A small silver vase, firmly packed with oasis, will safely display an arrangement of fresh flowers. The surface of the top tier is small, so allow a clear area in which to position the top decoration.

> *QUICK TIP*
> *Why not ask a florist to make the top arrangement for the cake? He or she will know the scale of flowers to use in proportion to the container and the cake and a professional arrangement will look beautiful.*

Guide to Cutting and Portion Control
As a general guide, if each slice of wedding cake is 2.5 cm (1 in) square, in theory a 25 cm (10 in) cake should yield 100 pieces – but it never does! Slightly larger portions may be cut or part of the cake may crumble, so count on approximately 80 pieces.

> *QUICK TIP*
> *To judge the approximate number of 2.5 cm (1 in) slices from a square cake, multiply the size of two sides together. Round cakes will always result in fewer slices.*

Cutting Cakes The responsibility for cutting the wedding cake usually rests with the caterers. The first cut is made by bride and groom. If there is not a lot of top decoration on the cakes, it is easier to turn the cake upside down on the board and cut it from the base. Use a large, sharp knife and wipe it frequently on a damp cloth to remove excess sugar. This way less icing is shattered.

Square Cakes: Cut across one third of the cake and remove it from the board. This allows space to cut the remaining cake. Cut the cake across in 2.5 cm (1 in) wide slices. As each slice is cut, lay it along the cake board and slice it again into 2.5 cm (1 in) sections.

Round Cakes: Do not need to be cut into wedges. They can be cut in the same way as square cakes, although the rounded sides will give some smaller pieces of cake.

Another method of cutting round cakes is to cut a circle, going right down to the cake board, about 3.5 cm (1½ in) in from the top edge of the cake. Cut this section of cake into 2.5 cm (1 in) sections. Repeat with the remaining cake.

American Cakes These are usually made from soft mixes or from a favourite recipe such as carrot cake. They are often iced in buttercream and frozen once the base coat is applied. The decoration is completed near the wedding day.

These soft cakes can be arranged in tiers using hollow pillars with dowels through the centre and separator plates to take the weight of the top cakes. Alternatively the cakes can be placed on thin cards of the same size, then stacked on top of each other. Each base layer of cake has four pieces of dowelling pushed through the cake down to the cake board, then cut level with the top surface of the cake. These take the weight of the upper cakes. Once in position any gaps in the icing around the bases of the cakes are filled and the remaining decoration completed.

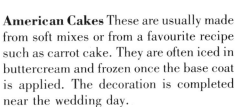

To remove the cakes, ease a knife carefully under the thin cake board of the top cake, then lift away the cake and board.

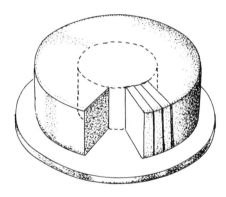

Cutting a round wedding cake

WRITING

Although writing on a cake becomes the focal point of the design, this is one skill that is rarely practised enough.

Space Consider carefully the amount of space available. Allow room on both sides of the name or message so that it stands out. If the message is long, start on the far left of the cake so that the whole width of the cake can be used. Decorate any excess space on the right of the cake with a small decoration, spray of flowers or a line ending consisting of tiny dots or scrolls piped level with the line of lettering.

Look at professional lettering and take note of the way it is achieved. Lettering on cakes often looks amateurish because of the wide spaces left between letters. The letters should be close to each other – almost touching – and the space left between words should be approximately the same size as the letter 'o'.

If the cake is large make the letters bigger. Runout letters look very attractive and they are easy to apply with tiny dots of icing. Keep the dots of icing small or they could ooze out from behind the lettering.

Centralizing a Name Count up the letters and divide the number in half. An odd number of letters is easier because the extra letter becomes the centre of the cake and the others are worked either side. Sometimes this does not work out satisfactorily as some letters take up more room than others. For instance, O occupies more space than I and two or three wide (or narrow) letters in a word can disrupt the spacing. Try practising the word before applying it to the cake. If not satisfied, measure the length of the piped word and start the piping on the halfway mark.

Style One of the most difficult forms of writing is piping on a cake in joined-up writing. Notice the lettering applied to cakes in shop windows: it is usually written in capital letters. Quick to pipe and easy to read, capitals can be large or small. Over half the capital letters in the alphabet are composed of straight lines that are always easier to pipe than curves.

SECRETS OF SUCCESS

When piping a long word or unusual name, have it written out for reference. It is so easy, when concentrating on piping to miss a letter.

Timing The writing is usually left as the last decoration to be applied to the cake. Reverse this procedure: pipe the message before the border decoration is worked. This means that it is far easier to pipe without worrying about damaging the top edge.

Overpiping writing in a strong colour gives a dramatic result

Direct Piping Practise writing directly on the cake surface without pricking out the shape of the letters first as this can often result in a maze of bewildering dots. They can be particularly eye catching if the piped line does not lie immediately over them.

Use icing the same colour as the cake to pipe the lettering. Then if you are not satisfied, the icing can easily be lifted off using a small palette knife, without leaving a coloured smudge. Once perfect, overpipe the letters in a deep or contrasting shade.

> QUICK TIP
> *Use a no. 2 icing tube (tip) for the base piping and overpipe using a no. 1.*

Icing Tubes (Tips) If piping directly on the cake, use a no. 1 icing tube (tip) which will give a fine outline and sufficient impact to be legible.

FREESTYLE LETTERING

1 Have all your equipment ready before you begin.

2 Place a small amount of icing in the bag and begin writing using firm but even pressure.

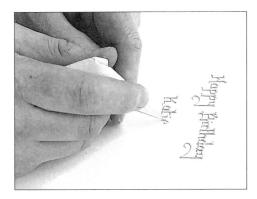

3 Take care to get the spacing even and ensure that all the tops and tails are of equal height.

4 Words on the second line should be spaced centrally below the first line.

RUNOUT LETTERING

1 Place the chosen lettering in a plastic file. Secure small pieces of waxed paper over the letters to be traced and iced.

2 Begin by outlining the letter using a no. 1 tube (tip).

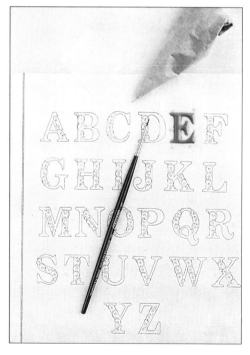

3 Flood the letter, brushing the icing into all parts until smooth and even. Use a fine paint brush.

4 The letters should be completely dry before transferring to the cake.

5 Peel the letters off the waxed paper and attach to the cake using small dots of icing.

Easy Alternatives
● Imprint a greeting on soft sugarpaste* using an embossing set. Once the paste is dry, pipe over the impression.
● Use an alphabet set of cutters to cut out the letters in sugarpaste or marzipan*. Good for children's cakes. Marzipan is stiffer and will be released from the cutters more easily than sugarpaste. If having difficulty, dip the cutter into icing (confectioners') sugar before using. The letters are made more interesting if the surface of the paste is textured with an embossed rolling pin first.

● Stencils* may be used to display a greeting. Place on a firmly iced surface of royal icing*, chocolate or sugarpaste.

● Pipe the greeting on a plaque*.

● Icing pens contain edible food colours and may be used to write on a strip of rice paper as well as on dry icing.

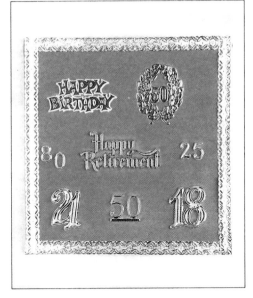

This plaque shows how to use plastic embossing script. Push the plastic piece into the paste covering of the cake or plaque within 15 minutes of coating, before a surface crust forms. Push into the paste in a straight movement – do not move the paste or you will get a distorted impression. Once pushed in, pull out straight to get a clean finish. When the impression is made you can leave it, or overpipe or outline the letters when the paste is dry.

This plaque shows a few of the many types of silver and gold plastic scripts and numerals available. These can be used on cakes or plaques. If you do not feel confident to write on a cake or are short of time these are an acceptable alternative.

DECORATED CAKES

This chapter highlights the variety of ways in which different cakes, fillings and coverings can be combined to suit many occasions. It is intended to lead you on from the basic instructions, methods, hints and tips explained previously towards exercising your skills and imagination to create finished cakes of all types. Hopefully, in using some of these cakes to practise certain techniques you will feel inspired to adventure further into the fascinating art of cake making and decorating.

Note Throughout the chapter, page references are not given for items which are included as entries in the previous section: simply look them up in their relevant alphabetical position, for example, marzipan or buttercream. However, page numbers are given for recipes which are included under a different main A–Z entry, for example, Quick Mix Sponge which is included under the entry on Cakes.

BLACK FOREST CAKE

Illustrated on page 17

1 quantity Whipped Ganache
250 g (8 oz/¾ cup) whole fruit morello
cherry jam
30 ml (2 tbsp) lemon juice
30 ml (2 tbsp) marashino syrup
1 × 20 cm (8 in) round Genoese Sponge,
see page 33
DECORATION
3 maraschino cherries
125 g (4 oz/4 squares) plain chocolate
60 g (2 oz/2 squares) white chocolate
3 small rose leaves

●

1 Make up ganache mixture; refrigerate for 1 hour before whisking. Meanwhile make chocolate decorations, following step-by-step instructions. Use dark chocolate for scrolls and white chocolate for cherries and leaves.

2 Combine jam, lemon juice and maraschino syrup in a saucepan. Stir over low heat until jam has melted. Brush melted jam liberally over both sponge layers to cover, then spoon out cherries remaining in saucepan and spread them over one of the cakes.

3 Whisk ganache until pale and doubled in volume. Spread one third of it over the cherries. Place second sponge on top, jam side down. Spread remaining ganache over top and side of cake and smooth over with a palette knife.

4 Press chocolate scrolls around side of cake and arrange half-dipped cherries and leaves on top. Chill cake before serving.

Melt white and plain chocolate separately. Drain maraschino cherries and dry on absorbent kitchen paper. Half dip them in warm white chocolate. Leave to dry on wax paper. Wash and dry rose leaves. Brush backs with white chocolate. Refrigerate, chocolate side up, until set, then carefully peel leaves off chocolate.

Spread melted plain chocolate smoothly over marble or clean smooth surface. Leave until dry. Use a long knife with a rigid blade. Hold knife at an angle of 45° to chocolate. Draw it lightly across to cut thin layers that curl into scrolls. Any small areas of melted chocolate may be used to make fans; make as for scrolls, but use the end of a round-bladed knife.

ROSE GATEAU

Illustrated on page 18

250 g (8 oz/8 squares) white chocolate
250 g (8 oz/8 squares) plain chocolate
vanilla essence (extract)
500 g (1lb/2½ cups) Basic
Buttercream
1 × 23 cm (9 in) round Genoese Sponge,
see page 33
pink dusting powder (petal dust/blossom
tint)
60 g (2 oz/4 tbsp) liquid glucose
green paste colouring
icing (confectioners') sugar

●

1 Melt the white and plain chocolate in two separate bowls over pans of hot, not boiling water. Beat vanilla essence (extract) to taste into the buttercream.

2 Sandwich together the sponge cakes using about one-third of the buttercream. Use the remaining buttercream to cover the top and sides of the cake. Draw a comb scraper around the sides, neaten the edges, then smooth the top of the cake using a palette knife.

3 Ladle a little melted white chocolate onto some greaseproof paper, flatten with a palette knife and flap the paper up and down to smooth and level. As soon as it is just set, cut out a small oval shape. Return the remaining chocolate to the bowl and colour it pink. Following the same procedure, cut out a larger oval plaque in pink.

4 Colour the remaining pink chocolate to a darker shade of pink then add an equal quantity of liquid glucose, mix with a wooden spoon. Turn out onto a clean surface and knead well. Cover and leave for about 15 minutes before making roses.

5 When the roses are complete, colour the remaining moulding chocolate green for the leaves. Flatten a walnut-sized knob of chocolate between the thumb and forefinger, place on a flat surface and stamp out a rose leaf using the cutter. Mark veins on leaves with a sharp knife. Refrigerate leaves if they are too soft to handle.

6 Make chocolate caraque from the plain chocolate. Fasten the small white plaque to the larger pink one and arrange the roses and leaves on top. Lift with palette knife onto the centre of the cake.

7 Mark the cake into four and arrange chocolate caraque on top. Cut very thin strips of paper and arrange on the rolls equidistant apart. Gently sieve the icing (confectioners') sugar over the top, then carefully remove paper strips. Place chocolate rose leaves in the corner of the caraque.

8 This gâteau is not suitable for refrigeration, as if exposed to alternate cold and warm air, condensation will form on the chocolate causing the flowers to droop and become sticky; the icing (confectioners') sugar will also dissolve. Store the gâteau in a large covered container in a cool place.

PETITS FOURS

Illustrated on page 19

These iced shapes provide the perfect opportunity for practising new skills. They may be filled with any butter icings or with fresh cream.

4-egg white American Sponge mixture,
see page 34
FILLING AND COATING
½ quantity Basic Buttercream
apricot glaze
double quantity Fondant
Sugar Syrup, see page 159
2.5 ml (¼ tsp) instant coffee dissolved in
2.5 ml (½ tsp) hot water
additional flavourings and colourings
as required
DECORATION
use any or all of the following:
marzipan, glacé (candied) cherries,
blanched almonds, stem (preserved)
ginger, crystallized rose petals or violets,
chocolate cutouts or piped chocolate
motifs

•

1 Preheat the oven to 180°C (350°F/Gas 4). Bake the cake in a lined and greased 20 cm (8 in) square cake tin (pan). Cool on a wire rack.

2 Warm fondant, dissolving it with sugar syrup to the consistency of thick cream. Flavour some of the fondant icing with the coffee and tint or flavour the rest as desired.

3 Cut up, ice and decorate the cakes, following the step-by-step instructions. When fondant has set, trim the base of each cake neatly with a sharp knife.

Cut cake in half horizontally, brushing off any loose crumbs. Spread cut halves with buttercream and sandwich back together again. Cut into neat rounds, squares or triangles, again brushing away loose crumbs. Coat with apricot glaze. A marzipan roll, nut or half glacé (candied) cherry may be placed on top of each cake, if liked.

Place cakes well apart on a wire rack over wax paper. Pour fondant icing slowly from a large spoon over the top of each cake, letting it trickle slowly down the sides. If free from crumbs, fondant that falls through onto the paper may be scraped up and used again. Decorate with nuts, ginger, crystallized rose petals, chocolate shapes or motifs.

CHESTNUT CREAM LOG

Illustrated on page 20

This may be served as an alternative to either Christmas pudding or the traditional rich cake.

2 quantities chocolate Swiss Roll mixture, see page 33
FILLING
1 quantity Crème Diplomate, see page 57
250 g (8 oz/1 cup) unsweetened chestnut purée
30 g (1 oz/2 tbsp) icing (confectioners') sugar
30 ml (2 tbsp) rum
DECORATION
1 quantity American Frosting
½ quantity American Parfait, coloured green, see page 29
small piece of marzipan, about 45 g (1½ oz)

●

1 Preheat oven to 220°C (425°F/Gas 7). Bake both cakes in lined and greased 20 × 30 cm (8 × 12 in) Swiss roll tins (jelly roll pans).

2 Roll up one of the chocolate cakes from the long side. Roll the other cake in the same way but over a rolling pin covered with greaseproof paper (parchment). Make several paper piping bags.

3 Make up the crème diplomate. Beat the chestnut purée, sugar and rum together and fold into the crème. Fill and roll the log, following the step-by-step instructions.

4 Chill for 30 minutes. Follow the step-by-step instructions for frosting and decorating. Keep the finished cake in a cool place and eat within two days.

Carefully unroll the thinner Swiss (jelly) roll. Spread half the chestnut cream over it, spreading it with a palette knife. Roll the cake up again and hold it for a few seconds with the join underneath so that the shape sets. Spread the roll with the remaining chestnut cream.

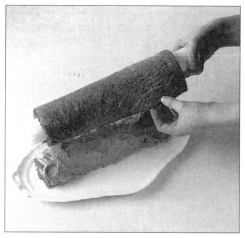

Carefully unroll the Swiss (jelly) roll from around the rolling pin and wrap it around the first roll, tucking the join underneath. Wrap the cake in greaseproof paper (parchment) and place it in the refrigerator for 30 minutes to set.

Make American frosting. Unwrap log, place on cake board and cover quickly with frosting; cover length of log first, then ends. As icing sets, swirl it with a warm dry palette knife or mark woodgrain down the length with a fork.

For trees, cut marzipan into three equal pieces. Mould each to a cone. Spoon green parfait into a piping bag fitted with a small ribbon tube (tip). Pipe small parfait ribbons around each cone, starting at the base. Bring tube sharply down and then sharply up and away from cone each time to break off parfait. Top each tree with an upright strand.

Place green parfait in a paper piping bag, snip off end and pipe ivy stems over the cake. Fill a second bag with parfait; snip end to 'V' shape. With tip of bag on ivy stem, apply pressure with your little finger. Squeeze bag, drawing it sharply away to form a leaf. Make remaining leaves in the same way.

If liked, the remaining marzipan may be used to make a greetings card. Roll marzipan to a 5 × 7.5 cm (2 × 3 in) rectangle and mark edges with fork or modelling tool. Pipe a greeting or design of leaves and berries, using the bag cut for piping the ivy stems. Alternatively, paint inscription with a fine paint brush dipped in green food colouring.

STRAWBERRY CHOCOLATE GATEAU

Illustrated on page 53

1 × 23 cm (9 in) round Genoese Sponge,
see page 33
strawberry jam
125 g (4 oz/¼ lb) strawberries plus 12
even sized strawberries for decoration
caster (superfine) sugar
kirsch
600 ml (1 pt/2½ cups) double (heavy)
cream
250 g (8 oz/8 squares) plain chocolate
small jar redcurrant jelly
icing (confectioners') sugar

●

1 Spread one of the sponge bases with strawberry jam. Wash, hull and quarter the strawberries. Place in a bowl and sprinkle with a little caster (superfine) sugar and a few drops of kirsch if required. Whip the cream to piping consistency and fold one-third into the strawberries.

2 Spread the strawberry cream onto jam and place the other sponge on top. Spread remaining cream on top and side of gâteau. Mark into 12 portions.

3 Melt chocolate and pour onto a sheet of greaseproof paper. When set, place the 23 cm (9 in) sponge tin (pan) on the chocolate and cut round the tin to produce a large circle. Using a long-bladed knife cut circle into 12 even triangles.

4 Melt some redcurrant jelly in a small saucepan adding just a little water to thin slightly. Wash and dry 12 even sized strawberries. Dip the strawberries into the jelly. Put onto greaseproof paper to set.

5 Place strawberries, thin edge to centre of the cake. Ease six chocolate segments off the paper and thickly dust with icing (confectioners') sugar. Arrange these on the cake, resting them on the strawberries and alternating with the triangles which are not dusted with icing sugar.

RASPBERRY VALENTINE CAKE

Illustrated on page 54

Fresh raspberries are used to flavour this special occasion cake, but other soft fruits would be equally acceptable.

6-egg Genoese Sponge mixture, see
page 33
125 g (4 oz/1 cup) pistachio nuts, finely
chopped
ICING
60 ml (4 tbsp) Sugar Syrup, see
page 159
125 g (4 oz/¼ lb) fresh raspberries,
sieved into a purée
1 quantity American Parfait, see
page 29
1 quantity Glacé Icing
small piece of marzipan, about
30 g (1 oz)
pink food colouring
icing (confectioners') sugar for
rolling out

●

1 Preheat oven to 180°C (350°F/Gas 4). Bake cake in two heart-shaped tins (pans). Cool on a wire rack. Make several paper piping bags.

2 Warm sugar syrup and pour it into a small bowl. Gradually stir in raspberry purée, then chill mixture until it is thick enough to just coat the back of the spoon. Make up parfait in a large bowl. Set aside 15 ml (1 tbsp) of the thickened raspberry purée for piping; gradually beat the rest into the parfait.

3 Using one third of the parfait, sandwich cakes together and then spread the rest around the side of the cake, bringing it well up to the top edge to form a shallow ridge. Press the pistachio nuts over the side of the cake.

4 Following the step-by-step instructions, ice the top of the cake with glacé icing and feather with raspberry purée. Decorate with marzipan hearts.

Put reserved raspberry purée in a piping bag. Have ready a skewer and a pin. Make up the glacé icing and immediately pour it onto the cake, starting in the centre and working towards the edge. The icing should flow over the cake. Use the skewer to tease it into any awkward corners. Prick any air bubbles with the pin.

Quickly pull the top of the skewer across the cake, through the coloured lines. Make a second drag line 1 cm ($\frac{1}{2}$ in) from the first, but in the opposite direction. Continue until feather pattern is complete.

Snip the point off the piping bag containing the raspberry purée. Pipe straight lines diagonally across the cake, 1 cm ($\frac{1}{2}$ in) apart. The glacé icing should still be so soft that the purée sinks into it.

Colour the marzipan pink. Roll it out on a surface lightly dusted with icing (confectioners') sugar to about 5 mm ($\frac{1}{4}$ in) thick. Cut out about 24 tiny hearts, using an aspic cutter, if you have one. Alternatively, make larger hearts, using a heart-shaped biscuit (cookie) cutter. Position hearts round rim of cake.

EASTER NEST

Illustrated on page 55

5-egg Madeira Cake mixture, see
page 35
almond essence (extract)
125 g (4 oz/¼ lb) marzipan
icing (confectioners') sugar for
rolling out
DECORATION
apricot glaze
375 g (12 oz/¾ lb) marzipan
125 g (4 oz/4 squares) plain chocolate

●

1 Preheat oven to 160°C (325°F/Gas 3). Grease and line a deep 20 cm (8 in) round cake tin (pan). Add almond essence (extract) to cake mixture, then place half the mixture in the prepared tin (pan).

2 On a clean surface dusted with icing (confectioners') sugar, roll out marzipan (almond paste) to a 20 cm (8 in) round. Place on top of cake mixture in tin (pan). Carefully smooth remaining mixture over the top.

3 Bake cake for 1½–1¾ hrs until firm to the touch, covering top with greaseproof paper if it begins to overbrown. Cool slightly before turning out on a wire rack.

4 When cold, brush top and sides of cake liberally with apricot glaze. Marzipan side of cake in two strips: measure around cake with a piece of string and cut to size. Measure depth of cake in the same way, adding on 1 cm (½ in) before cutting string.

5 Using 250 g (8 oz/½ lb) of the marzipan, roll out two sausages, each half the length of the longer piece of string. Roll and trim each sausage shape to a strip slightly taller than the cake, using smaller length of string as a guide. Press the fine side of a grater firmly onto both marzipan strips to make a pattern. Holding cake on its side, roll it onto one marzipan strip to fix it firmly in position. Repeat with second strip.

Smooth the joins carefully with a small palette knife, taking care not to spoil pattern on marzipan.

6 Roll out half of the remaining marzipan into two thin sausage strips, each the same length as the longer piece of string. Twist strips together to form a rope for the top edge of the cake. Fix it in position.

7 Melt most of the chocolate (reserving a little for piping the eyes of the chicks) and shave off small fan shapes as for making caraque, see page 42. When dry, sprinkle these over the top of the cake. Use remaining marzipan to make two Easter chicks.

Making Easter Chicks
Colour a pea-sized piece of marzipan red and the remainder yellow. Cut the yellow piece in half to make two chicks. Roll a small ball for each head and a larger ball for each body. Assemble the chicks, then make a snip on either side of each chick for the wings. Cut two red diamond shapes for the beaks and insert into the heads. Pipe chocolate eyes.

EASTER EGG CAKE
With Bas Relief Bunny

Illustrated on page 56
Templates on page 246

Bake the cake in a metal egg-shaped mould. If using an easter egg mould which does not have a stand, or legs, to support it, then prepare a 'nest' of crumpled foil on a baking tray to support the tin in a level position during cooking. Before removing cake, slice it across top, so that when turned out, the bottom will be flat.

15 × 23 cm (6 × 9 in) egg-shaped cake
apricot glaze
750 g (1¼ lb) marzipan
clear alcohol (gin or vodka)
750 g (1¼ lb) sugarpaste
selection of food colourings
125 g (4 oz/¼ lb) modelling paste
white vegetable fat (shortening)
pink dusting powder (petal dust/blossom tint)
royal icing
25 × 33 cm (10 × 13 in) oval cake board

●

1 Brush cake with apricot glaze and cover with marzipan. Brush with clear alcohol and coat with sugarpaste. Place on board. Trace door and cut a template from thin card. Place template on freshly coated cake, cut through sugarpaste coating and remove door portion, exposing marzipan. Dry for three days.

2 Colour some sugarpaste light brown. Roll out to same thickness as sugarpaste used for coating cake. Using template and scalpel, cut out door. Dampen back with water and place in gap on cake, siting it flush with sugarpaste coating. Add detail to door and make bas relief bunny directly on cake.

3 Pipe flower stalks around base of cake and next to door, using no. 1 tube (tip) and green royal icing. Using small and medium blossom cutters, cut flowers for side and top of cake from blue modelling paste. Dampen backs of flowers with water and fix to cake. Complete flowers by piping a dot of icing in each centre. Mould the larger leaves and flowers to the right of the door from modelling paste; attach to cake. Pipe a small shell border around base of cake, using no. 42 tube (tip) and green royal icing.

4 Make sugar ribbon and bow from pink modelling paste. Cut thinly rolled paste into 1 cm (½ in) wide strips. Attach one length over top of cake, offsetting it slightly to the left. Dampen lightly with water. Attach two shorter lengths for ribbon tails, cutting a V-shape in the end of each. Make two loops for the bow. Fix to cake, then cover centre of bow with another small strip of paste.

Template for bas relief bunny

Using template and scalpel, cut out door from brown paste; position on cake. Texture lines in door using veining tool. Paint a cross to represent window. Soften some white or pink modelling paste with vegetable fat, place in clay gun and extrude a length of paste for door edge; twist, dampen back and secure to door.

Pad body and head of bunny with modelling paste. Exaggerate eye, ear, arm and leg sockets, making hollows in paste with ball tool. Cut out back ear and arm from thinly rolled paste. Attach them to silhouette; texture fur (on back ear and arm only) with veining tool.

Smooth end of paste rope to neaten. Using food colouring and thin paint brush, paint basket of eggs directly on cake coating. Trace Easter bunny silhouette, ear, arm and jumper; cut out of thin card. Using template and scalpel, cut out bunny from thinly rolled modelling paste. Dampen back of paste; secure to cake.

Roll out some modelling paste. Using template and scalpel, cut out a second bunny silhouette about 2.5 mm ($\frac{1}{8}$ in) larger than the first. Dampen bunny on cake and place silhouette over padding, smoothing it into place and tucking it neatly into hollows. Mark small lines in direction of fur growth, using veining tool.

Using template, scalpel and blue modelling paste, cut out jumper. Place on bunny and reshape arm socket with ball tool. (Note that arm holes are avoided on bas relief figures where possible, to prevent raw edges showing).

Model arm, front ear and tail. Dampen back of paste and attach pieces to bunny. Dust the inside of the ear with pink dusting powder. Add texture to the tail by marking it with a veining tool. Make the eye and nose from tiny pieces of white paste, then paint in the eye detail with food colouring to complete the decoration.

MERRY CHRISTMAS PLAQUE CAKE

Illustrated on page 89
Template on page 246

1 × 20 cm (8 in) square rich fruit cake
apricot glaze
1 kg (2 lb) marzipan
1 kg (2 lb) sugarpaste
small piece of flower paste, about
30 g (1 oz)
non-toxic gold paint
yellow, red and blue paste colourings
small quantity royal icing
gum arabic glue
1 oval plaque, see 'Merry Christmas'
template for size
DECORATIONS
3 metres (3 yards) thin red ribbon
3 metres (3 yards) thin green ribbon
holly leaves
Christmas roses

●

1 Brush the cake with apricot glaze and cover with marzipan and white sugarpaste. When the surface is dry and firm, measure the centre point on each of the four sides of the cake and mark at the base. Secure one end of the thin red ribbon at this point with a dot of royal icing. Attach over the top corner and down the next side, attach at the marked point of the second side with royal icing. Continue in this fashion until all four sides have been covered with ribbon.

2 Repeat again using the green ribbon. This ribbon will have to be placed on top of the red ribbon at the centre points, but should be placed alongside the red ribbon at each corner allowing a small gap of about 2.5 mm ($\frac{1}{8}$ in) between the two ribbons.

3 The stars attached to the corners are quite small. To reduce the strain on the eyes and make painting easier, colour the flower paste to a pale yellow for the stars which are to be painted gold; very light blue for silver stars.

4 Roll out the yellow paste quite thinly and cut out small stars with a plunger cutter. Using gum arabic glue, attach the stars to the four corner areas created by the ribbons. When dry, paint with gold non-toxic paint.

5 Scribe the words 'Merry Christmas' onto the plaque using the template and paint in a dark red using a fine brush. Some of the red colours available are quite bright and garish. Burgundy is a much richer colour and can easily be mixed by adding a little blue to the red. When the lettering has been completed, attach the plaque to the centre of the cake using royal icing.

6 Make holly leaves and Christmas roses, as shown, and arrange in place along with three small simple ribbon loops and attach with royal icing.

Ribbon Loops

1 Make four figure-of-eight bows using both red and green ribbon. Holding the red ribbon in your left hand, bring it around your hand so that it lies flat and forms a loop. Repeat again in the opposite direction, but still keeping the ribbon flat so as to form a figure-of-eight. Cut off the ribbon so that the end is longer than the actual loop.

2 Repeat for the remaining ribbon loops. Bind the loops with wire. Lay the wire across the ribbon, then fold the ribbon in half and twist the wire to hold the loops in place. Trim the ends of the ribbon with either an angled or a swallow-tail cut. Cut off the excess wire. Place in position on the board and attach with royal icing.

Christmas Rose

1 Cut out a calyx using green paste. Cut five petals in white paste. Soften and thin the edges of the petals using a ball tool. Cup each petal onto foam.

2 Lightly grease a shallow dish (or an apple tray may be used). Place the calyx into the centre of the dish. Place the

petals, one at a time, onto the calyx and stick with egg white. The fifth petal should be placed overlapping the fourth and tucked under the first.

3 Pipe a small bulb of yellow-green royal icing into the centre of the flower. Insert yellow stamens around the bulb of icing, gently curving the stamen cotton with tweezers for a natural effect. When the paste is dry, lightly dust the base of the petals with green petal dust. The top edges of the rose can also be dusted a very pale pink.

Holly

1 Cut out the leaves in a dark green paste. Soften the edges using a ball tool. Mark a vein line down the centre of the leaf with a veining tool. Twist and dry over a spoon handle to create natural shapes.

2 The berries are made from small balls of red paste glazed with gum arabic, if required.

CHRISTMAS BAUBLE

Illustrated on page 90
Templates on page 247

*1 × 20 cm (8 in) round rich fruit cake
apricot glaze
1 kg (2 lb) marzipan
2 kg (4 lb) sugarpaste
cornflour (corn starch)
non-toxic silver colouring
grape, claret, blue, green, yellow and
skintone paste colours*

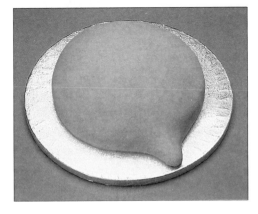

1 Carve away the top edge of the cake to create a rounded, domed shape, keeping it as rounded and smooth as possible. Model an extended point at the base of the bauble using marzipan taking care to keep the join smooth. Cover the entire cake with marzipan. The modelled base of the bauble and the rounded area of the cake should now appear as one shape. Cover the resulting cake with white sugarpaste and allow the surface to harden.

2 Colour 250 g (8 oz/½ lb) sugarpaste to a deep pink using claret paste colouring. Colour a further 250 g (8 oz/½ lb) of paste lilac using grape colouring.

3 Measure across the cake using a piece of string. Draw a band as long as the measurement taken and 3 cm (1½ in) wide. Curve the top and bottom edges of the band so that it will create a three-dimensional effect on the bauble.

4 Using the grape-coloured sugarpaste, roll out a strip of paste and cut out the curved band using your template. Using the diagram provided as a guide, place the band on the bauble in the appropriate place. Smooth and trim away any excess at the cake edge.

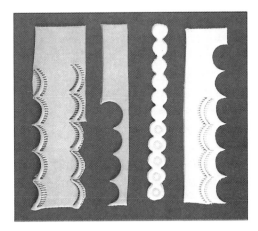

5 Use a no. 2 crimping tool to crimp near the top and bottom edge. Using a scalpel, cut away the excess paste near the crimped edge to give a smooth scalloped look.

6 Roll out the pink-coloured sugarpaste. Make a pattern and cut out a 3 cm (1¼ in) strip as for the previous band and again, using the diagram as a guide, place in an appropriate position on the cake. Crimp the scalloped pattern and trim as before. For the bottom edge, use the base of a piping tube to create the scalloped edging.

7 Arrange the two angels, in the stages and colours as shown, between the two bands. Measure the centre point between the two angels and add a cut-out star in white modelling paste. Continue to add the grape and pink bands using the pattern as a guide.

8 Cover the cake board with sugarpaste coloured a bluish green. This is more easily achieved by rolling out a strip of sugarpaste, cut one edge straight and gently roll up. Place the joining edge at the bottom of the bauble where the area between the edge of the bauble and the edge of the board is quite narrow. Carefully unroll the strip butting the straight cut edge to the side of the cake. Where the two joining edges meet, smooth gently with the hand to eradicate the joining line. Trim away the excess paste at the edge of the board. When the paste is dry, paint small silver stars onto the base with a fine brush.

9 Add the finishing touches to the angels with a fine brush and add the nose, lips and eyes. Darken the inside of the sleeve with a darker shade of grape. Darken the wings near the body. Paint the stars between the angels with the silver paint.

Assembling the angels

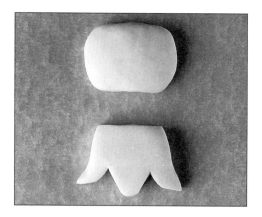

Bauble Top
1 Mould a piece of white sugarpaste, about 90 g (3 oz), into a rectangular shape. Round off the corners and, using the template provided, cut out the shape of the top. Round off the cut edges with the fingers smoothing the ends of the points so that they curve upwards until they fit snugly onto the curved shape of the bauble. Make a hole at the top edge fairly near the board so that the ring will fit inside.

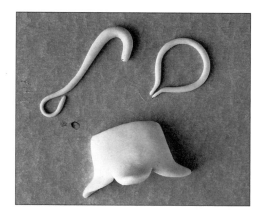

Ring and Hook
1 Roll a piece of modelling paste or sugarpaste into a thin rope and form into a circular shape as shown. Leave to dry, then place into the hole at the top of the bauble and secure with royal icing.

2 For the hook, make an elongated rope which gradually tapers at one end. Place the tapered end through the attached ring and close to form another ring. Curve the thicker end into a hook shape and support with foam until dry. Paint the top, ring and hook with non-toxic silver paint.

SANTA'S SLIDE

Illustrated on page 91
Templates below and overleaf

Any square firm sponge (creamed mixture, not whisked) or fruit cake would be suitable for this design.

1 × 15 cm (6 in) square cake, 5 cm
(2 in) deep
apricot glaze
750 g (1½ lb) marzipan
750 g (1½ lb/4 ¾ cups) royal icing
caster (superfine) sugar
runout icing
selection of food colourings

●

1 Cut the cake in half diagonally to form 2 triangles. Sandwich pieces together, using apricot glaze or marzipan, so that when stood on end, the cake forms a ramp shape. Brush cake with apricot glaze and cover with marzipan.

2 Using white royal icing, flat ice the sloping side, then rough ice the remaining sides to simulate snow. Sprinkle with caster (superfine) sugar. Coat the cake board with white royal icing. When the icing is dry, attach the cake to the board.

3 Using templates and following step-by-step instructions, make runout figures. When dry, pipe a line down the reverse side of each figure, using a no. 2 tube (tip) and white royal icing. Carefully position figures on cake.

4 Trace and scribe a 'Happy Christmas' inscription on cake board. Pipe lettering and exclamation mark, first using a no. 2 tube (tip) and white icing, then overpiping in red with a no. 1 tube. Trim board edge and complete scene with Christmas ornaments.

FIGURE PIPING
No dark outline is used, so the figures have a softer appearance. They also have more depth because certain areas are built up to give an effect reminiscent of half relief. They are not to be confused with freehand piped figures, which display even greater relief. The consistency of the icing for these figures needs to be almost that of soft peak: if you put a small sample on the work surface and brush it to a long point with a paint brush, the icing should stay put but lose the marks of the brush. As with all runout work, the icing should be coloured, if required, before being thinned to the correct consistency. No piping tubes (tips) are required; very small bags made with a sharp point will serve well.

The preparation of the icing can be time-consuming, so it is sensible to produce several figures at a time, working on one while another is drying. Keep one original drawing spare for reference. Look closely at the original drawing and note on it the order in which to work — a sort of 'Icing by Numbers', see step 2 overleaf.

SECRETS OF SUCCESS

When you are flooding a layer of icing on top of a previous layer dried under a lamp, always allow the first layer to cool before covering it. If you fail to do this, the second layer will dry on contact with the first and you will not have time to smooth it.

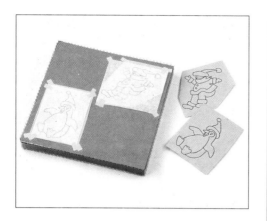

Prepare several drawings and tape or pin a piece of wax paper over each one. It is important not to move the paper once work commences. Keep your original drawing handy as it may be needed for reference. Have ready several bags of run-icing in appropriate colours, making sure that it is of the correct consistency.

When bulbs have crusted over, pipe a second layer on top. Continue flooding other areas, always working from background to foreground but avoiding areas adjacent to each other. Very dark colours should be allowed to dry completely before paler icing is piped next to them.

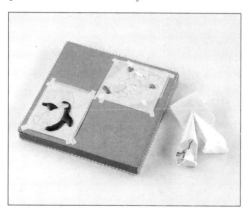

Start with those parts of the figure that appear to be furthest away. No outlining is necessary; simply push the icing to the shape required or use a paint brush to tease it into position. Parts like Santa's tummy, which need to be emphasized, can have a bulb of icing piped first to help accentuate the shape.

Some areas can be given a textured effect, either by stippling the surface with icing and a paint brush once the figure has dried or by using icing of full piping consistency, as for Santa's beard and the fur trim on his suit.

When each figure has dried, paint or pipe on any fine details. Allow to dry completely, then store figures carefully or use immediately.

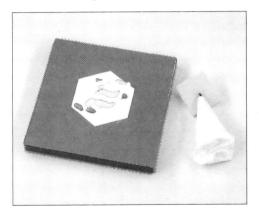

To fix a figure to a cake or plaque, turn it face down onto a piece of foam, peel off the backing paper, pipe some small bulbs of icing on the reverse, then carefully attach it where required.

SILENT NIGHT

Illustrated on page 92
Templates on page 249

Deep blue is not an easy colour to work with in food but its use in creating a natural-looking night sky does not detract from the appearance of this cake.

1 × 20 cm (8 in) square cake
apricot glaze
875 g (1¾ lb) marzipan
250 g (8 oz/½ lb) blue royal icing
500 g (1 lb) white royal icing
selection of food colourings
runout icing
caster (superfine) sugar
snowflake dusting powder
(petal dust/blossom tint)
about 1 m (1 yd 3 in) ribbon for cake side
about 1.25 m (1¼ yd) ribbon or paper band for board edge

●

1 Brush cake with apricot glaze and cover with marzipan. Coat top of cake with deep blue royal icing, then coat sides and board with white royal icing.

2 Using templates and technique for runout figures, see opposite, make runouts of village scene and fir bough. Flood lower part of fir bough first, using green icing, then flood upper part. When dry, pipe needle effect on green bough, using pale green royal icing and a no. 1 tube (tip). Add red berries, using a no. 1 tube. When top half of bough is dry, use white royal icing and a small shell tube to pipe on snow effect. Roughen texture with paint brush. Sprinkle with caster (superfine) sugar and allow to dry.

3 Flood houses and church in village scene in terracotta icing, then flood rooftops in white. When houses are dry, pipe on windows using yellow royal icing and a no. 1 tube. When rooftops are dry, brush them with snowflake dusting powder.

4 Pipe upright shell border around base of cake, using white royal icing and a no. 8 or 9 shell tube (tip). Overpipe with interlocking dropped loops, using a no. 2 tube.

5 Fix village runout on cake top, using a little icing on the reverse. With a no. 1 tube (tip) and yellow royal icing, pipe stars at random in the night sky. Pipe a crescent moon.

6 Carefully reverse fir bough runout on a block of foam. Pipe a line 5 mm ($\frac{1}{4}$ in) inside edge, using a no. 3 tube (tip). Allow line to dry, then overpipe using the same tube. Carefully position runout on cake top so that it stands a little proud of the surface.

7 Pipe a top border of simple shells with a no. 8 or 9 shell tube (tip) and white royal icing. Complete the cake with a red ribbon around the sides. Trim the board edge with ribbon or a paper band.

SECRETS OF SUCCESS

To keep cake edges clean when coating in two different colours, complete all coats in the deeper colour first, then coat in the lighter shade, taking care not to get too much icing on the dark section.

POINSETTIA

Illustrated on page 125
Templates on page 250

1 × 20 cm (8 in) round rich fruit cake
apricot glaze • 875 g (1$\frac{3}{4}$ lb) marzipan
1.5 kg (3 lb/10 cups) royal icing
cream, chocolate, red and green food colourings
about 1 m (1 yd 3 in) each narrow red and green ribbon for cake side
brown and green dusting powder (petal dust/blossom tint)
runout icing
about 1 m (1 yd 3 in) red velvet ribbon

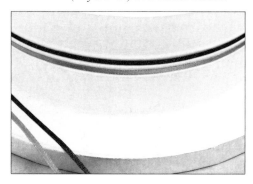

1 Coat the cake with apricot glaze, marzipan and cream-coloured icing. Coat the board with cream-coloured icing. For the final side coat use a cut scraper to create three lines. When dry insert red and green ribbons between the grooves securing with small dots of icing.

2 Using a no. 2 tube (tip) and chocolate-coloured icing, pipe twigs onto waxed paper. Pipe oval bulbs with red icing for holly berries. Add a small chocolate-coloured icing dot to each berry.

3 Make pine branches using a no. 1 tube and green icing. Side spikes are pulled out to a point while piping. When dry use a dry brush with edible petal dust to apply brown and green tones.

4 Trace the three poinsettia petals onto drawing paper. Place a piece of waxed paper over the drawing and outline the petals using a no. 0 tube (tip) and white icing. Flood in, place on a curved former and leave to dry. Paint the petals with the same food colouring used on the cake top to ensure a good colour match. Prepare a few runout holly leaves, drying them over a curved former.

5 Transfer petal, holly leaf and pine branch outline to cake top. Block in the red and green base colours.

6 Paint shading and detail on petals and leaves using a no. 1 or no. 0 paint brush. Complete with a fine brown outline using a no. 0 paint brush.

7 Using small dots of base colour icing, fix runout holly leaves, poinsettia petals and pine branches to the lower area of the painting.

8 Pipe twig and berries onto top area of painting.

9 To make top and base border decoration, pipe shells onto waxed paper using a no. 44 tube (tip) for top shells and a no. 32 tube (tip) for base shells. Pipe enough shells to fit around the cake. When dry pipe around the shell as shown using a no. 2 tube (tip) for the small shells and a no. 3 tube (tip) for the larger ones. Let dry. Pipe a long roped C-shape around half of each shell using a no. 1 tube (tip) and green icing. Finish each shell with a small red dot using a no. 1 tube (tip).

10 Transfer 'Christmas' inscription to cake top, pipe using a no. 2 tube (tip) and base colour. Overpipe the lettering using a no. 1 tube (tip) and chocolate coloured icing.

11 Remove shells from waxed paper and attach to cake top edge and base board using small bulbs of icing. Make sure shells are positioned at an angle to the cake as shown. Attach a red velvet ribbon to the cake board edge.

Karen's Cake
see page 213

Birthday Cake with Appliqué Train
see page 215

Perfect Posy
see page 216

Daisy Cake
see page 217

LANTERN CAKE

Illustrated on page 126
Templates on pages 251–252

1 × 20 cm (8 in) square rich fruit cake
apricot glaze
1 kg (2 lb) marzipan
1.25 kg (2½ lb/8¾ cups) royal icing
lemon, chocolate, black, green, gold
and red food colouring
runout icing
2 pieces leaf gelatine
green dusting powder (petal dust/
blossom tint)
about 1 m (1 yd 3 in) gold ribbon for
board edge

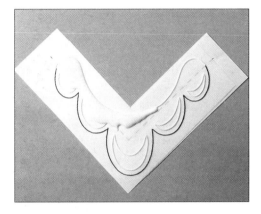

1 Coat the cake with apricot glaze, marzipan and lemon-coloured icing. Coat the board with icing. For the final side coating use a cut scraper to create a combed texture on the lower half. Make four top corner runout collars; using a no. 1 tube (tip) outline all lines in base colour icing except the outside curved edges which are outlined in chocolate-coloured icing. Flood in with base colour runout icing.

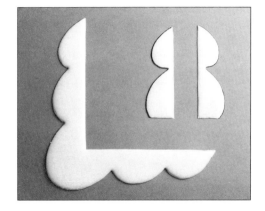

2 Make four base corner runout collars. Outline using a no. 1 tube (tip) and base colour icing, flood in and let dry. Make four side corner sections; outline the two straight sides in base colour icing, and the curved edges in chocolate-coloured icing, using a no. 1 tube (tip). Flood in; let dry. Remove the side corner sections from waxed paper, turn over and repeat outlining and flooding in. Allow to dry.

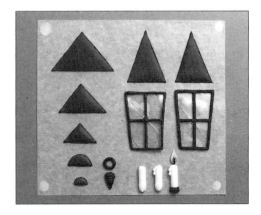

3 Make runout pieces for lantern. The window sections are piped directly onto pieces of leaf gelatine, cut to the correct size and shape from the drawing. The candle is piped using a no. 4 tube (tip) and white icing. Pipe two tiny bulbs to represent running wax. Using a no. 1 tube (tip) and chocolate-coloured icing pipe three lines around the base of the candle. Pipe the flame in yellow icing, or in white icing and paint yellow when dry. Pipe the black candle wick. Allow to dry.

4 Trace inscription 'Greetings' onto drawing paper. Place a piece of waxed paper over the drawing and outline with a no. 1 tube (tip) for the sections to be flooded, and a no. 2 tube (tip) for the single strokes. Flood in with green runout icing. When dry, apply green shading using petal dust or an airbrush.

5 Assemble lantern using chocolate-coloured icing; let dry. Leave brown, or paint gold. Colour a small area of the cake top yellow. Fix the piped candle in position. Position and attach the lantern. Pipe branches using a no. 1 tube (tip) and chocolate icing. Pipe holly leaves and berries onto the branches. A few holly leaves, piped onto waxed paper and allowed to dry, could be attached to give more depth. Complete the lantern by piping on white icing and sprinkling with granulated sugar to create a frosty effect. Attach a tiny red ribbon bow as shown. Remove the lettering from the waxed paper, arrange it in position, then attach to the cake top with small dots of the base colour icing.

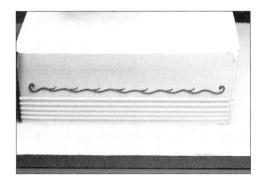

6 For the side decoration, pipe a wavy chocolate-coloured line along each side, just above the comb scraping. Follow the drawing for the wavy line. Pipe holly leaves and berries.

7 Fix base collars and side corner sections using base colour icing. Where the base collar joins the cake side, pipe a small shell using a no. 3 tube (tip), then pipe a small shell down each corner section using a no. 42 tube (tip); use base colour for shells.

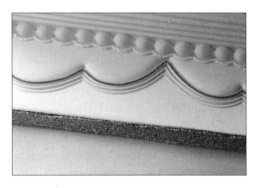

8 Pipe 3.2.1. linework on the cake board alongside the runout edge. Pipe the top line in chocolate-coloured icing using a no. 1 tube (tip).

9 Attach top collars. Pipe 3.2.1. linework on cake surface around inside edge of collars. Pipe the top line in chocolate-coloured icing using a no. 1 tube (tip). Attach a gold ribbon to the board.

SAINT NICHOLAS BAS RELIEF

Illustrated on page 127
Templates on page 253

This is a cake for the more confident cake decorator.

1 × 20 cm (8 in) oval rich fruit cake
apricot glaze
1 kg (2 lb) marzipan
500 g (1 lb) white sugarpaste
750 g (1½ lb) blueberry blue-coloured
sugarpaste
750 g (1½ lb) modelling paste
dark blue, flesh-coloured, red, black,
mint green and brown paste colouring
gold food colouring
small quantity royal icing
gum arabic
1 metre (1 yd 3 in) blue velvet ribbon

●

1 Coat the cake with apricot glaze and marzipan. Roll out the dark blue sugarpaste along with a smaller quantity of the white sugarpaste. Slightly thin one edge of both pieces and place the blue edge over the white edge. Roll together making sure that the joined edge is quite smooth; the overall paste should be of the same

thickness and be handled as one piece. Place over the cake and board making sure that the sky line is placed in the right position. Continue to cover the cake in the usual way.

2 Draw the outline of the figure onto a piece of wax paper. Keeping within the outline, gradually build up the body using sugarpaste. Make depressions where the arm, neck and sack are to be placed. On the face, make a smaller depression for the eye socket.

3 Transfer the figure carefully onto the cake using a palette knife. Cover the top of the head with a small cap shape for the hat. Cover the right arm with a small piece of red paste. Make sure the edge of the modelling paste is sealed to the cake surface with a modelling tool to give a smooth finish. Roll out a small piece of skin-coloured paste and place over the face. Smooth into the indentations.

4 The eye socket and other facial details should be indented using a ball tool, exaggerating the features as they will lose shape when covered with paste.

5 Use a small piece of black paste to cover the shoe shapes. Using the template provided, cut out the coat in red modelling paste. The coat is larger than the drawn outline of the figure to allow for the added body paste. Moisten and drape over the sugarpaste figure. Then use a modelling tool to mould the paste around the body carefully and to shape the folds and creases. Round the cut edge so that the clothes appear to continue all way around the figure.

6 Roll out some brown paste and cut out the inside and back part of the sack. Glue in position. Make the top part of the sack by drawing the shape onto silicone paper as for the main figure. Keep the paste fairly thick at the base of the sack where it would be filled with gifts.

7 Use a small rolling pin and gradually thin the sack towards the top edge. Cut out the shape of this top edge using the template. Thin the edge with the fingers and fold it back to create the natural effect of soft fabric sacking. Glue the sack in place on the figure.

8 Using red modelling paste, roll out the furled back coat shape using the template provided. Glue in place and support with foam until dry. Cut out the gown front panel. Glue to the coat side edge and roll paste over the touch finished coat shape. This will give quite a rounded three-dimensional effect to the figure. Make the arm from red paste as shown and attach in position with glue.

9 The hands are basic shapes because of their sideways position. Make a fairly thick, narrow strip in black paste and bend into position as shown. Flatten out the wrist area and glue in position. For the left hand, make a flat, square shape. Make a hole where the base of the thumb should be with a modelling tool. The strap for the sack can be pushed into this hole so that the figure appears to be holding the strap in the hand.

10 The squirrel is made from small pieces of brown and white paste, as illustrated. The tail is piped on at the same time as the figure's beard.

11 Apply the beard and hair by forcing modelling paste through a clay gun or by using rough-textured royal icing. Make the fur for the collar, cuffs and gown edge by pushing sugarpaste through a metal tea strainer to give a soft, textured effect. This will be much softer than the strands created when using a clay gun (this may also be used for the beard).

12 Measure the circumference of the cake, cut out a strip of tracing paper the same length. Fold the paper equally into five sections. Cut a deep scallop out of the top edge of the folded strip. Open the strip and attach all around the cake. Mark the five scallops into the cake surface using a scriber.

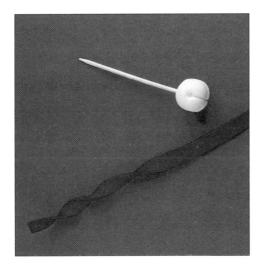

13 Roll out some mint-green-coloured paste. Cut into five long, thin strips. Twist the strip and glue each end into position at the top of each scallop. Cut off any excess paste.

14 Make bells by rolling small balls of paste each about the size of a seedless grape. Make two cuts in the top of the ball using a sharp knife. At each end of the cuts, indent a small hole with a tiny ball tool or a glass-headed pin. When dry, paint the bells gold using a non-toxic paint. Make a small hole above the twisted green paste with a cocktail stick or toothpick. Roll a fine strand of paste and insert into the hole; loop it over the twisted strips and glue to the cake side directly under the strips. Attach the gold balls with royal icing under the loops. Paint the loops gold when dry.

15 Pipe in the trees with brown royal icing and a no. 1 tube (tip). When dry, pipe snow onto the branches using white royal icing. Place velvet ribbon around the cake board to trim.

BASKET CAKE
with Brush-embroidered Appliqué Flowers

Illustrated on page 128
Templates on page 254

The technique used for the appliqué flowers can be adapted for a variety of different blooms, such as roses, sweet peas or peonies. Try cutting the flowers from white paste and using different colours for the brush embroidery.

20 × 15 cm (8 × 6 in) oval cake
apricot glaze
1 kg (2 lb) marzipan
clear alcohol (gin or vodka)
1.25 kg (2¼ lb) sugarpaste
small amount of royal icing
selection of food colourings
flower paste
clear piping gel
egg white
confectioners' glaze
8 pink and yellow sugar carnations

●

1 Brush cake with apricot glaze. Cover with marzipan and brush with clear alcohol. Coat cake and board with sugarpaste, smooth and leave for 3 days to dry.

2 Scribe and pipe the stems for the flowers on the side of the cake. Using a no. 3 piping tube (tip) and dark green royal icing, pipe a border on the cake base.

3 Trace one flower from template and cut out of thin card. Colour small pieces of flower paste pink and yellow. Working with one colour at a time, roll out paste. Using template and scalpel, cut out flowers for side of cake. Colour flower paste green and cut out and attach ivy leaves.

4 Mix royal icing with clear piping gel and embroider all ivy leaves and flowers. When duplicate flowers are dry, attach them to cake.

5 Trace 'Best Wishes' inscription and scribe it on top of cake. Using a no. 0 tube (tip) and green royal icing, pipe lettering. Trace basket template and cut out of thin card. Colour some flower paste brown and mould a small cushion to pad out the basket shape. Dampen back with water and secure it to cake. Using template, accurately cut out silhouette of basket base. Dampen and attach to cake over paste cushion.

6 Soften some brown flower paste with vegetable fat, and extrude it through a clay gun, twisting paste to form a rope. Paint egg white along top and bottom edge of basket and secure paste rope trim, then extrude another piece of paste, about 10 cm (4 in) long for handle. Fix it in place, allow basket to dry, then varnish with confectioners' glaze. Arrange sugar carnations and reserved ivy leaves in basket, attaching them with royal icing.

SECRETS OF SUCCESS

To slow down speed at which royal icing sets, mix it with clear piping gel in the proportion 250 ml (8 fl oz/1 cup) icing to 5 ml (1 tsp) gel.

Measure height and circumference of cake and make a greaseproof paper (parchment) template for side. Trace stem design only onto paper template, repeating design and adjusting length if necessary. Scribe design on cake. Using no. 0 piping tube (tip) and dark green royal icing, pipe small shells for stems.

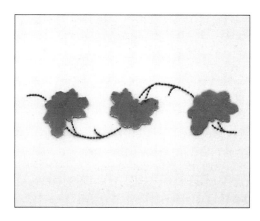

Roll out suitably tinted flower paste on a lightly greased board. Using template and scalpel, cut out flowers for side of cake. Dampen backs lightly with water and attach to stems on side of cake. Cut out duplicate set of flowers; leave on a flat board to dry.

Using green food colouring with a small amount of black, colour some flower paste a dark mossy green. Roll out paste as thinly as possible on a lightly greased board. Cut out leaves for side of cake, using ivy leaf cutter. Attach to stems while still pliable.

Cut out nine extra leaves for top of cake; reserve on a board.

Mix royal icing with piping jelly. Brush embroider flowers and leaves on side of cake; also reserved flowers and leaves. Work on one flower or leaf at a time, as icing will not brush smoothly once it begins to dry. It is also important to use piping gel to prevent rapid drying. Begin by piping outline of flower or leaf, using a no. 1 piping tube (tip); apply firm pressure for larger flowers.

Using a damp paint brush, brush icing onto petals or centre of leaf, leaving icing thicker around the edge and brushing it thinly enough to allow the colour of the flower or leaf to be seen through the icing. Keep brush clean and damp; if too wet it will be difficult to brush icing without dissolving it. Always brush from edge to centre.

When all brush-embroidered flowers and leaves have dried, attach duplicate set of flowers to cake. Pipe a small bulb of well-beaten icing onto the back of each flower. Marry it to its partner, fixing it to the cake at a slight angle to create a three dimensional effect. Reserve remaining brush embroidered leaves for top of cake.

RUSTIC WEDDING

Illustrated on page 161
Templates on page 255

Decorated with corn poppies and ears of wheat encircled by a pair of gold wedding rings, this cake is perfect for a late summer country wedding.

large oval fruit cake
apricot glaze
1.4 kg (3 lb) marzipan
1.4 kg (3 lb) sugarpaste
apple green, black, Christmas red,
Cornish cream and moss
green food colouring
350 g (12 oz/3 cups) royal
icing for piping
piping gel
2 gold plastic wedding rings
pack of edible gold leaf or gold flake
5 red sugar poppies
•

1 Brush the cake with apricot glaze and cover with marzipan. Leave to dry.

2 Colour the sugarpaste with a little Cornish cream colouring the day before you intend to ice the cake. When the sugarpaste is ready, first use it to cover the board, trimming the edge with a sharp knife. Impress scallops around the edge with a no. 4 crimper, then press a crescent-shaped embossing tool against the sugarpaste to create a pattern above the crimped scallops.

3 Cover the cake in the normal way, making sure it has a clean edge. Place it in the centre of the cake board and leave for at least 48 hours, to allow the sugarpaste to harden before marking out the patterns for the sprays of poppies and ears of wheat.

4 Make templates of the embroidery designs from the patterns provided, then scribe them on the sides and top of the cake. Create the flowers on the sides of the cake, and the background leaves and daisies on the top using the brush embroidery technique.

5 Pipe the half-relief ears of wheat directly on the sides and top of the cake using a no. 1 tube (tip) for the stems and a no. 2 tube (tip) for the wheat itself, and royal icing tinted with Cornish cream colouring to match the sugarpaste. Pipe the stems first, then the two rows of offset pointed beads, or teardrops, of icing to represent the grains. The grains are arranged in lines so that the bulbous end of each bead is only just touching its opposite neighbour. Work all the way around the cake, piping these first two rows. Then, when they are dry, pipe another row down the centre, between the two earlier rows, and finish the line with a grain piped directly on to the icing. Six to eight grains are sufficient for each row.

6 The miniature wheatsheaf, around which the wedding rings are placed, is prepared in much the same way, except that the beads, or grains, of icing are piped on long stalks of thin-covered wire which are laid on a sheet of waxed paper. When

the first three rows of grains are dry, carefully lift the whole stalk off the paper, turn it over, then repeat the process on the back. When each one is finished and dried, it is three-dimensional, with the grains of wheat completely covering the wire.

7 Pipe about twelve ears of wheat and leave to dry, then thread them through the two gold rings, sticking them into position on the cake with a small dot of royal icing.

8 To make the gold ribbon that is used to tie the bunch of flowers together on top of the cake, flood Cornish cream-coloured royal icing in sections on to the top of the cake, working without piped outlines. Leave to harden before gilding it with gold leaf or gold flake.

9 Gilding is not easy, as the material is so fine that it can tear very easily, it may float about and it usually sticks wherever it lands. Moisten the surface of the icing very carefully with a little water, or with piping gel placed on a second paintbrush, and touch the dry gilding brush against it. Pick the gold from its vial with the tip of a very soft paintbrush and smoothly transfer it to the area to be treated. The gold will instantly adhere to the dampened area. If any of the gold overlaps the intended area, pick it off with a fine scalpel. Then burnish the surface by brushing the gold in one direction with a gentle stroking motion.

10 Pipe a tiny trail of beading around the bottom of the cake, using a no. 0 tube (tip) and cream-coloured royal icing. Pipe a continuous herringbone band of teardrops, to represent wheat grains, around the sides of the cake using a no. 2 tube (tip). Fix the sugar poppies to the embroidery on the top of the cake.

SUMMER ROSES

Illustrated on page 162
Templates on page 256

The cakes are covered with sugarpaste, which must be of a high quality and free from gritty lumps, so that it will remain flexible and won't crack while being moulded. It must also remain workable and soft enough to accept the design that is impressed into the sides of the cakes. The cake yields 170–180 portions.

small oval fruit cake
medium oval fruit cake
large oval fruit cake
apricot glaze
3 kg (6 lb) marzipan
clear alcohol (gin or vodka)
3.1 kg (6 lb 10 oz) sugarpaste
60 g (2 oz/½ cup) royal icing for piping
small piece of pastillage, about 60 g (2 oz)
burgundy and rose food colourings
plum dusting powder (petal dust/
blossom tint)
gum arabic
25 cm (10 in) oval cake board
30 cm (12 in) oval cake board
40 cm (16 in) oval cake board
3 × 7.5 cm (3 in) white octagonal cake
pillars
3 × 8.75 cm (3½ in) white octagonal
cake pillars
5 metres (5½ yards) 3 mm (⅛ in)
double-sided burgundy satin ribbon
2½ metres (2¾ yards) 3 mm (⅛ in)
double-sided pink satin ribbon
3 metres (3⅜ yards) 8 mm (⅜ in) white
acetate satin ribbon
4 sugar rosebuds
5 white sugar blossom sprays with pink
stamens
3 white sugar blossom sprays with pearl
stamens

•

1 Coat the cakes with apricot glaze and cover with marzipan, then position each one on its board and cover both the board and the cake with sugarpaste, making sure it doesn't crack. Avoid any interruptions or the sugarpaste may dry out before you finish work. Smooth the sugarpaste down over each cake, across each board and down over its sides.

2 Trim the edge of the sugarpaste with scallop-shaped crimpers to create a fluted effect against the sides of the board. You can use different sizes of crimper to create additional interest.

3 The pattern is applied to the sides of the cakes by marking the sugarpaste with a stencil made from a sheet of thin card. Cut it to the correct size, then gently press it against the sugarpaste to provide a bare outline. This is accentuated with the scalloped crimpers.

4 Using the three sizes of plain-ended, not serrated, crimpers, press them gently against the icing but don't penetrate it fully. As they begin to bite, withdraw them slightly and then release the pressure on the jaws as they are withdrawn completely. If they seem to stick and drag at the icing, dip the jaws into a little icing (confectioners') sugar. Follow the pattern around the cake, working continuously so the sugarpaste will not dry out before you have finished.

5 With an oval template, mark a line where the sugarpaste rim is to be positioned on the top of each cake, and dampen the line with water. Roll out a sausage of sugarpaste to about the diameter of a pencil and press it gently on to the dampened sugarpaste. Taking care only to partially close the jaws of the crimpers, form the oval into scalloped curves.

6 Trace over the outlines for the simple icing embroidery to make a template, then use it to mark the sides of each cake. Pipe the stems and leaves in plain white royal icing, and the forget-me-not flowers in plum-coloured royal icing, both with a no. 1 tube (tip).

7 To make the other flowers for the sides of the cakes, roll out some plum-coloured pastillage, then stamp out flowers with small, medium and large blossom cutters. To make the pink flowers on the sides of each cake, roll out some pink-coloured pastillage, then stamp out heart shapes using the small, medium and large cutters. Each flower is made from five hearts, which are immediately glued to the cake with a mixture of one part gum arabic to three parts water.

8 Pipe a dot of plum-coloured royal icing into the centre of each flower. Dust a narrow line of plum dusting powder around the scalloped edge of each board, then brush it off to create a gently diffused effect. Then secure the plum-coloured flowers between the scallops around the sides of each board with a dot of royal icing.

9 Wrap burgundy ribbon around each cake, securing it with a dot of royal icing. Cover the join with a small bow. The top cake tier is decorated with a mixture of moulded sugar roses and sprays of blossom flowers, some of which have been tinted with plum dusting powder.

10 Curl toning pink and plum-coloured florist's ribbons by running a blunt knife or the edge of a pair of scissors along their length, then arrange them amongst the flowers on the top tier to give extra height and fullness to the arrangement. Satin ribbon will not curl, so make up a series of ribbon loops and assemble with the sugar flowers into a walnut-sized piece of sugar paste.

ROSES ALL THE WAY

Illustrated on page 163
Templates on page 257

Single-tier petal-shaped cakes are very popular because they offer scope for so many different types of decoration. Here, most of the classic sugarpaste techniques are used – the delicate double frill, the flowing embroidery and the use of a large spray of sugar roses and stephanotis with rose buds, leaves and ribbon loops. The cake yields about 50 portions.

1 × 25 cm (10 in) petal-shaped rich
fruit cake
apricot glaze
750 g (1½ lb) marzipan
clear alcohol (gin or vodka)
1.1 kg (2 lb 2 oz) sugarpaste
125 g (4 oz/¾ cup) royal icing for
piping
apple and moss green food colourings
moss green and yellow dusting powder
(petal dust/blossom tint)
yellow dusting colour for flowers
125 g (4 oz/¼ lb) pastillage (optional)
37.5 cm (15 in) petal-shaped cake board
7 large white sugar roses
5 medium white sugar roses
3 small white sugar roses
12 very small white sugar roses
6 white sugar rose buds
20 sugar rose leaves of various sizes
18 sugar stephanotis flowers
6 sugar blossoms
9 metres (10 yards) 2.5 mm (⅛ in)
double-sided moss green satin ribbon
2 metres (2¼ yards) 2.5 mm (⅛ in)
double-sided white satin ribbon
1 metre (1⅛ yards) 12 mm (½ in) white
satin ribbon

●

1 Coat the cake with apricot glaze and marzipan. Reserve 250 g (8oz/½ lb) of the sugarpaste, then use the rest to cover the cake. The sugarpaste must be applied extremely carefully and smoothly over the base layer of marzipan. Pay particular

·attention to the concave sections where the petals meet, if necessary erasing any marks by rubbing them away with the fleshy part of your thumb or the base of your palm. The friction and warmth of your hand will be enough to make the surface smooth again. Leave the cake for at least 24 hours.

2 Position the cake on the board. Make a template of the embroidery from the pattern provided, then scribe it on to the cake – the pattern is used three times around the sides of the cake.

3 Using a no. 1 tube (tip) and white royal icing of a piping consistency, pipe a beaded border around the base of the cake. Pipe over the scribed outlines with a no. 0 tube (tip) and white royal icing. On the parts of the design where the icing pattern broadens out to represent garlands or ribbons, increase the pressure on the piping bag and use a fine paint brush to smooth and shape the icing.

4 The two rows of frills are made from the remaining sugarpaste, which can be mixed with up to 125 g (4 oz/¼ lb) pastillage to give a firmer finish. To make the lower frill, colour half the sugarpaste with equal amounts of moss green and apple green food colourings until you achieve a deep and even colour.

5 When positioning the frills, leave about 5 mm (¼ in) between the lower green one and the upper white one. There are several ways to disguise the join where the frill meets the cake, and here the rounded end of a no. 1 dogbone modelling tool has been used to press the top edge of the frill into the sugarpaste. If the cake covering is still fresh and soft, you can use crimpers, such as the no. 2 scallop or the no. 6 vee, to make the distinctive line at the join. This creates an effect similar to stitches on a piece of needlepoint.

6 The large triangular spray of flowers, leaves and ribbons is attached to the top of the cake with a block of sugarpaste.

BON VOYAGE

Illustrated on page 164
Templates on page 258

Since accurate square edges are required for this design, it is recommended that only royal icing be used for coating. The design is for a 20 cm (8 in) square cake; if a larger cake is required, it will be necessary to adjust the size of the templates.

20 cm (8 in) square rich fruit cake
apricot glaze
875 g (1¾ lb) marzipan
625 g (1¼ lb) royal icing
selection of food colourings
runout icing
about 1.25 m (1¼ yd) ribbon or paper
band for board edge

•

1 Brush the cake with apricot glaze and cover with marzipan. Coat with pale blue royal icing. Coat the board with white icing. When the final coat on the cake is dry, attach it to board.

2 Using the templates, run out 8 large cloud sections, 8 small cloud sections, 2 balloons and 2 baskets, following the step-by-step instructions. Copy the illustration on page 164 or use your own colour scheme for balloons. Trace the inscription and scribe it on cake top. Trace treetop pattern; scribe on each side of the cake.

3 Using tweezers to hold a 5 mm (¼ in) piece of foam, dip it into a little green royal icing. 'Paint' treetops on each side of the cake, using a dabbing action to achieve a textured effect. Two or more shades of green look particularly effective.

4 Using a no. 2 tube (tip) and white royal icing, pipe a line 5 mm (¼ in) from the edge on reverse side of large balloon. Fix piece in place on cake top. Repeat this process with small balloon, baskets and 4 small cloud sections, positioning each piece as illustrated. Fix the large and remaining cloud sections to the cake sides.

5 If the cake edges are not quite square and there are gaps where the off-pieces meet, pipe white icing into the gaps and carefully smooth off with a paintbrush.

6 Scribe inscription on cake top, then pipe using a no. 1 tube (tip) and white royal icing. Pipe a small shell edge, using a no. 2 tube (tip) and pale blue royal icing, between the clouds at the base of the cake where it meets the board. Finally, using a no. 1 tube (tip) and brown royal icing, pipe birds on side of cake. Trim board edge.

Trace the design for the cloud pieces, using the templates or drawings of your own choice. Fix the tracings securely to a flat surface with either masking tape or drawing pins. Cut a piece of wax paper for each piece required, plus some spares in case of breakages. Pipe bulbs of icing on drawing or the wax paper reverse. Place wax paper flat over the tracing.

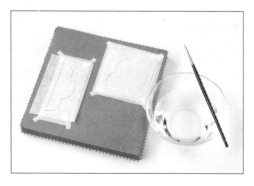

Have ready enough runout icing to flood all the pieces, plus a bag of royal icing fitted

with a no. 1 tube (tip). Using the royal icing, outline the design, using a damp paintbrush to neaten if necessary.

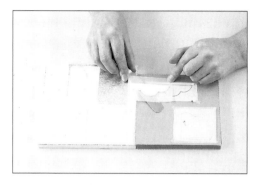

Flood the first pieces with runout icing. Slip a small palette knife under the wax paper. Slide the knife along, vibrating it gently – this will help to level the icing. Carefully slide the wax paper onto a drying board. It is important to do this before a crust starts to form on the runout.

Make another off-piece in exactly the same way. Dry complete pieces under an angled desk lamp. When all the pieces are dry, pipe on any embellishments required.

KAREN'S CAKE

Illustrated on page 197

For a birthday, christening or any special celebration, this simple cake is easy to prepare and charming. For a boy's Christening cake, use blue instead of pink and a teddy motif.

6 egg Madeira Cake mixture, see
page 35
2.5 ml ($\frac{1}{2}$ tsp) mixed spice
125 g (4 oz/$\frac{2}{3}$ cup) raisins
125 g (4 oz/1 cup) mixed chopped peel
60 g (2 oz/$\frac{1}{2}$ cup) ground almonds
ICING
1 quantity Buttercream Paste
pink and green food colouring
almond essence (extract)
1 quantity American Parfait, see
page 29
apricot glaze

●

1 Preheat oven to 160°C (325°F/Gas 3). Grease and line a 20 cm (8 in) square cake tin (pan). Make up cake mixture, sifting spice in with flour and folding raisins, peel and ground almonds in at the end. Mix to a soft dropping consistency, level in the tin (pan) and bake for 1$\frac{3}{4}$–2 hours. Leave to cool in tin.

2 Prepare several paper piping bags, fitting one with a writing tube (tip) and snipping end of another to a 'V' shape.

3 Make up buttercream paste, kneading in one or two drops of pink colouring with almond essence (extract) to taste. Place paste in a polythene bag. Make up parfait. Set aside 180 m (12 tbsp) for piping and colour the rest pale pink, a shade or two lighter than the buttercream paste. Set aside 90 ml (6 tbsp) pink parfait for piping.

4 Invert the cake on a cake board. Brush the top with apricot glaze. Cover with buttercream paste and decorate with parfait, following the step-by-step instructions given right.

Having glazed cake, knead buttercream paste on a surface dusted with icing (confectioners') sugar. Roll it out thickly to a 20 cm (8 in) square, using short, light movements. Run a knife around paste to loosen it, then slide hands underneath and lift it onto cake. Smooth gently with the palm of your hand.

Spread parfait over sides of cake, working it up and down so that it comes well up to buttercream paste topping. Hold a serrated scraper at 45° angle to the cake. Starting at a corner away from you, quickly and firmly draw scraper towards you and up to a nearer corner in one movement. Clean scraper; repeat along remaining sides.

Place some reserved white parfait in a paper piping bag fitted with a small star tube (tip). Make border on top of cake. Holding tube at an angle of 90° to the cake, press out a little parfait to form a star. Remember to stop squeezing the bag before you lift the tube to make the next star, otherwise all the stars will finish in points.

For flowers, fill piping bag cut to a 'V' end with white parfait. Place tube (tip) on cake, near a corner, and squeeze bag. Stop squeezing; sharply pull up tube at an angle of 45°. The parfait should form a raised petal. Pipe four more petals, then, with pink parfait, pipe centre. Pipe green leaves in same way.

Write child's name boldly on a 20 cm (8 in) square of greaseproof paper, place on cake and pinprick out word. Using piping bag with writing tube (tip) and white parfait, pipe name. If preferred, refer to the final section of this book for letters instead of writing freehand.

Adapting the design: for a boy's christening or birthday cake, use blue buttercream paste and parfait. Trace a teddy or similar motif and make a cardboard template. Make templates for each letter of child's name. Knead the buttercream paste trimmings, then roll out thickly; cut around teddy and letters. Lift shapes, brush backs with gin; put on cake. Smooth edges.

BIRTHDAY CAKE
With Appliqué Train

Illustrated on page 198
Templates on page 259

This attractive design can be adapted to use on any number or letter shaped cake.

number three shaped cake
apricot glaze
1 kg (2 lb) marzipan
clear alcohol (gin or vodka)
1.75 kg (3½ lb) sugarpaste
selection of food colourings
small amount of royal icing
185 g (6 oz/⅓ lb) modelling paste

●

1 Brush cake with apricot glaze. Marzipan top and sides in separate pieces. Dampen marzipan with alcohol. Colour half sugarpaste pale blue; roll out and cover cake. Gently tuck sugarpaste into sides and smooth. Cover board with white sugarpaste. When dry, attach cake to board.

2 Trace train templates and cut out of thin card. Colour half the royal icing black. Using a no. 3 piping tube (tip), pipe a line around the base of cake. Pipe bulbs of icing on the piped line about 1 cm (½ in) apart to represent the track.

3 Brightly colour small pieces of modelling paste, leaving some white. Working with one colour at a time, roll out modelling paste on a lightly greased board. Using templates and scalpel, cut out basic engine shape and suffient carriages to go all around the cake. Neaten wheel arches with end of a piping tube (tip). Dampen back of paste shapes with water and secure to side of cake.

4 Cut out funnel and carriage motifs from thinly rolled modelling paste, varying motifs if liked. Make wheels by cutting paste circles with the end of a piping tube (tip). Texture each wheel with an embossing tool or textured button. Dampen

funnel, carriage motifs and wheels and fix to cake.

5 Make smoke clouds by cutting large flowers from white modelling paste. Stretch shapes by gently rolling them with a non-stick rolling pin. Attach shapes to top of cake. Finally, finish top of cake by piping a scroll border using a no. 1 tube (tip) and white royal icing.

Cutting a Number Three Shape
If you don't have a tin (pan) in the shape of a three, you can cut out the required shape from a 20 cm (8 in) round cake and a 15 cm (6 in) square cake. Cut the square cake in half, cut a wedge off one end of each half and position on the cake board, following the diagram. Cut a circle out of the centre of the round cake, then cut a wedge from one side to form a horseshoe and place at the base of the pieces you have already assembled. Alternatively, bake the second cake in a 23 cm (9 in) ring tin. Sandwich the pieces together with buttercream, or layers of jam and buttercream. Apricot glaze may be used to assemble fruit cake if the cake is made for a formal third anniversary or similar occasion requiring a three-shape cake.

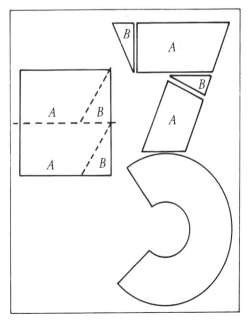

PERFECT POSY

Illustrated on page 199
Templates on page 254

This attractive, unusual, cake is ideal for many festive occasions. The cake can either be a Madeira or a fruit cake mixture. It is baked in a spherical tin (pan) of the type originally intended for traditional Christmas puddings. The tin (pan) consists of two halves, one of which is completely filled with the cake mixture, and then clamped to its partner, which is half-filled and secured on a simple stand. There is usually a hole in the top of the upper half through which moisture is released as the cake is cooked and the mixture expands to fill the void. When the cake is ready it must be released from the tin (pan) while it is still hot. The interior should be brushed with fat and dusted with flour.

spherical cake
700 g (1 lb 8 oz/1½ lb) marzipan
apricot glaze
1.1 kg (2 lb 8 oz/2½ lb) sugarpaste
50 g (2 oz/½ cup) royal icing for piping
lemon yellow and violet food colouring
120 2.5 cm (1 in) silk buttercups or daisies
1 metre (1⅛ yards) lacelon frill
½ metre (½ yard) yellow decorette
ribbon

●

1 When the cake has cooled, fill any gaps or irregularities in its surface with pieces of marzipan. If the cake has been standing on a flat surface for more than a few hours, it will have developed a flat area about 10 cm (4 in) across, which must be disguised with a piece of marzipan, cut to the same shape, and stuck over the cake with a little apricot glaze.

2 Roll out a large piece of marzipan into a circular shape, the diameter of which is roughly equivalent to the circumference of the cake less the piece of marzipan already attached. Measure the cake tin to determine the approximate size.

3 Brush the exposed surface of the cake with apricot glaze, then drape the marzipan over it, smoothing it down and compressing it towards the base where the marzipan is already in position. Mould it into shape by smoothing and warming it with the palms of your hands until it follows the ball shape, then trim off any excess pieces. The easiest way to do this is to turn the cake upside down and trim off any surplus, making sure there is a good join to the original marzipan circle. Leave to harden for at least 24 hours.

4 Repeat this technique using sugarpaste, this time brushing the marzipan with a little alcohol or water first. Place the cake on a thin piece of cake card, 10 cm (4 in) in diameter.

5 Begin decorating the cake from the base, securing each flower and leaf to the cake with tiny beads of royal icing. Do not stick any wires into the sugarpaste if the cake is to be eaten. When you have completed the first two rows, place the cake on a piece of lacelon frill and position it on the cake board. Complete the decoration by covering the entire cake with flowers and leaves. Fix a loop of ribbon to the top of the cake for a handle.

6 To make the butterflies, flood them on to waxed paper placed over templates traced from the patterns provided. To thicken the bodies of the butterfly, use a no. 1 tube (tip) and pipe a second coating of icing on the undersides, once they have been removed from the paper. Make the bodies from yellow or brown icing and paint on their markings with food colouring.

7 Insert stamens into the icing while it is still wet to represent the antennae, and leave to dry. The insects can be stuck directly on the cake with royal icing, or mounted on to a piece of wire or the tip of a wooden cocktail stick (toothpick).

8 To cut the cake, slice it in half, then remove it from its board, place it on its flat side and cut it as though it were a loaf.

DAISY CAKE

Illustrated on page 200

1 quantity Quick Mix Sponge mixture,
see page 32
ICING AND DECORATION
1 quantity Basic Buttercream
15–30 ml (1–2 tbsp) lemon juice
green, yellow and orange food colouring
125 g (4 oz/1⅛ cups) fine desiccated
coconut
1 quantity Glacé Icing
60 g (2 oz) marzipan
mimosa balls, optional
125 g (4 oz/4 squares) plain chocolate,
chopped

•

1 Preheat oven to 180°C (350°F/Gas 4). Bake cake in a lined and greased 20 × 30 cm (8 × 12 in) cake tin (pan). Cool on a wire rack. Make a thin cardboard template of a petal 8.5 cm (3½ in) long. Prepare a 56 × 38 cm (22 × 15 in) cake board.

2 Make up buttercream, slackening it with lemon juice. Colour 30 ml (2 tbsp) of the buttercream green and set it aside. Colour remaining buttercream yellow.

3 Put two thirds of the coconut into a bowl. Add a few drops of yellow food colouring and stir until evenly coloured. Colour remaining coconut orange. Alternatively, coconut can be coloured by placing in a polythene bag, adding colour and closing tightly, then shaking well to distribute colour evenly.

4 Cut out parts for daisy, coat in buttercream and coconut and assemble cake on a board, following step-by-step instructions.

5 Make up glacé icing and colour it yellow. Flood top of each petal with glacé icing, using the same technique as for Raspberry Valentine Cake on page 182. Knead green food colouring into marzipan. Roll it to a long sausage for the daisy stem. Sprinkle chocolate around base of daisy.

Cut 10 cm (4 in) circle from corner of cake for daisy centre. Using template and sharp knife, cut out 13 petal shapes (12 petals and 1 leaf). Brush away any loose crumbs on the sides of the petal shapes, using a dry pastry brush. Assemble the daisy on the cake board.

Spread side and top of daisy centre liberally with buttercream. Roll in orange coconut. Coat sides of petals only in buttercream, making sure it comes above the top edge; roll in yellow coconut. Colour remaining yellow coconut green. Use with green buttercream to coat leaf.

GRANDMA'S 80TH BIRTHDAY CAKE

Templates on page 259

Frosted fresh flowers are perfect for a special celebration. Choose flowers with thin petals such as violets, primroses and sweet peas. The flowers should be frosted the day before to allow time for drying. Inedible flowers should be removed before cutting the cake.

1 × 23 cm (9 in) Victoria Sandwich Cake
FILLING AND TOPPING
2 quantities Meringue Buttercream, see page 29
4 pieces stem (preserved) ginger, finely chopped
1 quantity Buttercream Paste
icing (confectioners') sugar for rolling out
60 g (2 oz/2 squares) white chocolate
food colouring to match flowers
FROSTED FLOWERS
fresh flowers
egg white, beaten
caster (superfine) sugar
●

1 Split each cake in half horizontally. Place all the layers cut side up. Make several paper piping bags.

2 Make up one quantity of meringue buttercream and divide it between three of the cut layers. Sprinkle chopped ginger on top of each. Layer cake with plain sponge on top, place on a plate and leave to set for 30 minutes.

3 Make up buttercream paste. Knead it until smooth, then place in a polythene bag. Make up second quantity of meringue buttercream. Spread a thin layer on the top of the cake. On a surface lightly dusted with icing (confectioners') sugar, roll out buttercream paste to a 23 cm (9 in) round. Run a knife under the round to loosen it, slide both hands under and lift onto cake.

4 Spread remaining meringue buttercream around side of cake. Mark design on side of cake and make runout 80 below and frosted flowers, following step-by-step instructions. When dry, fix runouts and flowers to cake.

Smooth buttercream around the side by placing cake on a turntable or upturned cake tin. Hold a cake scraper or palette knife at an angle of 45° to the side of the cake and rotate cake with other hand until a complete circuit has been made. Repeat with a serrated scraper or use a fork to mark a vertical design, working from base to top.

To make runout numerals, trace the 8 and the 0, making several copies of each on the same piece of paper. Secure tracing paper to

a flat surface with wax paper on top. Pipe outlines with coloured chocolate. Set for 1 minute, then fill in, moving bag to and fro. Use a cocktail stick (toothpick) to tease chocolate into corners.

Spread flowers for frosting on absorbent kitchen paper. Leave for 30 minutes, then shake gently upside down to dislodge any insects. Swish leaves through cold water, shake and dry on absorbent kitchen paper. Beat egg white lightly with 15 ml (1 tbsp) water. Brush all over front and back of each petal/leaf and down into any crevices.

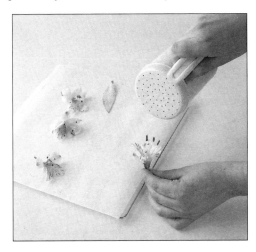

Lightly sprinkle flowers/leaves with caster (superfine) sugar, gently shaking off any excess. Spread flowers out on wax paper. When dry, they will be firm and brittle and

may be stored for a few days in tissue paper in a cardboard box. Always frost twice as many flowers or leaves as needed as some may not dry properly.

Arrange the runout 80 and flowers on the finished cake, adding the flowers just before serving, or presenting, the cake.

QUICK TIP

A ginger-flavoured meringue buttercream would be particularly delicious on this cake. Follow recipe for Quick Meringue Frosting. When meringue is stiff, remove from heat and gradually whisk in 30 ml (2 tbsp) ginger syrup (from a jar of stem/preserved ginger) in a slow steady stream. When incorporated and meringue is stiff again, gradually fold into softened butter.

TUXEDO PLAQUE

Illustrated on page 233
Template below

Enlarge this plaque to make an attractive novelty cake for a man. Use double the quantity of sugarpaste for a cake. Alternatively, set the plaque into the top of a sugarpaste-coated cake.

125 g (4 oz/$\frac{1}{4}$ lb) sugarpaste
black and silver food colouring
1 sugar carnation
10 × 12.5 cm (4 × 5 in) cake board

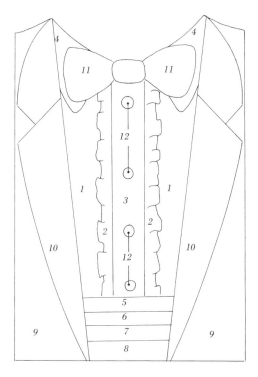

1 Trace tuxedo diagram and make a thin card template of the silhouette. Make individual templates of the various parts. Cut board to same shape as silhouette and cover with sugarpaste.

2 Cut out two Garrett frills and frill edge of each with a cocktail stick (toothpick). Attach to the covered board with water, as shown. Cut another paste strip wide enough to cover the inner edge of each frill. Fix it in place. Before frills dry, cut out and attach collar so that it lies neatly against shirt.

3 Make cummerbund from three strips of paste, attaching it to the plaque as shown. Colour some paste black and roll it out. Using templates and scalpel, cut out jacket and lapels. Dampen backs lightly and attach pieces carefully to shirt, taking care not to stretch paste.

4 Make bow tie from black paste and attach it in the same way. Lastly make buttons from four small balls of white sugarpaste. When buttons are dry, paint with silver food colour and attach to shirt with royal icing. To finish the plaque, attach sugar carnation.

SECRETS OF SUCCESS

Do not roll sugarpaste too thin or the layer beneath may show through.

GARDEN TRUG

Illustrated on page 234

1 quantity Quick Mix Sponge mixture,
see page 32
Marmalade Glaze, see page 13
2 quantities Basic Buttercream
juice of 1 orange
DECORATION
750 g (1$\frac{1}{2}$ lb) white marzipan
125 g (4 oz/4 squares) plain chocolate
yellow, green, orange, red and brown
food colouring
●

1 Preheat oven to 180°C (350°F/Gas 4). Bake sponge cake in a lined and greased 20 × 30 cm (8 × 12 in) cake tin (pan). Cool on a wire rack. Make several paper piping bags.

2 Cut cake as shown. Brush sections with glaze. Make up one quantity of the

buttercream and stir in the orange juice to slacken. Using buttercream, layer the main sponge pieces for the trug. Leave to set for 30 minutes.

3 Finish making trug and mould the marzipan vegetables, following step-by-step instructions. When trug is complete and icing is dry, arrange moulded vegetables on top as shown in the illustration on page 234.

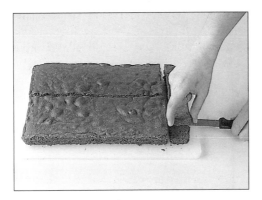

Have ready warm apricot glaze and buttercream. Cut a 4 cm (1½ in) strip from one short side of cake. Split strip in half horizontally, then assemble pieces side by side for base, using glaze and buttercream. Cut remaining piece of cake in half lengthwise, sandwich with glaze and icing and attach to base to make trug.

Having cut and assembled cake, trim front and back to make trug shape. Use trimmed wedge-shaped pieces to build up top edge of trug. Brush with apricot glaze. Roll 125 g

(4 oz/¼ lb) marzipan to a sausage; fit around top of trug. Melt chocolate; pour over top of cake.

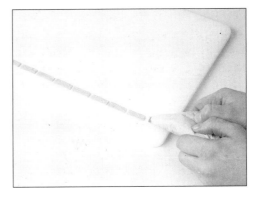

Coat thinly with buttercream. Put some buttercream in a piping bag with a basket tube (tip). Spoon a smaller amount of buttercream into another bag, with a plain no. 2 writing tube (tip). Pipe a row of ribbon strips, each 2.5 cm (1 in) long, horizontally along the top edge of one side of trug, leaving a small gap between each.

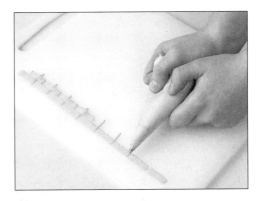

Using bag with writing tube (tip) pipe a line down between each ribbon strip to a point where a second line of ribbon would end. Pipe another row of ribbon, this time starting in the middle just below the first one. Pipe over first vertical line and end under the middle of the next ribbon, brick-wall fashion. Continue to build up pattern.

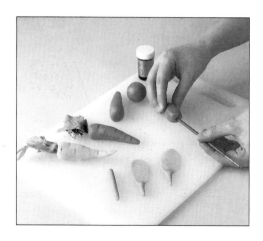

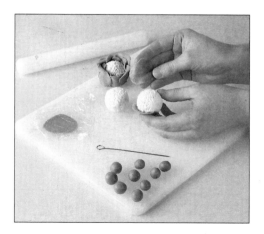

Carrots and Parsnips *Colour marzipan allowing 30 g (1 oz) for each carrot/parsnip and 15 g (½ oz) for leaves. Mould main pieces to 6.5 cm (2½ in) cones. Mould each green piece into two 5 cm (2 in) thin rolls. Flatten out at one end and snip down each side then ease apart to feather out the tops. Push thin ends into the vegetable tops; brush the vegetables with brown food colouring, as shown, for realistic results.*

Cauliflower *Allow 30 g (1 oz) marzipan for head; colour 15 g (½ oz) green for leaves. Roll plain marzipan to a ball; mark floret pattern with skewer. Roll green marzipan into pea-sized balls of varying sizes. Roll out thinly between plastic wrap. Using small leaves first, wrap around florets, slightly overlapping. Smooth.*

SECRETS OF SUCCESS

To whiten marzipan for cauliflower, knead in some food grade whitening powder, available from cake decorating shops.

WISE OWL

Illustrated on page 235
Templates on page 260

Tomatoes and Radishes *Colour some marzipan, allowing 30 g (1 oz) for two tomatoes or four radishes and 15 g (½ oz) for radish leaves. You will also need a pea-sized piece of green marzipan for the calyxes. Roll main pieces into balls. Cut a star for each calyx and push each one into a tomato. Make the radish leaves as for the carrot tops.*

1 Prepare the basic sponge cake shape using the template provided. Coat all sides of the shape with chocolate buttercream.

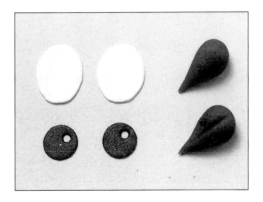

2 Using a no. 57, 58 or 59 petal tube (tip), pipe petal shapes in regular rows over the sides of the coated cake to represent the feathers of the owl.

4 Thinly roll out some white sugarpaste and cut out two oval shapes for the eyes. Also cut out two small circles of black-coloured sugarpaste, removing a small hole for a highlight. The circle can be cut using the wide end of a piping tube (tip), and the highlight using the narrow end of a no. 2 or 3 tube (tip). Stick the black circles onto the white ovals with egg white. Model a beak from egg-yellow-coloured marzipan, and indent a line of the beak using a small knife or modelling tool. Two tiny balls of black marzipan inserted with the point of a cocktail stick complete the beak.

3 Using the same tube and cream, pipe two wings on the front of the owl by building-up rows of petal shapes to form the finished triangular shape.

5 Mould six small carrot-shaped pieces of egg-yellow-coloured marzipan and attach together in two sets of three, as shown, to make the claws. Set the claws on a small piece of drinking straw to allow them to dry with a curve.

6 Model the spectacles from a thin rope of marzipan. The circular shape can be easily formed by positioning the marzipan around the wide ends of two piping tubes, securing the join with egg white. When the spectacles are dry, paint them with gold or silver food colouring.

7 Make the mortar board by cutting out a square of thinly rolled black sugarpaste or marzipan, using the templates provided as a guide to the size. Make the base of the mortar board from a ball of black paste cut in half and allowed to dry. Model a few thin strands of black paste and attach together with a little egg white to create a tassel. When dry, stick all the various parts together.

8 Attach the eyes and beak to the owl with a dab of buttercream.

9 Attach the mortar board and claws.

10 Model a small pencil from sugarpaste or marzipan along with a sugarpaste plaque on which you can pipe a name or inscription of your choice.

MINIATURE ROCKING HORSE

Illustrated on page 236
Templates on page 261

Just like the real thing. This original cake idea will appeal to all ages; and it is easier to make than it appears!

Instructions for the basic preparation of miniature cakes are included under the A–Z entry on Novelty Cakes. Similar to the jolly clown, the design can be adapted for making a larger cake by enlarging the templates proportionally. Either trace the templates on squared paper or use a photocopier to enlarge the designs.

1 First prepare the covering paste. Partly mix together a small amount of grey-coloured sugarpaste (use edible black food colouring to make grey) and some white sugarpaste; do not fully mix thereby creating an interesting mottled effect. Roll out the paste and press some small balls of black-coloured sugarpaste into the flattened surface. Continue to roll out the paste pressing the black balls flat to create a sheet of spotted sugarpaste.

2 Cover the basic cake shape with marzipan and then cover with the prepared, spotted sugarpaste. Cover the narrow top first.

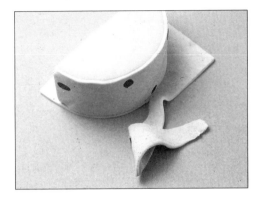

3 Next, cover the semi-circular side shapes with marzipan and sugarpaste.

4 Roll out some red-coloured marzipan, then re-roll with a boxwood roller to create an interesting texture and pattern. Using an orchid flower cutter or the template provided, cut out the two saddle sides.

5 Using the same red, boxwood-rolled marzipan, cut out the saddle top using the template as a guide.

6 Attach the saddle pieces to the horse's body with egg white.

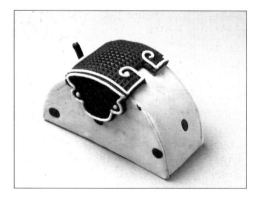

7 Model a small black tail piece and insert it into the body of the horse. Using a no 2 tube (tip), carefully pipe the pattern detail on the saddle, then allow it to dry. When the pattern is dry, paint with gold food colouring.

8 Roll out some white sugarpaste to about 9 mm ($\frac{3}{8}$ in) thickness. Using the template provided, cut out the head shape. Allow to dry for several hours until firm. When firm enough to handle, paint on the eyes, nose and mouth with black food colouring and a fine paint brush. To make the ears, cut out small triangle shapes of thinly rolled white sugarpaste. Tint the triangles with pink edible petal dust using a dry paint brush. Pinch two ends of a triangle together to form the ear shape. Attach the ears to the horse with egg white.

9 To make the horse's mane, press a small amount of black-coloured marzipan through a clay gun, fine sieve or tea-strainer, leaving it attached to the sieve. Brush the back of the prepared head with egg white, then use a small knife to lift off tufts of the black marzipan from the sieve and position them on the horse's head. A small tuft of the same marzipan is attached to the end of the tail piece. Attach the finished head to the horse using icing.

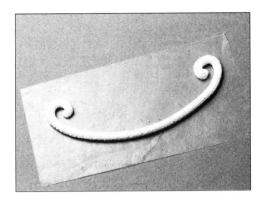

10 Using the template provided underneath a piece of waxed paper, pipe out two rockers using a no. 44 tube (tip) and white royal icing. Allow to dry.

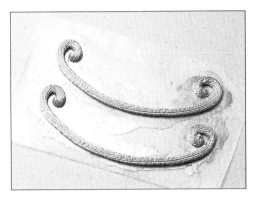

11 When dry, paint the rockers with gold food colouring and allow them to dry. Attach the finished rockers to the horse with royal icing.

LITTLE WITCHY CHOCOLATE CAKE

Illustrated on page 269
Templates on page 262

Delicious chocolate cake masquerading in the guise of a witch. Let the children have a go at making their own quick-to-decorate Hallowe'en treats.

Follow the instructions for preparing miniature cakes, given in the A–Z entry on Novelty Cakes.

1 Prepare a chocolate cake base to the size of the template provided. Two witches can be made from one long oblong sheet of cake, by simply reversing the template. Coat the cake in chocolate by placing the cake on a wire rack with wax paper beneath, spread the back with melted chocolate and allow to set. Turn the cake over and cover the sides and the top with melted chocolate, then tap the wire to encourage the excess chocolate to drain away. Allow the chocolate to set partially, then remove the cake from the wire. Place onto waxed or greaseproof paper to finish setting.

2 Pipe chocolate drops onto waxed paper using the template provided as a size guide. Allow to set, then cut in half.

3 Dip the straight edge of the chocolate drop halves into melted chocolate and attach them to the witch's body. Place a row of drops around the base and another row about one-third of the way down from the point to give the appearance of a hat.

4 Roll out some green-coloured sugar-paste to about 2.5 mm ($\frac{1}{8}$ in) thick; adding

a touch of blue colour in with the green gives a better colour for the witch's face. Cut out a circle using a round cutter of the required size. Indent the eyes with a modelling tool and using a ball modelling tool, press a small ball of red marzipan in place for the mouth. Add a pointed nose, attaching it with egg white, then pipe in the eyes with white and brown-coloured royal icing. The hair is made by pressing egg-yellow-coloured marzipan through a fine sieve, tea-strainer or clay gun. Attach two tufts of hair, using a little egg white to secure them.

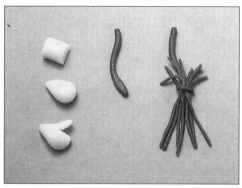

5 Model a hand from a pear-shaped piece of green marzipan, making a cut to represent the thumb; allow to firm-up. Model the broom from thin strands of brown marzipan attached together with a little egg white and allowed to dry. Attach the prepared face, broom and hand to the witch's body with royal icing. A small, sugarpaste star and moon motif attached to the hat with royal icing may also be added.

VALENTINE CHOCOLATE BOX

Illustrated on page 270
Templates on page 263

A miniature Valentine gift for a loved one to treasure. This simple-to-make sugarpaste chocolate box features embossed and painted roses.

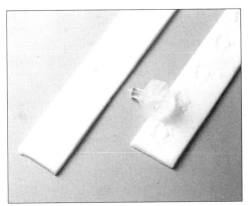

1 Roll out a long strip of white sugarpaste about 2.5 mm ($\frac{1}{8}$ in) thick. The width of the sugarpaste will be determined by the depth of your heart-shaped food cutter. The length of the strip can be calculated by holding a piece of string around the heart-shaped cutter. Using an embossing tool, mark indentations along the length of the strip. Use a rose pattern if possible, working quickly before the paste dries.

2 Immediately after completing the embossing, roll up the strip like a Swiss roll and place into the heart-shaped cutter lined with waxed paper. Unravel the roll of paste and position it neatly around the inside of the cutter, gently pressing into the corners to create a neat finish. Allow the paste to firm up before continuing to work on this section.

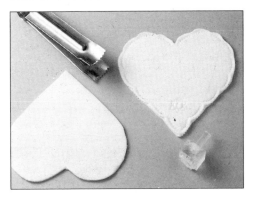

3 Using a slightly larger heart-shaped cutter than the one used previously, cut out a lid and a base for the chocolate box. The paste for the lid and base needs to be the same thickness as for the sides. Crimp the edges of both the lid and base to make a pretty decorative edge. On the lid, emboss a single rose pattern at the base of the heart near to the point.

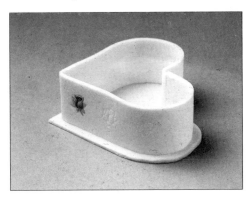

4 When all the prepared sugarpaste sections are dry, remove the cutter from the heart shape and position the shaped paste on the heart-shaped base. Secure with white royal icing; use a fine paint brush or small plastic scraper to remove any excess icing and to tidy the join.

5 Using a fine paint brush and edible pink, green and brown food colourings, paint the detail on each rose. Mix edible brilliant white powder to each colour to produce delicate, pale tints of colour; the white powder also produces a better consistency of paint with which it is easier to work. Paint the rose design on the prepared sugarpaste lid.

7 Decorate the lid with a fine, roped line piped on the edge of the crimper work, use a no. 1 tube (tip) with pink royal icing. Pipe the inscription 'With Love' on the lid using a no 1 or no. 0 tube (tip) with brown royal icing.

6 Using a no. 1 tube (tip) with white royal icing, pipe a tiny plain shell along the edge where the side joins the base. Overpipe the white border with a fine line piped in pink royal icing using a no. 0 tube (tip).

8 Half fill the finished box with shredded red or pink coloured tissue paper and arrange three truffles or chocolates on top. Position the lid onto the box and present in a gift box. A greeting message on an edible gift tag personalizes the gift.

MAKING CLASSIC CAKES

This section provides a glossary-style guide to making selected favourite, classic cakes. A system of symbols is used to indicate the basic cake-making technique which applies in each case, so that the step-by-step information on basic methods, such as whisking or folding in, may be checked if necessary. For traditional, basic cakes suitable for decorating, refer to the alphabetical entry on cakes and on rich fruit cake, where a chart provides ingredients for cakes of different sizes. Methods of covering cakes with marzipan, sugarpaste or royal icing are explained under the relevant alphabetical entries.

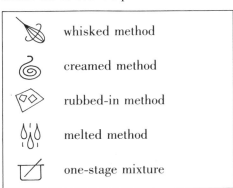

whisked method

creamed method

rubbed-in method

melted method

one-stage mixture

ANGEL CAKE

Preheat oven to 190C°/375°F (Gas 5). Have ready an ungreased 25 cm (10 in) ring tin (tube pan). Sift 125 g (4 oz/1 cup) plain (all-purpose) sponge (cake) flour with 125 g (4 oz/$\frac{3}{4}$ cup) icing (confectioners') sugar. In a large, perfectly clean bowl, whisk 12 egg whites with 1.25 ml ($\frac{1}{4}$ tsp) salt until foamy, then add 7.5 ml (1$\frac{1}{2}$ tsp) cream of tartar and continue whisking until the whites form soft peaks. Stir in 5 ml (1 tsp) vanilla essence (extract) and 2.5 ml ($\frac{1}{2}$ tsp) almond essence (extract), then sift the flour mixture over

and fold in. Turn the mixture into the tin and bake for 45 minutes. Invert the cake in its tin over the neck of a bottle or large up-turned metal funnel and leave until cold. Use a spatula to loosen when cold.

APPLE CAKE, ENGLISH

Preheat the oven to 180°C (350°F/ Gas 5) and grease an 18 cm (7 in) square cake tin (pan). In a large bowl, mix 250 g (8 oz/$\frac{1}{2}$ lb) peeled cored and grated apple, 155 g (5 oz/$\frac{2}{3}$ cup) margarine, 185 g (6 oz/$\frac{3}{4}$ cup) caster (superfine) sugar, 60 g (2 oz/$\frac{1}{3}$ cup) currants, 60 g (2oz/$\frac{1}{2}$ cup) pine nuts and 2 beaten eggs. Sift in 280 g (9 oz/2$\frac{1}{4}$ cups) plain (all-purpose) flour and 5 ml (1 tsp) each of bicarbonate of soda (baking soda), ground cinnamon and grated nutmeg. Add 2.5 ml ($\frac{1}{2}$ tsp) ground cloves. Beat mixture for 1–2 minutes, until thoroughly combined and glossy. Spoon into tin. Bake for 65–70 minutes. Cool in tin 5 minutes, then on rack.

APPLE SAUCE CAKE

Preheat oven to 180°C (350°F/Gas 5). Line and grease a 23 × 33 cm (9 × 13 in) tin (pan). Mix 280 g (9 oz/2$\frac{1}{4}$ cups) plain (all-purpose) flour), 10 ml (2 tsp) bicarbonate of soda (baking soda), 5 ml (1 tsp) ground cinnamon and 2.5 ml ($\frac{1}{2}$ tsp) each ground cloves, grated nutmeg and salt. Add 2 beaten eggs, 185 g (6 oz/$\frac{3}{4}$ cup) softened butter, 125 g (4 oz/$\frac{1}{2}$ cup) sugar, 250 g (8 oz/1 cup) light brown sugar and 410 ml (13 fl oz/1$\frac{2}{3}$ cups) unsweetened apple purée (apple sauce). Beat until well blended, about 2 minutes, then stir in 185 g (6 oz/1 cup) raisins and 60 g (2 oz/$\frac{1}{2}$ cup) chopped walnuts. Turn into tin and bake for 30–35 minutes. Cool in tin.

BANANA LOAF CAKE

Preheat the oven to 180°C (350°F/ Gas 5). Base line and grease a 1 kg (2 lb) loaf tin (pan). Rub 125 g (4 oz/¼ lb) butter into 250 g (8 oz/2 cups) self-raising flour. Stir in 125 g (4 oz/½ cup) sugar, 90 g (3 oz/½ cup) sultanas (white raisins), 2 small chopped bananas, 60 g (2 oz/½ cup) chopped walnuts or pecans. Add 2 beaten eggs and mix well. Turn into tin (pan) and bake for 1–1¼ hours. Cool on a wire rack. Banana loaf cake is good warm, with pure maple syrup or a little honey for those with a sweet tooth, or chocolate spread for chocoholics. It keeps well in an airtight container.

BATTENBURG CAKE

Prepare an 18 cm (7 in) square cake tin (pan) by dividing it in half with a piece of greaseproof paper. Fold the paper four layers thick, then crease about 2.5 cm (1 in) double thickness of paper out along the base on both sides to stand the strip steadily. Base line and grease both halves of the tin (pan). Prepare an 18 cm (7 in) Madeira Cake mixture, see page 35, place half in one side of the tin (pan). Colour the second half pink, then place it in the second side. Bake following the recipe instructions and cool on a wire rack. Trim the top and sides of the cake neatly, then cut both pieces in half lengthways. Sandwich the strips of cake together into a loaf-shaped cake, brushing with apricot glaze* and placing alternate colours next to and above each other in a harlequin pattern. Roll out 500 g (1 lb) marzipan large enough to wrap around the cake without covering the ends. Brush the middle of the marzipan with apricot glaze, place the cake on it and brush with more glaze, then wrap the marzipan around the cake to enclose it completely. Neaten the edges, pinching them or marking with a fork. Sprinkle with caster (superfine) sugar.

BLUEBERRY AND APPLE CAKE

Preheat the oven to 180°C (350°F/ Gas 5). Line and grease a 20 cm (8 in) round cake tin (pan). Place 125 g (4 oz/ ¼ lb) butter, 5 ml (1 tsp) vanilla essence (extract), 170 g (5½ oz/¾ cup) caster (superfine) sugar, 2 eggs, 185 g (6 oz/1½ cups) self-raising flour and 125 ml (4 fl oz/ ½ cup) buttermilk or milk in a bowl and beat until thoroughly combined. Have ready 220 g (7 oz) well-drained canned or fresh blueberries. Spoon half the mixture into the tin (pan). Top with half the blueberries, then add the remaining mixture and the second portion of blue-berries. Mix 20 ml (4 tsp) caster (super-fine) sugar and 5 ml (1 tsp) ground cinnamon, then sprinkle this over the fruit. Bake for 55–60 minutes, or until a skewer inserted into the cake comes out free of mixture. Leave in the tin (pan) for 10 minutes, then cool on a wire rack.

BROWNIES

Preheat the oven to 180°C (350°F/ Gas 5). Base line and grease a 23 cm (9 in) square cake tin (pan). Beat together the following until thoroughly combined: 155 g (5 oz/⅔ cup) softened butter, 170 g (5½ oz/½ cup) warmed honey, 20 ml (4 tsp) water, 2 beaten eggs, 220 g (7 oz/1¾ cups) self-raising flour, 125 g (4 oz/⅔ cup) soft brown sugar and 125 g (4 oz/4 squares) cooled, melted plain chocolate. Turn the batter into the tin and bake for 30–35 minutes. Leave to cool in the tin (pan), then cut into squares.

BUTTERFLY CAKES

Make a batch of cup cakes. When cool, slice the tops off the cakes and cut each slice across in half. Pipe a swirl of buttercream* on the top of each cake. Dust the top of the cut lids with icing

Tuxedo Plaque
see page 220

Garden Trug
see page 220

Wise Owl
see page 223

Miniature Rocking Horse
see page 225

(confectioners') sugar, then stick them at a slight angle into the swirl of buttercream, placing the rounded sides in. These can be made with any flavour cake and corresponding buttercream.

CARROT CAKE

Preheat the oven to 160°C (325°F/ Gas 3). Base line and grease a 23 cm (9 in) round cake tin (pan). Heat the following in a large saucepan until butter has melted, stirring gently: 250 g (8 oz/$\frac{1}{2}$ lb) finely grated carrots, 125 g (4 oz/$\frac{3}{4}$ cup) raisins, 60 g (2 oz/$\frac{1}{3}$ cup) chopped figs, 125 g (4 oz/$\frac{1}{2}$ cup) caster (superfine) sugar, 125 g (4 oz/$\frac{1}{4}$ lb) unsalted butter, 185 g (6 oz/$\frac{1}{2}$ cup) clear honey and 155 ml (5 fl oz/$\frac{2}{3}$ cup) orange juice. Allow to cool. Sift 250 g (8 oz/2 cups) self-raising flour and 5 ml (1 tsp) ground mixed spice over mixture, then mix well, adding 1 beaten egg. Place in tin (pan) and bake for 60–70 minutes. Cool on a wire rack.

CHERRY CAKE

Prepare ingredients and tin (pan) for the basic Madeira Cake, see page 35. Wash and drain 155 g (4 oz/$\frac{3}{4}$ cup) quartered glacé (candied) cherries. Dry on absorbent kitchen paper, then dust with a little of the measured flour. Make the cake, folding in the cherries last. Bake as usual.

CHIFFON CAKE

Preheat the oven to 160°C (325°F/ Gas 3). Have an ungreased 25 cm (10 in) ring tin (tube pan) to bake the cake. Mix 250 g (8 oz/2 cups) plain (all-purpose) flour, 15 ml (3 tsp) baking powder, 5 ml (1 tsp salt) and 375 g (12 oz/1$\frac{1}{2}$ cups) sugar. Make a well in the middle, then pour in 125 ml (4 fl oz/$\frac{1}{2}$ cup) vegetable oil, 6 egg yolks, 185 ml (6 fl oz/$\frac{3}{4}$ cup) fresh orange juice, 15 ml (1 tbsp) grated orange rind

and 10 ml (2 tsp) vanilla essence (extract). Beat well until thoroughly blended. Whisk 6 egg whites separately until stiff but not dry, then fold these into the mixture. Pour the batter into the tin (pan) and bake for about 1 hour 10 minutes, until a skewer inserted into the cake comes out clean. Leave to cool in the tin, then use a spatula to free the cake.

CHOCOLATE CHIP BUNS

Make and bake as for Rock Cakes, stirring in 125 g (4 oz/4 squares) chopped plain chocolate (or use chocolate chips) to the dry ingredients.

CHOCOLATE FUDGE CAKE

Preheat the oven to 160°C (325°F/ Gas 3). Base line and grease two 20 cm (8 in) round sandwich tins. Sift 125 g (4 oz/1 cup) self-raising flour and 45 ml (3 tbsp) cocoa into a bowl. Stir in 60 g (2 oz/$\frac{1}{2}$ cup) ground almonds and 155 g (5 oz/$\frac{2}{3}$ cup) caster (superfine) sugar, then make a well in the middle. Add the following: 125 ml (4 fl oz/$\frac{1}{2}$ cup) sunflower oil beaten with 3 egg yolks, and 125 ml (4 fl oz/$\frac{1}{2}$ cup) boiling water. Beat to a smooth batter. Whisk egg whites until stiff, then fold in. Divide mixture between tins. Bake for 20–25 minutes. Cool on a wire rack. Sandwich together and coat with Chocolate Fudge Icing, see page 44.

COCONUT CAKES

Make as for Rock Cakes, adding 60 g (2 oz/$\frac{2}{3}$ cup) desiccated coconut to the dry ingredients. Stir in an extra 30 ml (2 tbsp) milk to soften. Bake as usual.

COFFEE SANDWICH CAKE

Make a coffee-flavoured Victoria Sandwich Cake, see page 31. Sandwich together and top with coffee-flavoured buttercream* or use fresh coffee cream. For fresh coffee cream, whip 315 ml (10 fl oz/1¼ cups) double (heavy) cream with 60 ml (4 tbsp) very strong, cold black coffee and 60 ml (4 tbsp) icing (confectioners') sugar.

COFFEE WALNUT CAKE

Make a coffee-flavoured Victoria Sandwich Cake, see page 31, stirring in 250 g (8 oz/2 cups) finely chopped walnuts after the flour. Bake as usual. Sandwich and top the cake with American frosting*, coffee buttercream* or with fresh coffee cream, as above. Decorate with walnut halves.

CUP CAKES

Preheat the oven to 180°C (350°F/ Gas 5). Place paper cake cases in 24 patty tins (pans). Make 1 quantity basic Victoria Sandwich Cake, see page 31 and divide it between the paper cases. Bake for 15–20 minutes. The cakes may be topped with glacé icing*, or the mixture may be flavoured with chocolate and the tops of the cakes coated with melted chocolate. Feather icing* looks attractive on cup cakes.

DEVIL'S FOOD CAKE

Preheat the oven to 180°C (350°F/ Gas 5). Base line and grease two 23 cm (9 in) sandwich tins (pans). Beat 155 g (5 oz/⅔ cup) softened butter with 125 g (4 oz/½ cup) caster (superfine) sugar, then continue to beat, adding a further 185 g (6 oz/1 cup) soft brown sugar. Beat in 3 eggs, 5 ml (1 tsp) vanilla essence (extract) and 90 g (3 oz/3 squares) melted plain chocolate. Sift together 250 g (8 oz/2 cups) plain (all-purpose) flour, 10 ml (2 tsp) baking powder and 2.5 ml (½ tsp) bicarbonate of soda (baking soda). Gradually fold the dry ingredients into the mixture, adding 250 ml (8 fl oz/1 cup) milk alternately. Divide the mixture between

the tins (pans) and bake for 30–35 minutes. Cool on a wire rack. Sandwich and coat the cakes with American frosting* or whipped cream.

DUNDEE CAKE

Make a Light Fruit Cake, see page 35, adding 125 g (4 oz/1¼ cups) ground almonds with the flour and stirring in 250 g (8 oz/½ lb) chopped blanched almonds. When the mixture is in the tin (pan), top with concentric circles of blanched almonds before baking.

FAIRY CAKES

Another name for small plain cakes, baked as for plain cup cakes. Sometimes 90 g (3 oz/½ cup) mixed dried fruit is added to the mixture with the flour.

GENOA CAKE

Follow the recipe for Madeira Cake, see page 35, adding 185 g (6 oz/1⅔ cups) ground almonds with the flour. Top with a layer of chopped blanched almonds before baking. Fruit is sometimes added to this classically plain almond cake: 125 g (4 oz/¾ cup) chopped, washed and dried glacé (candied) cherries, 90 g (3 oz/½ cup) chopped candied peel and 250 g (8 oz/1½ cups) raisins may be added with the flour, if wished. In place of the chopped almonds, a more elaborate topping of candied fruit may be added after baking. Apricot glaze* is usually used to finish fruit-topped cakes.

GINGERBREAD

Preheat the oven to 180°C (350°F/ Gas 4). Line and grease an 18 cm (7 in) square tin. Mix 375 g (12 oz/3 cups) plain (all-purpose) flour, 5 ml (1 tsp) ground cinnamon, 15 ml (1 tbsp) ground ginger and 1 tsp (5 ml) bicarbonate of soda. Heat the following together until the

238

butter melts, stirring occasionally: 125 g (4 oz/¼ lb) butter, 125 g (4 oz/¾ cup) soft brown sugar, 125 g (4 oz/⅓ cup) black treacle (molasses) and 4 tbsp (60 ml) milk. Make a well in the dry ingredients and add 2 beaten eggs, then gradually beat in the melted ingredients to make a smooth batter. Turn into the tin and bake for about 1¼ hours. Allow to cool in the tin.

LEMON CAKE

Make 1 quantity Victoria Sandwich Cake, see page 31, adding the grated rind of 2 lemons to the creamed mixture. Fold in the juice of 1 lemon with the flour. Sandwich the cooked cakes together with good-quality lemon curd. Dust the top with icing (confectioners') sugar or top with lemon glacé icing*.

MADELEINES, ENGLISH

Thoroughly grease 12 dariole moulds and set the oven at 180°C (350°F, Gas 4). Make up 2-egg quantity Victoria Sandwich Cake mixture, see page 31. Divide the mixture between the tins (pans) and bake for about 20 minutes. Cool on a wire rack. Trim the tops off any domed cakes so they sit neatly. Coat with warmed strawberry or raspberry jam, then roll the cakes in desiccated coconut. Top each with half a glacé (candied) cherry and two angelica leaves.

MARBLE CAKE

A cake made of two different coloured and/or flavoured mixtures, cooked together in the same tin (pan). Flavoured Victoria Sandwich Cake mixture, see page 31, or Madeira Cake mixture, see page 35, may be used, the latter for larger, deep cakes. Make up the mixture following the recipe, and to suit the chosen tin (pan) size, then divide it into two portions.

Leave one portion plain, then flavour the second portion chocolate or coffee; a combination of chocolate and coffee mixtures marble well. To add flavouring when the cake has been mixed, dissolve the cocoa or instant coffee in a little boiling water first, then fold into the mixture. Drop spoonfuls of the prepared mixtures into the tin at random to cover the base evenly. Use a pointed knife or skewer to slightly drag the mixtures – do not marble them together at this stage or they will run into each other as they melt during the first stages of cooking. Bake as usual.

MERINGUE GATEAU

Lightly grease and base line two 20 cm (8 in) sandwich tins (pans) with non-stick baking paper. Sprinkle 10 ml (2 tsp) finely chopped hazelnuts around the sides of the tins to coat them. Preheat the oven to 180°C (350°F/Gas 4). Mix 5 ml (1 tsp) orange flower water with 2.5 ml (½ tsp) cream of tartar and 5 ml (1 tsp) cornflour (corn starch). In a clean bowl, whisk 4 egg whites until stiff and dry, gradually add 250 g (8 oz/1 cup) caster (superfine) sugar, whisking all the time. Whisk in cornflour (corn starch) mixture until meringue is stiff and glossy. Carefully fold in 125 g (4 oz/½ cup) finely chopped hazelnuts. Divide between the tins (pans) and bake for 45–50 minutes. Cool in tins (pans), turn out and remove paper. Sandwich together with whipped cream and fresh fruit, such as raspberries, then spread more whipped cream around side and press on toasted chopped hazelnuts. Decorate with swirls of whipped cream and more fruit.

OIL SPONGE

Good-quality vegetable oil, preferably sunflower oil which has a light flavour, can be used to make light cakes. The Chiffon Cake, in this guide, is made from an oil-based mixture using the whisked-sponge method. The following one-stage method gives a result similar to a creamed mixture. Preheat the oven to 180°C (350°F/Gas 4). Base line and grease two 15 cm (6 in) sandwich tins (pans). Sift 125 g (4 oz/1 cup) self-raising flour and 5 ml (1 tsp) baking powder into a bowl. Add a good pinch of salt. Make a well in the middle, then add 125 g (4 oz/½ cup) caster (superfine) sugar, 2 beaten eggs, 5 ml (1 tsp) vanilla essence (extract) and 90 ml (6 tbsp) oil. Beat well, until thoroughly combined, preferably using an electric beater. Bake for 35–40 minutes. Cool in the tins for 5 minutes.

PASSION CAKE

Carrot cake, usually with walnuts and raisins added, coated in American frosting* or cream cheese icing*.

POUND CAKE

Preheat oven to 180°C (350°F/Gas 4). Base line and grease a 1 kg (2 lb) loaf tin (pan). Cream 220 g (7 oz/1 cup) butter with 410 g (13 oz/1¾ cups) sugar. Gradually beat in 5 eggs, 10 ml (2 tsp) lemon juice and 2.5 ml (½ tsp) grated lemon rind. When thoroughly beaten, sift 345 g (11 oz/2¾ cups) self-raising flour with 5 ml (1 tsp) baking powder, 2.5 ml (½ tsp) salt and 1.25 ml (¼ tsp) ground mace. Gradually fold in the sifted ingredients. Turn it into the tin. Bake for about 1 hour. Cool for 10 minutes in the tin.

QUEEN CAKES

Another name for small cakes made from Victoria Sandwich mixture.

ROCK CAKES

Place twelve paper cases in patty tins (pans). Preheat the oven to 200°C (400°F/Gas 6). Sift 250 g (8 oz/2 cups) self-raising flour into a bowl. Rub in 125 g (4 oz/¼ lb) butter and stir in 125 g (4 oz/½ cup) sugar. Add 60 g (2 oz/⅓ cup) mixed dried fruit and beat in 2 eggs. Divide between the paper cases and bake for about 20 minutes.

SACHERTORTE

Base line and grease a 23 cm (9 in) cake tin (pan). Preheat the oven to 200°C (400°F/Gas 6). Cream 125 g (4 oz/¼ lb) butter with 155 g (5 oz/⅔ cup) caster (superfine) sugar. Beat in 5 egg yolks. In a separate, perfectly clean bowl, whisk 5 egg whites until stiff but not dry. Stir 125 g (4 oz/4 squares) melted plain chocolate into the creamed mixture. Working quickly, fold in 125 g (4 oz/1¼ cups) ground almonds, and 60 g (2 oz/½ cup) very fine, dry white breadcrumbs, then fold in the egg whites. Turn the mixture into the tin and bake for about 30 minutes. Allow to cool in the tin. When cold, coat with apricot glaze* or melted redcurrant jelly, then leave to set. Coat completely with melted chocolate, unwhipped chocolate ganache* or chocolate-flavoured fondant*.

SEED CAKE

Madeira Cake, see page 35, with caraway seeds added. Allow 45 ml (3 tbsp) caraway seeds to 1 quantity basic mixture and bake as usual.

SIMNEL CAKE

Rich fruit cake* with a layer of marzipan in the middle. Baked for Easter, half the mixture is put in the tin, then a neat layer of rolled-out marzipan*, about 2.5 cm (1 in) thick, is placed on top before the remaining cake mixture is added. The cake is baked in the usual way. The top is finished with a marzipan cover and eleven balls of marzipan are added around the edge. The marzipan topping is browned under the grill.

TEMPLATES

For A to Z Section and Decorated Cakes

This section includes all templates for designs and decorations referred to throughout the alphabetical section and within the recipes for the decorated cakes. Trace the outlines carefully to avoid errors and follow the instructions for their use. Shapes may be enlarged or reduced by tracing on squared paper and copying on a larger or smaller scale. An easier method is to have the finished tracing enlarged or reduced on a photocopying machine.

When following intricate patterns, for example for floral decorations, it may be easier to trace different sections of the design on separate sheets of paper. Staple or tape the required number of sheets together on one side, use paper clips to keep them firmly in position over the design as you work, then draw the different areas on individual sheets (two or three are a practical number). When all the areas are drawn, the different sheets may be laid one on top of another to reproduce the complete design. Alternatively, use different coloured pens or pencils to outline different areas on one sheet.

❧

Chocolate rice paper
cutouts: Three Kings,
see page 43

DIAGRAM OF POSITIONS FOR CAKE PILLARS

For round tiered cakes, *follow positions marked on the black lines*
For square tiered cakes, *follow positions marked on the pale grey lines*
For heart, hexagonal and petal-shaped cakes, *follow positions marked on the dark grey lines. Centre a full-size template on the bottom tier. Mark the relevant positions on the icing by pricking through the tracing paper with a scriber. Repeat the procedure for the remaining tiers. It is not necessary to enclose the template in a square or circle.*

(Diagram is quarter size.)

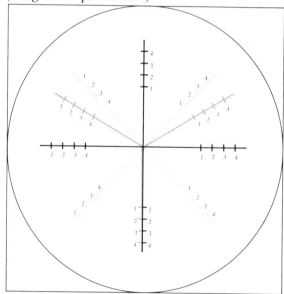

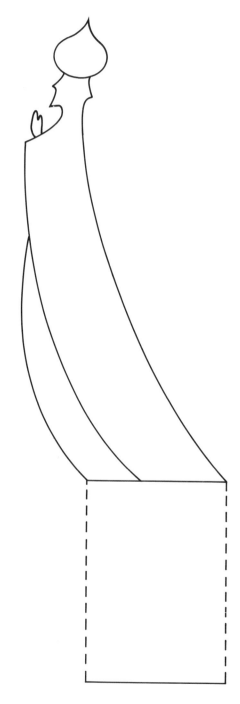

1 = *positions for 20 cm (8 in) diameter cake*
2 = *positions for 25 cm (10 in) diameter cake*
3 = *positions for 30 cm (12 in) diameter cake*
4 = *positions for 35 cm (14 in) diameter cake*
30 cm/12 in square frame

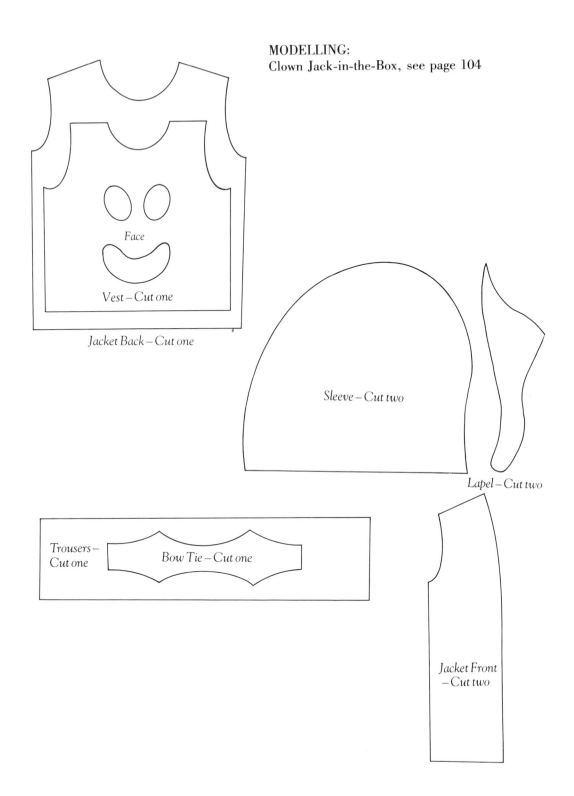

MODELLING:
Clown Jack-in-the-Box, see page 104

Face

Vest – Cut one

Jacket Back – Cut one

Sleeve – Cut two

Lapel – Cut two

Trousers – Cut one

Bow Tie – Cut one

Jacket Front – Cut two

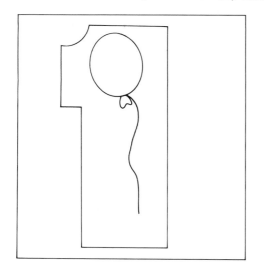

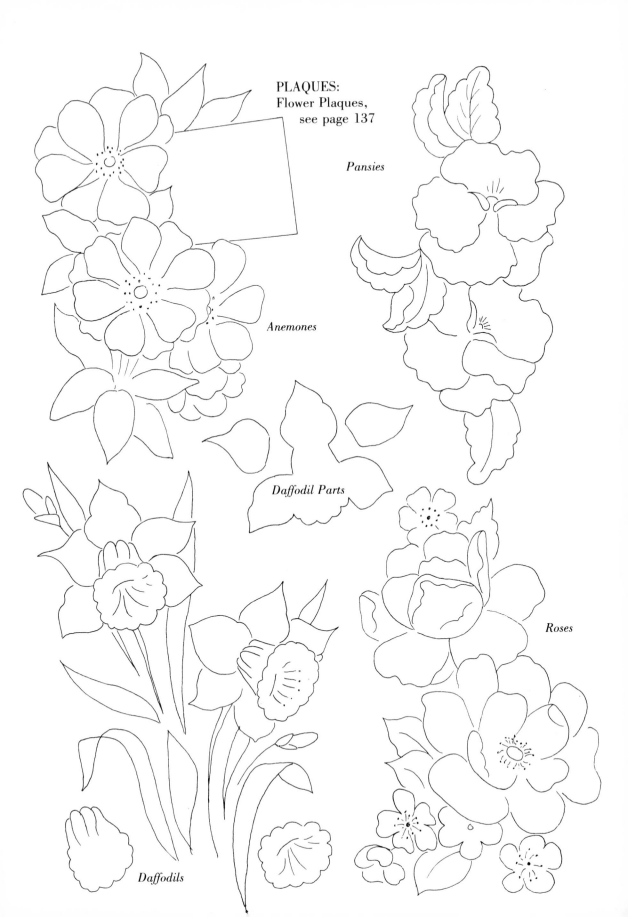

PLAQUES:
Flower Plaques,
see page 137

Pansies

Anemones

Daffodil Parts

Daffodils

Roses

EASTER EGG CAKE,

see page 185

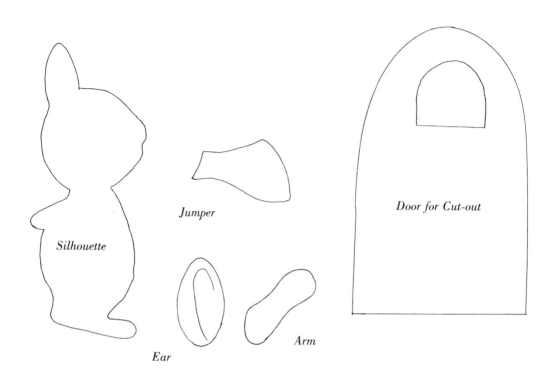

Silhouette

Jumper

Ear

Arm

Door for Cut-out

MERRY CHRISTMAS PLAQUE CAKE,
see page 187

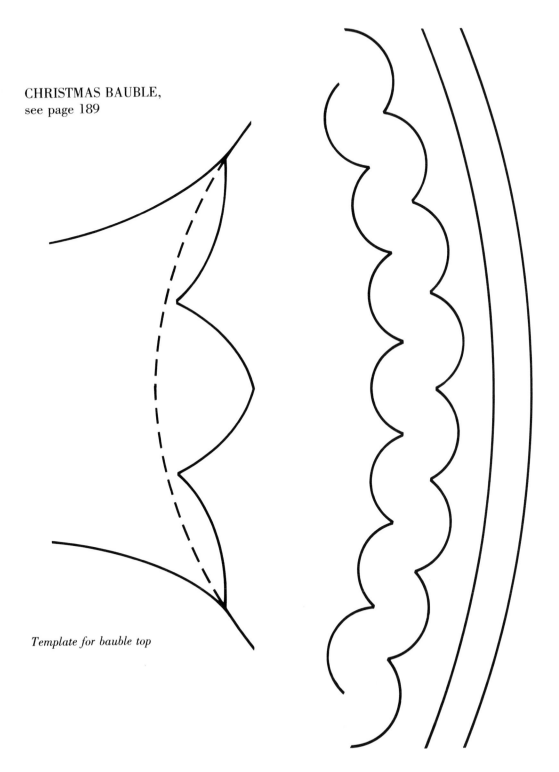

CHRISTMAS BAUBLE,
see page 189

Template for bauble top

CHRISTMAS BAUBLE, continued

Christmas Bauble: decorating diagram

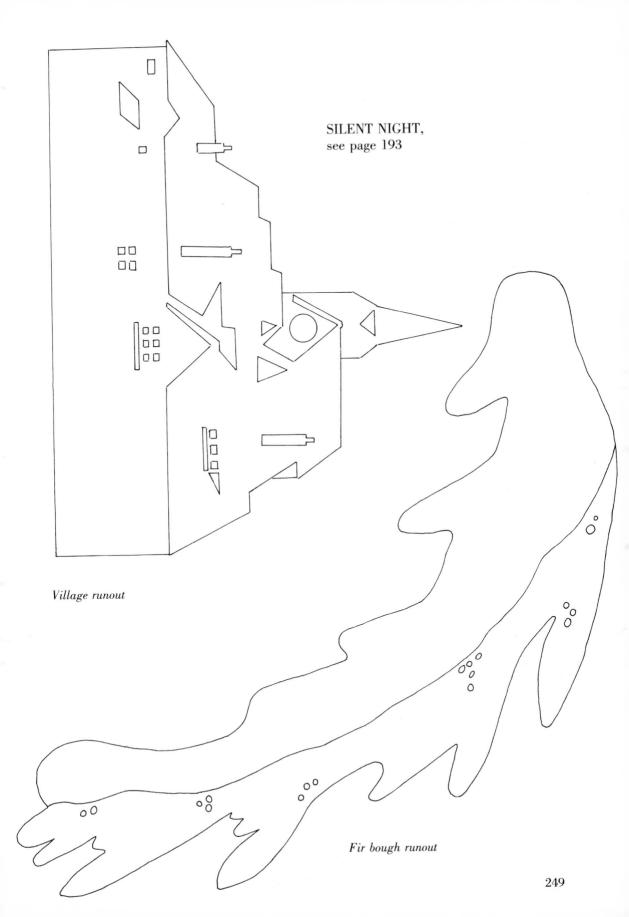

SILENT NIGHT,
see page 193

Village runout

Fir bough runout

POINSETTIA
see page 194

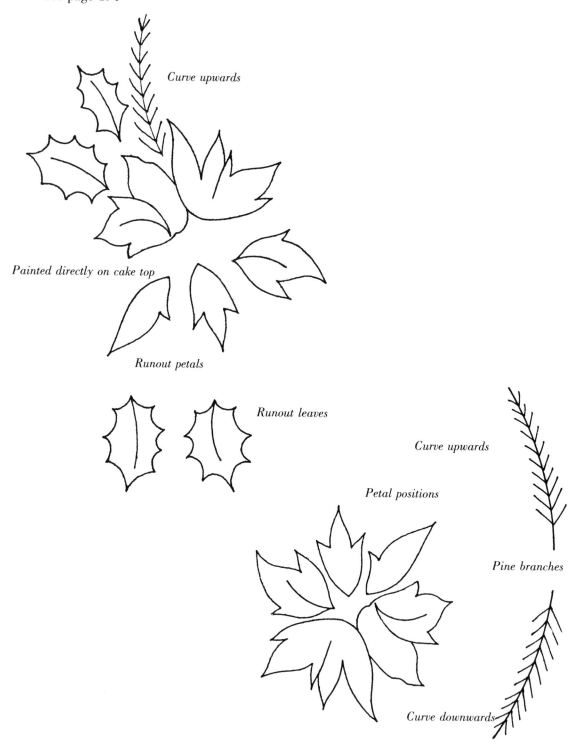

Curve upwards

Painted directly on cake top

Runout petals

Runout leaves

Petal positions

Curve upwards

Pine branches

Curve downwards

Greetings

Chocolate-coloured line ends here

Runout corner templates:
outline curved edges in
chocolate-coloured icing

Template for wavy line on cake sides

Template for runout top collar:
make four

Outside line piped in chocolate-coloured icing

251

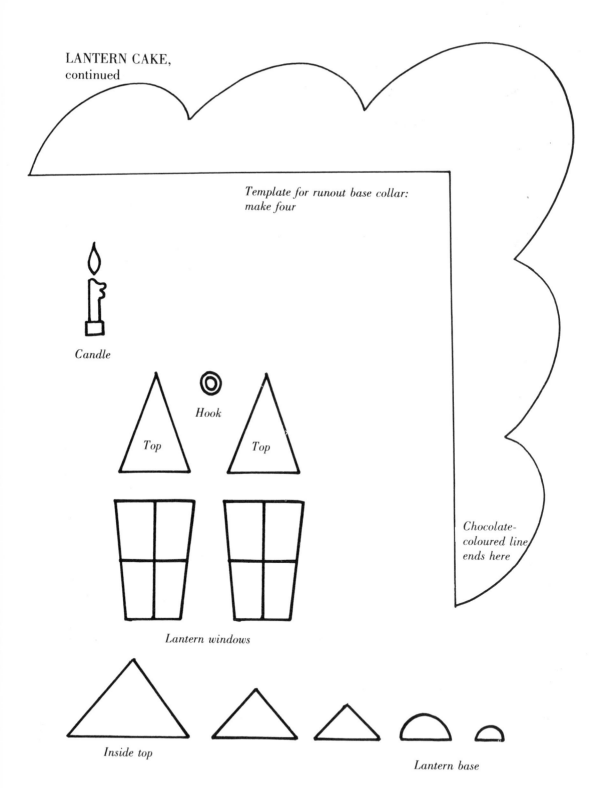

*Template for runout base collar:
make four*

Candle

Hook

Top

Top

*Chocolate-
coloured line
ends here*

Lantern windows

Inside top

Lantern base

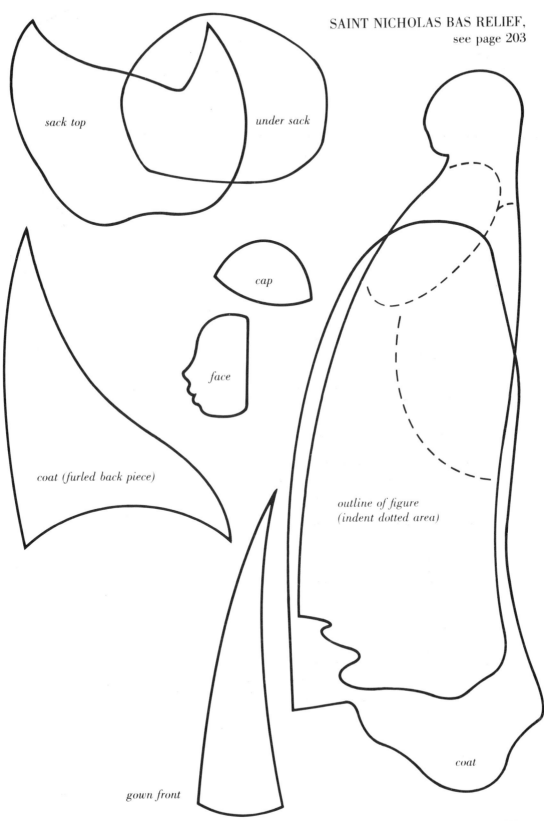

sack top

under sack

cap

face

coat (furled back piece)

outline of figure
(indent dotted area)

coat

gown front

BASKET CAKE,

see page 205

Best

Wishes

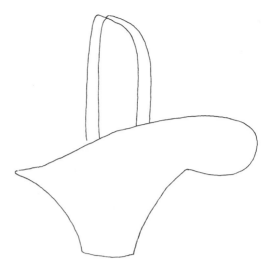

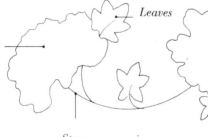

Flowers

Leaves

Stems

PERFECT POSY,

see page 216

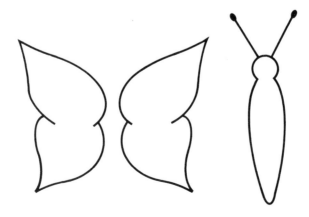

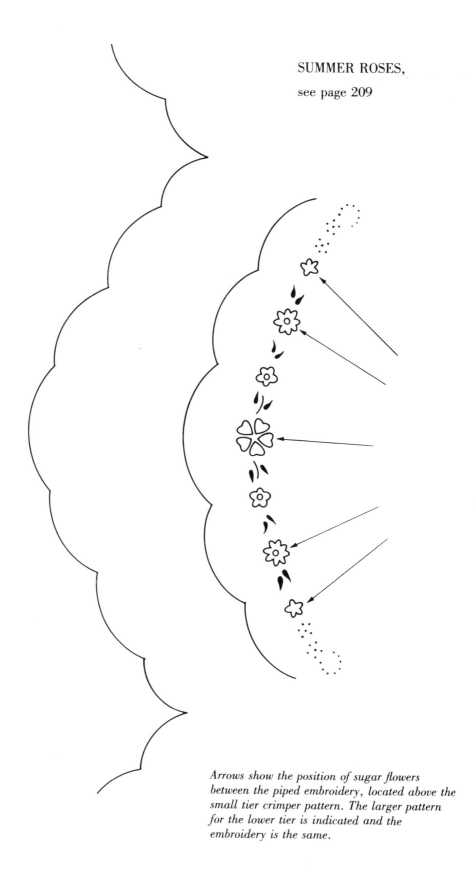

SUMMER ROSES,

see page 209

Arrows show the position of sugar flowers between the piped embroidery, located above the small tier crimper pattern. The larger pattern for the lower tier is indicated and the embroidery is the same.

ROSES ALL THE WAY,

see page 210

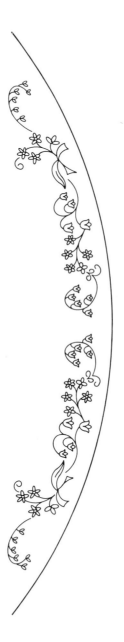

BON VOYAGE,
see page 211

Template of tree outlines

Side and top runouts: make 8

Side runout: make 8

Balloon and basket runouts: make 2 of each

Inscription

BIRTHDAY CAKE
with Applique Train,
see page 215

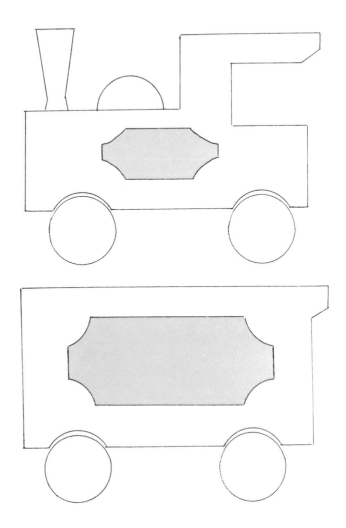

GRANDMA'S 80TH BIRTHDAY CAKE,
see page 218

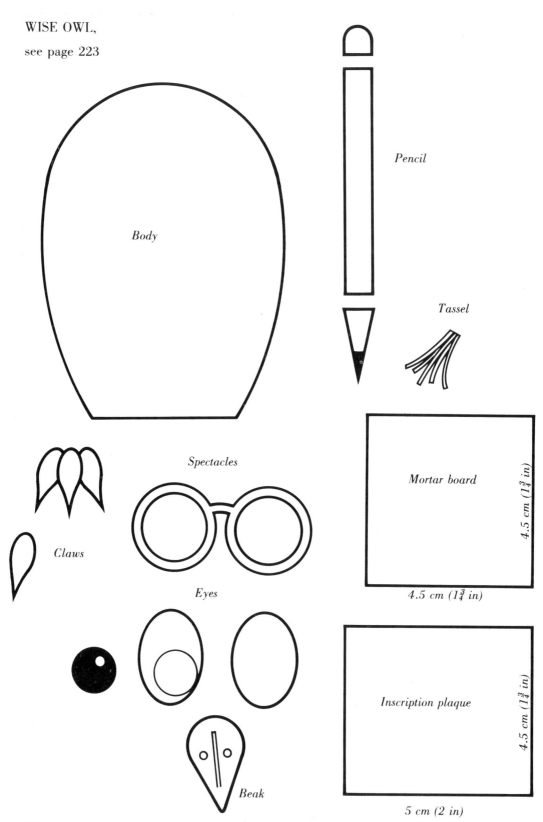

WISE OWL,
see page 223

Body

Pencil

Tassel

Claws

Spectacles

Mortar board

4.5 cm (1¾ in)

4.5 cm (1¾ in)

Eyes

Inscription plaque

4.5 cm (1¾ in)

Beak

5 cm (2 in)

MINIATURE ROCKING HORSE,
see page 225

Cake board

Head and face

14 cm ($5\frac{1}{2}$ in)

Saddle side: make 2

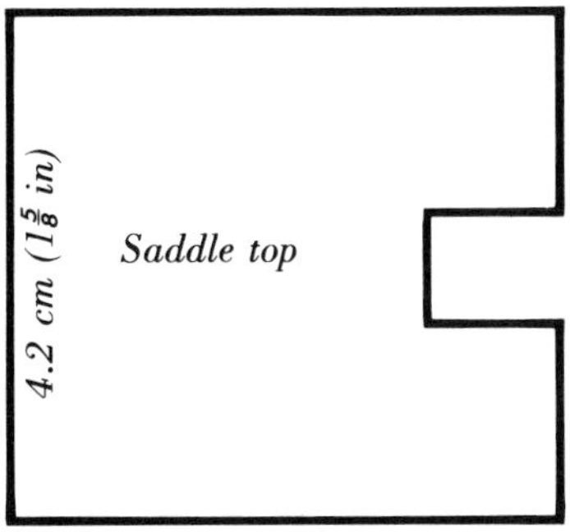

Saddle top

4.2 cm ($1\frac{5}{8}$ in)

4.5 cm ($1\frac{3}{4}$ in)

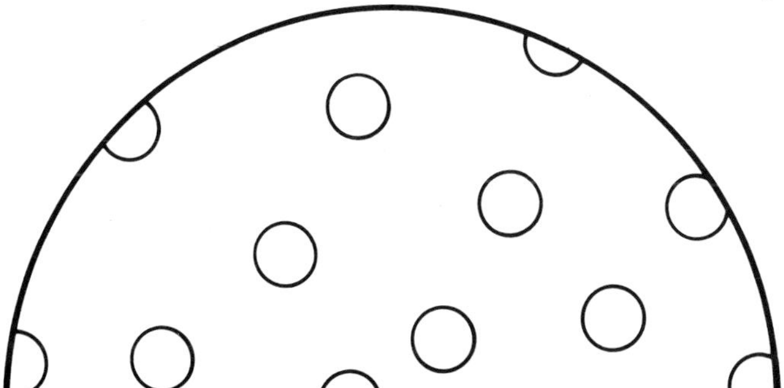

9 cm ($3\frac{1}{2}$ in)

Ears

Side of body

Rocker: make 2

261

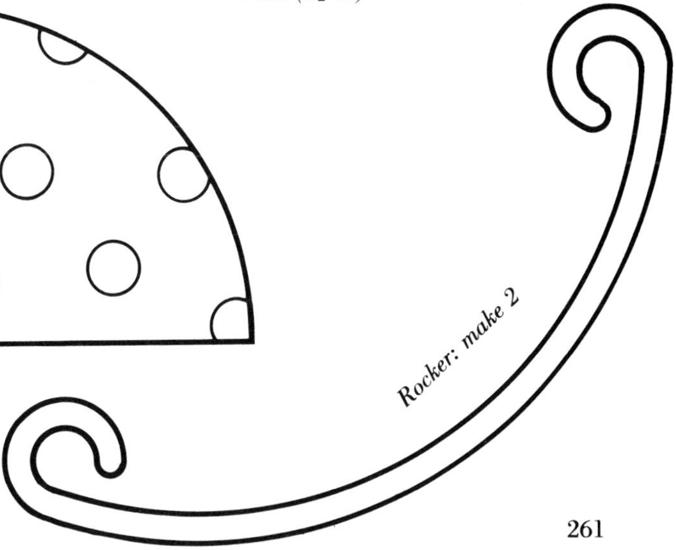

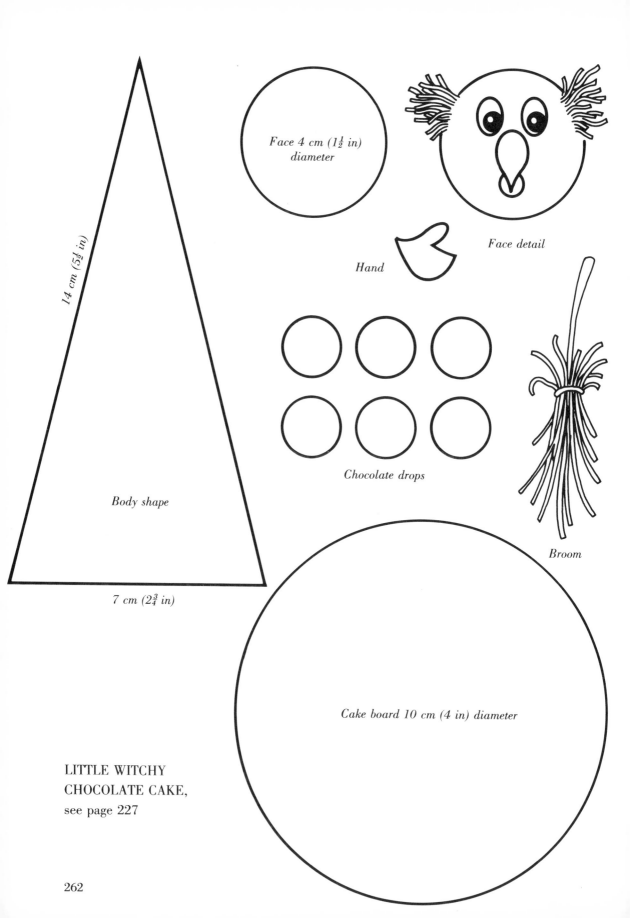

Face 4 cm ($1\frac{1}{2}$ in) diameter

Face detail

Hand

14 cm ($5\frac{1}{2}$ in)

Body shape

Chocolate drops

Broom

7 cm ($2\frac{3}{4}$ in)

Cake board 10 cm (4 in) diameter

LITTLE WITCHY
CHOCOLATE CAKE,
see page 227

262

VALENTINE CHOCOLATE BOX,

see page 229

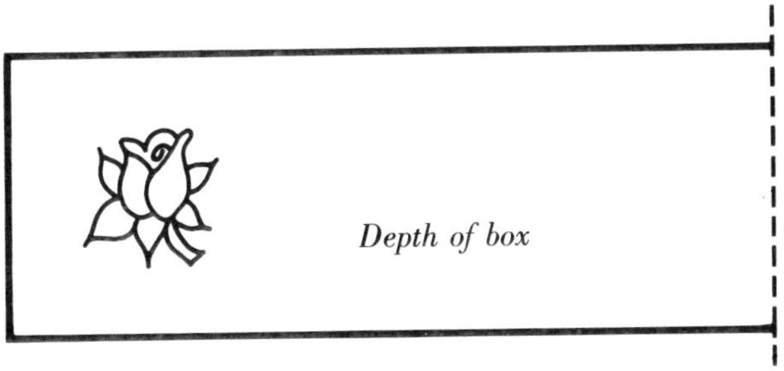

Depth of box

3 cm (1⅛ in)

Lid and base: make 2

With Love

Lettering

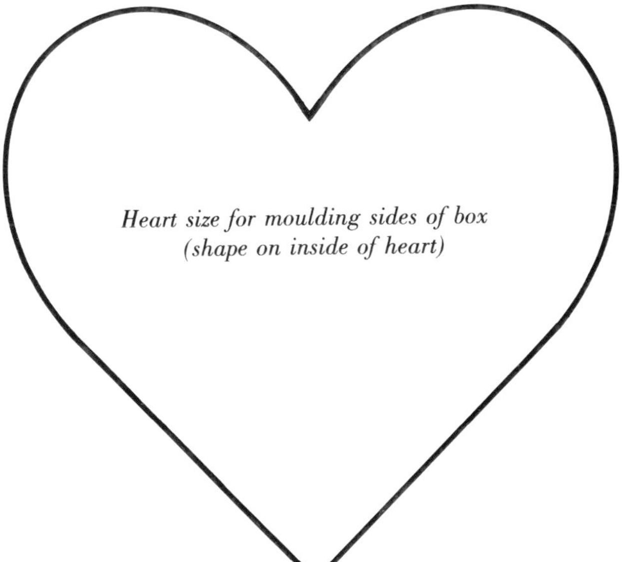

*Heart size for moulding sides of box
(shape on inside of heart)*

263

ADDITIONAL USEFUL TEMPLATES

This section provides a selection of versatile templates which may be used individually or incorporated into elaborate cake designs.
The first group of shapes is for numerals and letters — always useful when including a message, name, date or number on a cake.
Remember that they may be enlarged or reduced by using squared paper when tracing, or by photocopying. When arranging letters and numerals, consider the spacing carefully as well as the position of the group on the cake. Often, the message or the number should form the focal point for the top decoration, so bad placing or poor spacing can ruin the result. Practise first on a piece of paper cut to the size of the cake, trying different positions and designs until you are happy with the result.
Next you will find a small selection of collars. These may be made more elaborate by tracing, then drawing around them to vary the shapes. There is also a selection of filler ideas included for the open collar. Fillers may be worked in the same or contrasting colours, or the piping may be tinted with gold or silver which can be dramatic on the right cake and for the right occasion.
Lastly, there is a collection of general patterns and shapes, including a useful guide to cutting cakes in order to create different numbers.
Many of the shapes and patterns in this chapter may be worked in several ways. They may be used as a guide for cutting out shapes in sugarpaste or as shapes for runouts. In some cases they may be used as a base for brush embroidery. There are ideas for side piping on a cake, or for using as a border or in small sections to complete the corner decoration.
One of the most important functions of this type of information is to spark off new and individual ideas by arousing enthusiasm. Look through the pages, trace samples and experiment by combining different patterns, using complementary cake decorating mediums and various shades and depths of different colours.

ABCDEF
FGHIJKL
MNOPQR
STUVWX
YZ 1234
456789

a b c d e f g h

i j k l m n o p

q r s t u v w

x y z

Happy
Birthday

D P P A R Q

1234567890

1234567890

Merry Christmas

1234567890

12345

678

90

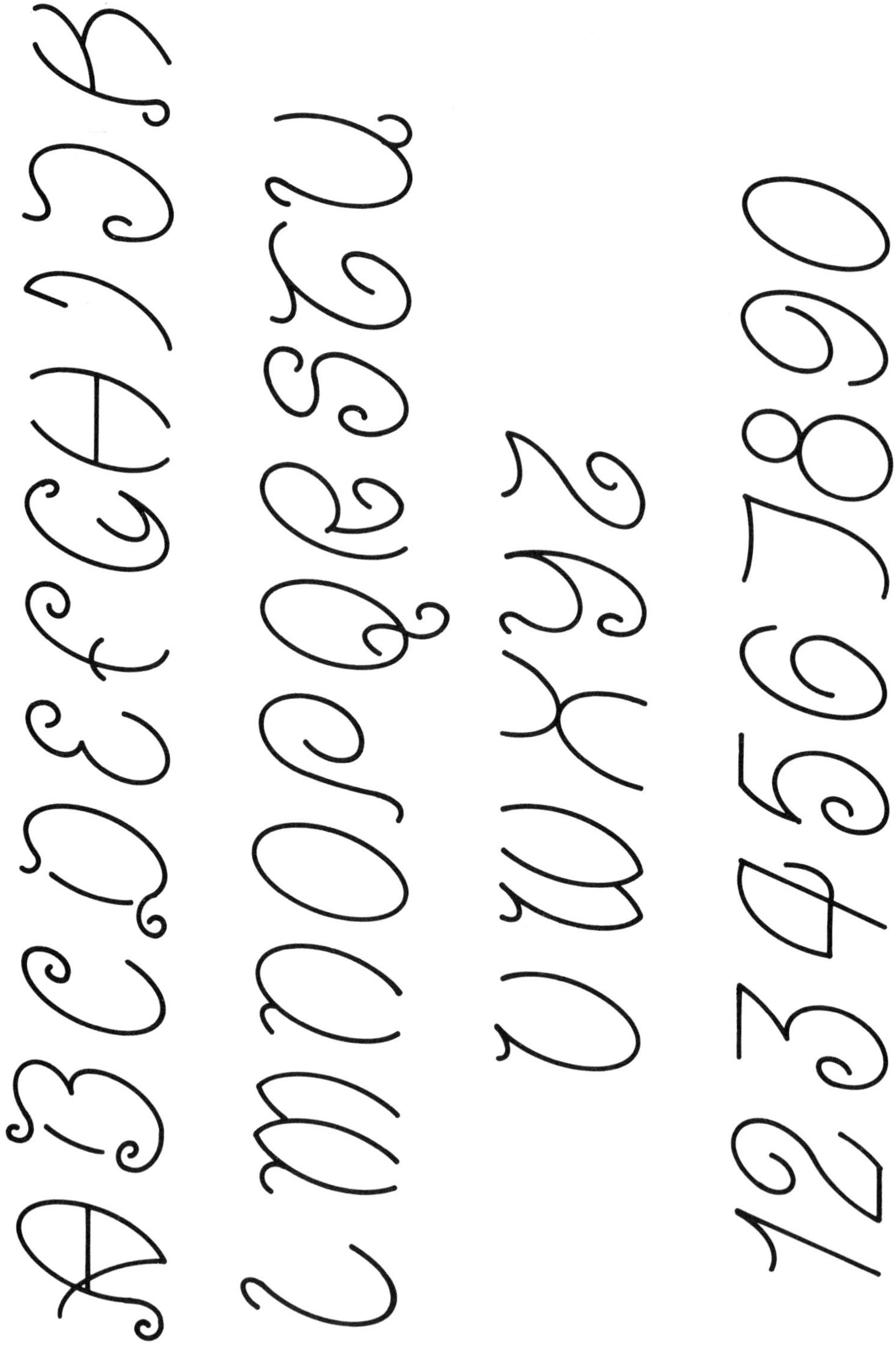

Little Witchy Chocolate Cake
see page 227

Valentine Chocolate Box
see page 229

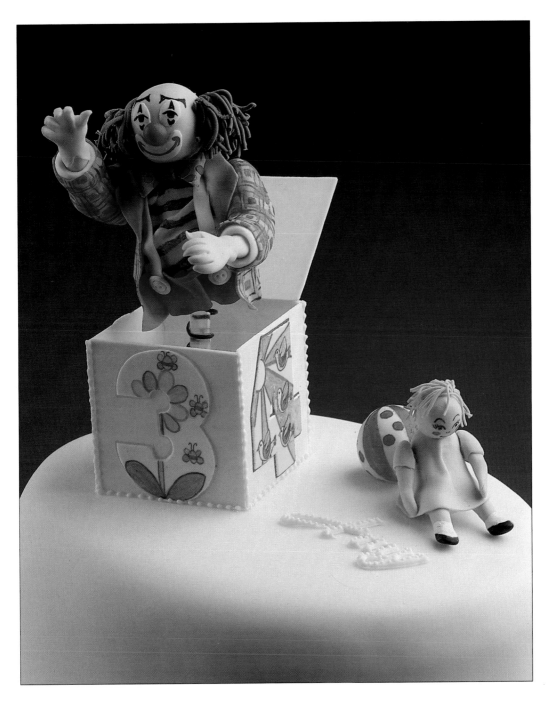

Clown Jack-in-the-Box
see page 104

Flower Plaques
see page 137

ABCDEFGHIJ
KLMNOPQRS
TUVWXYZ
ABCDEFGHIJKLM
NOPQRSTUVWXYZ

N·O·E·L

SEASONS

GREETINGS

HAPPY
BIRTHDAY

Happy

Birthday

50 18

25 50

21 50

Congratulations

Happy
Retirement

Happy

Anniversary

25yrs

E·A·S·T·E·R

GREETINGS

MOTHER

Happy
Father's Day

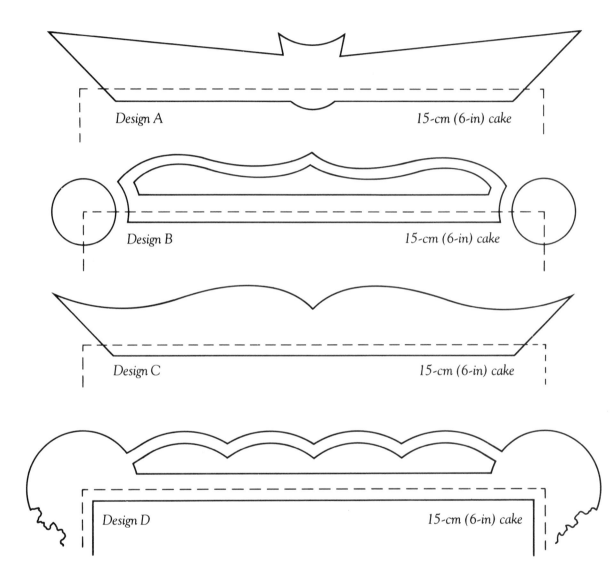

Design A   15-cm (6-in) cake

Design B   15-cm (6-in) cake

Design C   15-cm (6-in) cake

Design D   15-cm (6-in) cake

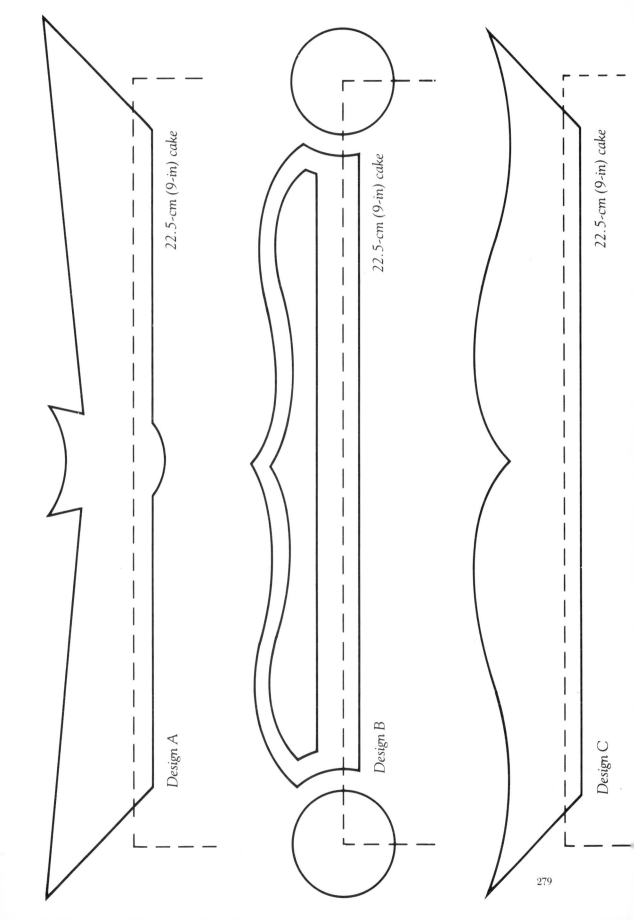

22.5-cm (9-in) cake

22.5-cm (9-in) cake

22.5-cm (9-in) cake

Design A

Design B

Design C

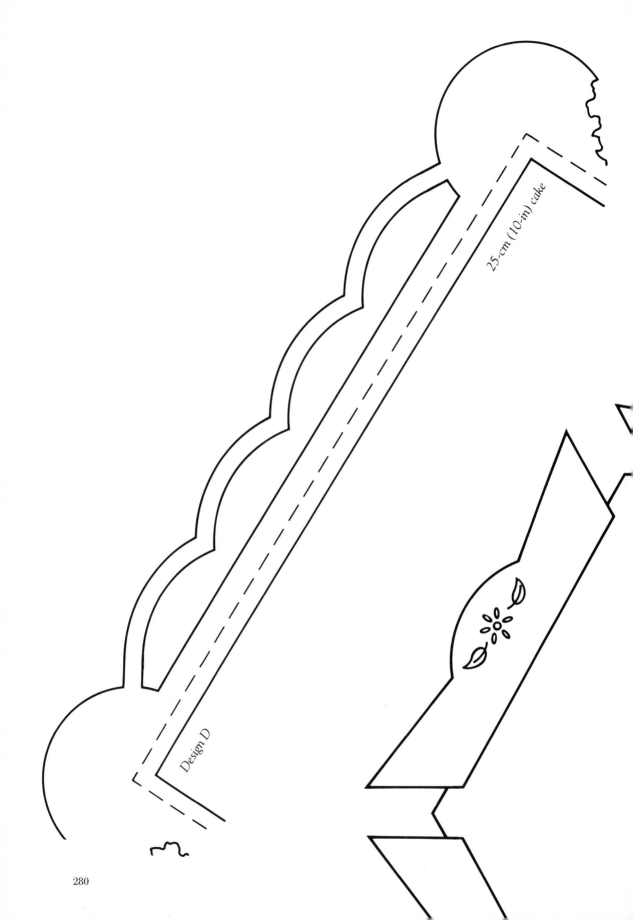

25-cm (10-in) cake

Design D

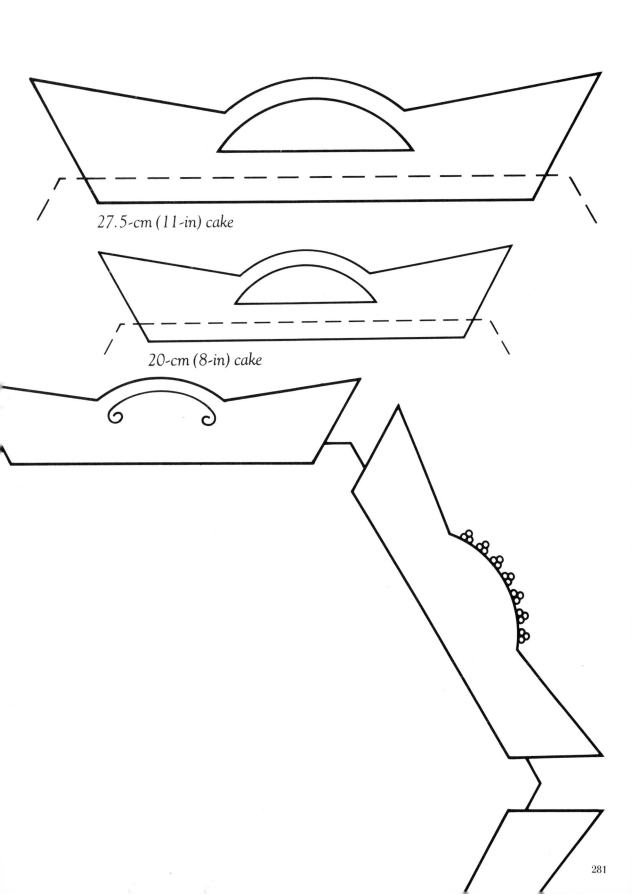

27.5-cm (11-in) cake

20-cm (8-in) cake

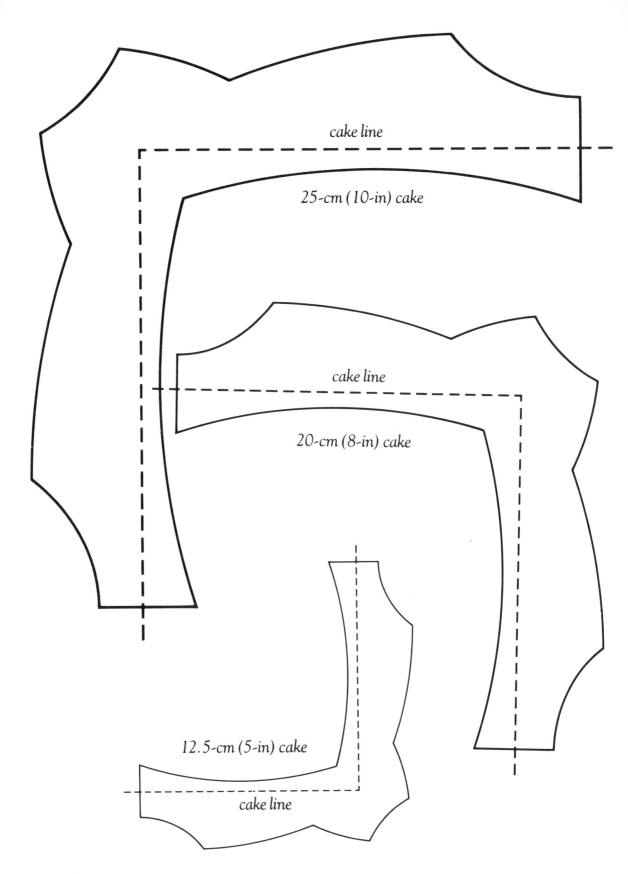

cake line

25-cm (10-in) cake

cake line

20-cm (8-in) cake

12.5-cm (5-in) cake

cake line

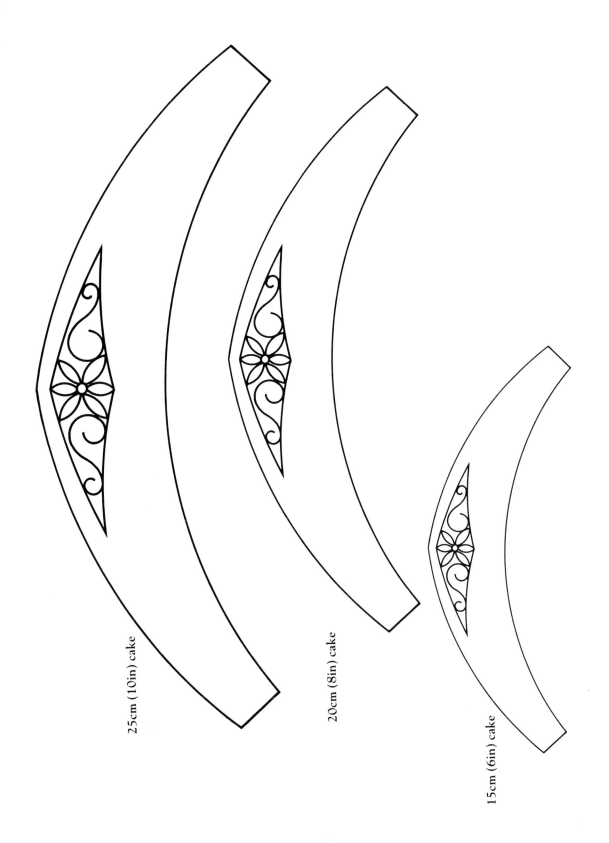

25cm (10in) cake

20cm (8in) cake

15cm (6in) cake

285

288

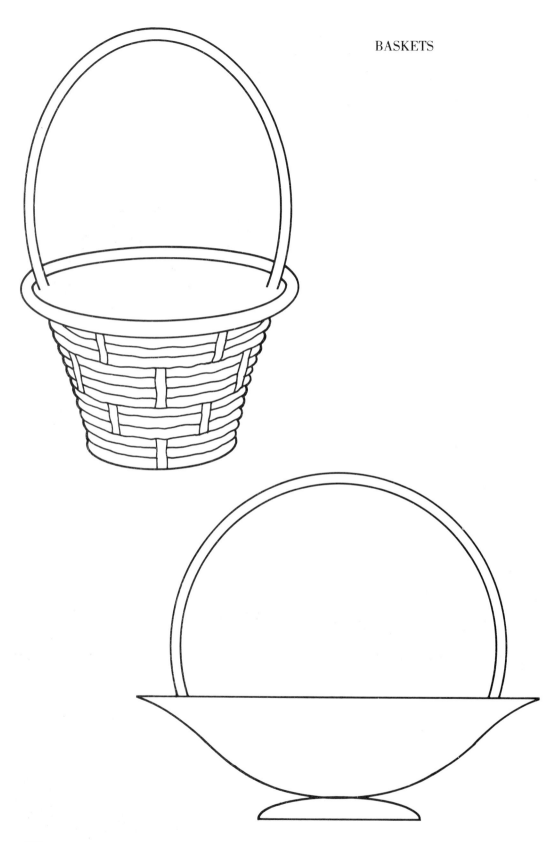

NUMBER CAKES

The general instructions for each of the following cakes is the same. Trim the tops so that all cakes to be used for the one number are the same depth. Use the illustrations to cut the cakes to the correct shape and size. Place the cut cakes upside down on a board and assemble as shown. Join pieces using a little icing or apricot glaze and decorate.

YOU WILL NEED
☐ 2 bar cakes

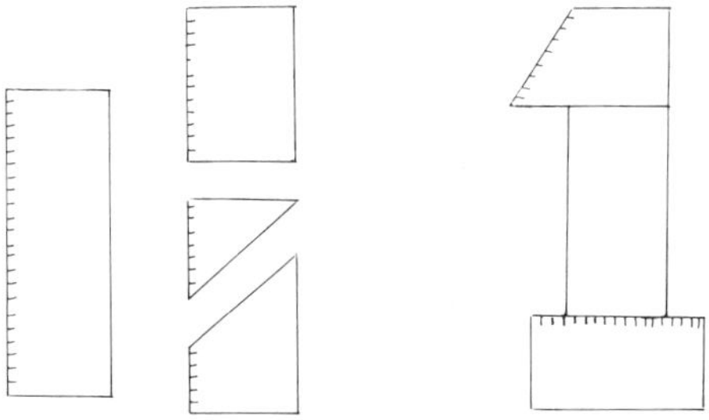

YOU WILL NEED
☐ 1 bar cake
☐ 1 slab cake

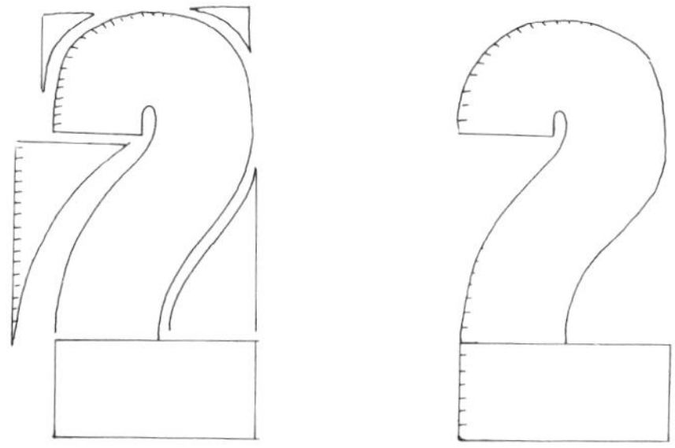

YOU WILL NEED
☐ 2 x 22 cm (8¾ in) ring cakes

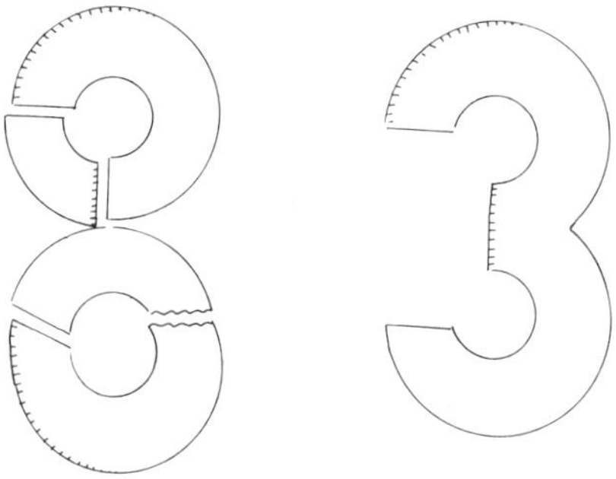

YOU WILL NEED
☐ 3 bar cakes

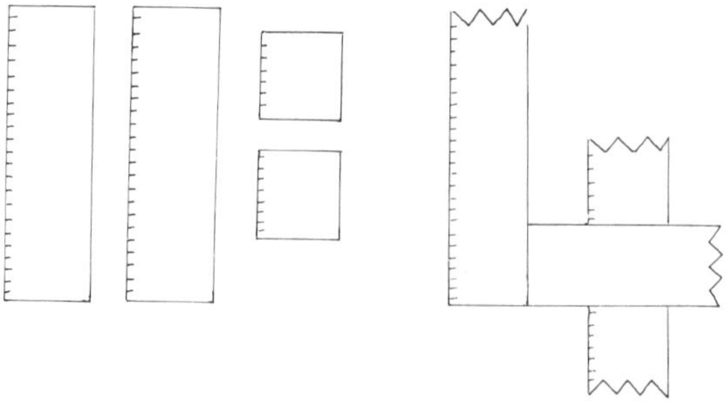

5

YOU WILL NEED
- ☐ 1 bar cake
- ☐ 1 x 22 cm (8¾ in) ring cake

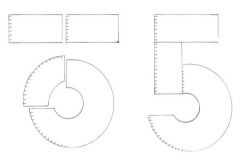

6

YOU WILL NEED
- ☐ 1 bar cake
- ☐ 1 x 22 cm (8¾ in) ring cake

(This cake can be turned upside down to make 9.)

7

YOU WILL NEED
- ☐ 2 bar cakes

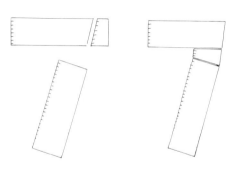

8

YOU WILL NEED
- ☐ 2 x 22 cm (8¾ in) ring cakes

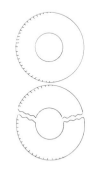
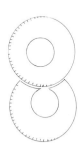

10

YOU WILL NEED
- ☐ 2 bar cakes
- ☐ 1 x 22 cm (8¾ in) ring cake

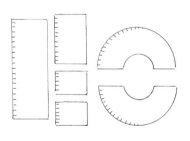
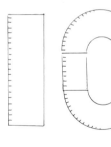

AN A–Z GUIDE TO SOME COMMON AMERICAN TERMS

UK	AMERICAN
Baking tin	pan
Biscuit (cutter)	cookie (cutter)
Black treacle	molasses
Blue tac	plastic adhesive
Cake tin (springform)	cake pan
Candied fruit	glacé fruit
Caster sugar	superfine sugar
Chocolate, plain	chocolate, dark (comes in unsweetened or sweetened)
Chocolate vermicelli	chocolate sprinkles
Cocktail stick	toothpick
Cotton	thread
Desiccated coconut	shredded coconut
Double saucepan	double boiler
Essence	extract
Flour, plain	flour, all-purpose
self raising	self rising
Glacé icing	water icing
Golden syrup	a substitute light corn syrup
Greaseproof paper	waxed paper
Hazelnuts	filberts
Icing sugar	confectioners' sugar
Jam	jam or conserve
Liquid glucose	clear corn syrup
Loaf tin	loaf pan (size is usually given in dimensions rather than weight)
Marzipan	almond paste
Muslin	cheesecloth
Non-stick silicone paper	parchment paper
Self-raising, see flour	
Swiss roll	jelly roll
Swiss roll tin	jelly roll pan
Sweets	candies
Tin (cake)	pan (cake)
Fairy bun tin	tart pan
Vanilla essence, see essence	vanilla extract
White vegetable fat	vegetable shortening

LENGTH

$\frac{1}{8}$ inch	2.5 mm
$\frac{1}{4}$ inch	5 mm
$\frac{1}{2}$ inch	1 cm
1 inch	2.5 cm
2 inch	5 cm
3 inch	7.5 cm
4 inch	10 cm
5 inch	13 cm
6 inch	15 cm
7 inch	18 cm
8 inch	20 cm
9 inch	23 cm
10 inch	25 cm
11 inch	28 cm
12 inch	30 cm
13 inch	33 cm
14 inch	36 cm
15 inch	38 cm

OVEN TEMPERATURES

110°C	(225°F/Gas $\frac{1}{4}$)
120°C	(250°F/Gas $\frac{1}{2}$)
140°C	(275°F/Gas 1)
150°C	(300°F/Gas 2)
160°C	(325°F/Gas 3)
180°C	(350°F/Gas 4)
190°C	(375°F/Gas 5)
200°C	(400°F/Gas 6)
220°C	(425°F/Gas 7)
230°C	(450°F/Gas 8)
240°C	(475°F/Gas 9)
260°C	(500°F/Gas 10)

LIQUID MEASURES

For accuracy, measure in teaspoons and tablespoons up to 2 fl oz

Metric	Imperial	American Cups
30 ml	1 fl oz	(6 teaspoons)
60 ml	2 fl oz	$\frac{1}{4}$ cup
75 ml	$2\frac{1}{2}$ fl oz	$\frac{1}{3}$ cup
90 ml	3 fl oz	
100 ml	$3\frac{1}{2}$ fl oz	
125 ml	4 fl oz	$\frac{1}{2}$ cup
140 ml	$4\frac{1}{2}$ fl oz	
155 ml	5 fl oz	$\frac{2}{3}$ cup
170 ml	$5\frac{1}{2}$ fl oz	
185 ml	6 fl oz	$\frac{3}{4}$ cup
200 ml	$6\frac{1}{2}$ fl oz	
220 ml	7 fl oz	
250 ml	8 fl oz	1 cup
280 ml	9 fl oz	
315 ml	10 fl oz	$1\frac{1}{4}$ cups
345 ml	11 fl oz	$1\frac{1}{3}$ cups
375 ml	12 fl oz	$1\frac{1}{2}$ cups
410 ml	13 fl oz	$1\frac{2}{3}$ cups
440 ml	14 fl oz	$1\frac{3}{4}$ cups
470 ml	15 fl oz	
500 ml	16 fl oz	2 cups
530 ml	17 fl oz	
560 ml	18 fl oz	$2\frac{1}{4}$ cups
595 ml	19 fl oz	$2\frac{1}{3}$ cups
625 ml	20 fl oz	$2\frac{1}{2}$ cups
655 ml	21 fl oz	$2\frac{2}{3}$ cups
690 ml	22 fl oz	$2\frac{3}{4}$ cups
720 ml	23 fl oz	
750 ml	24 fl oz	3 cups
785 ml	25 fl oz	
815 ml	26 fl oz	$3\frac{1}{4}$ cups
845 ml	27 fl oz	$3\frac{1}{3}$ cups
875 ml	28 fl oz	$3\frac{1}{2}$ cups
910 ml	29 fl oz	$3\frac{2}{3}$ cups
940 ml	30 fl oz	$3\frac{3}{4}$ cups
970 ml	31 fl oz	
1 litre	32 fl oz	4 cups

WEIGHT

Metric	Imperial
7 g	$\frac{1}{4}$ oz
15 g	$\frac{1}{2}$ oz
22 g	$\frac{3}{4}$ oz
30 g	1 oz
45 g	$1\frac{1}{2}$ oz
60 g	2 oz
75 g	$2\frac{1}{2}$ oz
90 g	3 oz
100 g	$3\frac{1}{2}$ oz
125 g	4 oz
140 g	$4\frac{1}{2}$ oz
155 g	5 oz
170 g	$5\frac{1}{2}$ oz
185 g	6 oz
200 g	$6\frac{1}{2}$ oz
220 g	7 oz
250 g	8 oz
280 g	9 oz
315 g	10 oz
345 g	11 oz
375 g	12 oz
410 g	13 oz
440 g	14 oz
470 g	15 oz
500 g	1 lb
625 g	$1\frac{1}{4}$ lb
750 g	$1\frac{1}{2}$ lb
875 g	$1\frac{3}{4}$ lb
1 kg	2 lb
1.25 kg	$2\frac{1}{2}$ lb
1.5 kg	3 lb
1.75 kg	$3\frac{1}{2}$ lb
2 kg	4 lb
2.25 kg	$4\frac{1}{2}$ lb
2.5 kg	5 lb
2.75 kg	$5\frac{1}{2}$ lb
3 kg	6 lb

INDEX